RAMAKRISHNA-VIVEKANANDA CENTER
OF NEW YORK
17 East 94th Street, New York, N.Y. 10128

PUBLICATIONS

By Swami Nikhilananda

HINDUISM: Its Meaning for the Liberation of the Spirit

HOLY MOTHER: Being the Life of Sri Sarada Devi, Wife of Sri Ramakrishna
    and Helpmate in His Mission

MAN IN SEARCH OF IMMORTALITY: Testimonials from the Hindu Scriptures

VIVEKANANDA: A BIOGRAPHY

Translated by Swami Nikhilananda

THE BHAGAVAD GITA

THE BHAGAVAD GITA (Pocket Edition)

THE GOSPEL OF SRI RAMAKRISHNA

THE GOSPEL OF SRI RAMAKRISHNA (Abridged Edition)

SELF-KNOWLEDGE (Atmabodha)

THE UPANISHADS   Volumes I, II, III, and IV

By Swami Vivekananda

INSPIRED TALKS, My Master and Other Writings

JNANA-YOGA

KARMA-YOGA AND BHAKTI-YOGA

RAJA-YOGA

VIVEKANANDA: THE YOGAS AND OTHER WORKS
(Chosen and with a Biography by Swami Nikhilananda)

VIVEKANANDA

VIVEKANANDA

A Biography

by

SWAMI NIKHILANANDA

NEW YORK

RAMAKRISHNA-VIVEKANANDA CENTER

VIVEKANANDA: A Biography

Copyright © 1953, by Swami Nikhilananda
Trustee of the Estate of Swami Vivekananda

PRINTED IN THE UNITED STATES OF AMERICA

Paperback Edition Second Printing

ISBN 0-911206-25-6

ISBN 978-0-911206-25-8

Library of Congress Catalog Card Number: 53-7851

PREFACE

SWAMI VIVEKANANDA's inspiring personality was well known both in India and in America during the last decade of the nineteenth century and the first decade of the twentieth. The unknown monk of India suddenly leapt into fame at the Parliament of Religions held in Chicago in 1893, at which he represented Hinduism. His vast knowledge of Eastern and Western culture as well as his deep spiritual insight, fervid eloquence, brilliant conversation, broad human sympathy, colourful personality, and handsome figure made an irresistible appeal to the many types of Americans who came in contact with him. People who saw or heard Vivekananda even once still cherish his memory after a lapse of more than half a century.

In America Vivekananda's mission was the interpretation of India's spiritual culture, especially in its Vedāntic setting. He also tried to enrich the religious consciousness of the Americans through the rational and humanistic teachings of the Vedānta philosophy. In America he became India's spiritual ambassador and pleaded eloquently for better understanding between India and the New World in order to create a healthy synthesis of East and West, of religion and science.

In his own motherland Vivekananda is regarded as the patriot saint of modern India and an inspirer of her dormant national consciousness. To the Hindus he preached the ideal of a strength-giving and man-making religion. Service to man as the visible manifestation of the Godhead was the special form of worship he advocated for the Indians, devoted as they were to the rituals and myths of their ancient faith. Many political leaders of India have publicly acknowledged their indebtedness to Swami Vivekananda.

The Swami's mission was both national and international. A lover of mankind, he strove to promote peace and human brotherhood on the spiritual foundation of the Vedāntic Oneness of existence. A mystic of the highest order, Vivekananda had a direct and intuitive experience of Reality. He derived his ideas from that unfailing source of wisdom and often presented them in the soul-stirring language of poetry.

The natural tendency of Vivekananda's mind, like that of his Master, Ramakrishna, was to soar above the world and forget itself in contemplation of the Absolute. But another part of his personality bled at the sight of human suffering in East and West alike. It might appear that his mind seldom found a point of rest in its oscillation between contemplation of God and service to man. Be that as it may, he chose, in obedience to a higher call, service to man as his mission on earth; and this choice has endeared him to people in the West, Americans in particular.

v

In the course of a short life of thirty-nine years (1863-1902), of which only ten were devoted to public activities—and those, too, in the midst of acute physical suffering—he left for posterity his four classics: *Jnāna-Yoga, Bhakti-Yoga, Karma-Yoga,* and *Rāja-Yoga,* all of which are outstanding treatises on Hindu philosophy. In addition, he delivered innumerable lectures, wrote inspired letters in his own hand to his many friends and disciples, composed numerous poems, and acted as spiritual guide to the many seekers who came to him for instruction. He also organized the Ramakrishna Order of monks, which is the most outstanding religious organization of modern India. It is devoted to the propagation of the Hindu spiritual culture not only in the Swami's native land, but also in America and in other parts of the world.

Swami Vivekananda once spoke of himself as a "condensed India." His life and teachings are of inestimable value to the West for an understanding of the mind of Asia. William James, the Harvard philosopher, called the Swami the "paragon of Vedāntists." Max Müller and Paul Deussen, the famous Orientalists of the nineteenth century, held him in genuine respect and affection. "His words," writes Romain Rolland, "are great music, phrases in the style of Beethoven, stirring rhythms like the march of Handel choruses. I cannot touch these sayings of his, scattered as they are through the pages of books, at thirty years' distance, without receiving a thrill through my body like an electric shock. And what shocks, what transports, must have been produced when in burning words they issued from the lips of the hero!"

NIKHILANANDA

Ramakrishna-Vivekananda Center
New York
January 5, 1953

CONTENTS

Preface v

Illustrations ix

Note on Pronunciation x

Vivekananda 1

Appendix 181

Glossary 211

ILLUSTRATIONS

Vivekananda in Meditation .... *facing page*   1
The Temple of Kāli at Dakshineswar .... *following page*   28
Śri Ramakrishna 28
The Holy Mother 28
The Cossipore Garden House 28
Narendranath at the Cossipore Garden 36
Vivekananda as a Wandering Monk 36
Vivekananda as Hindu Teacher 128
Brahmananda, Premananda, Saradananda 128
Jogananda, Niranjanananda, Advaitananda, Adbhutananda 128
Shivananda, Ramakrishnananda, Turiyananda,
    Trigunatitananda 128
Akhandananda, Subodhananda, Vijnanananda, Abhedananda 128
Śri Ramakrishna Monastery at Belur 128
Miss J. MacLeod, Mrs. Ole Bull, Vivekananda,
    Sister Nivedita 146
Trigunatitananda, Shivananda, Turiyananda,
    Vivekananda, Brahmananda, Sadananda 146
Vivekananda, the Wandering Monk 180
Vivekananda Temple at the Belur Math 180
The Belur Math 180

Cover Illustration:
  Swami Vivekananda

NOTE ON THE PRONUNCIATION OF
SANSKRIT AND VERNACULAR WORDS

a	has the sound of				o in come.
ā	"	"	"	"	a in far.
e	"	"	"	"	e in bed.
i	"	"	"	"	ee in feel.
o	"	"	"	"	o in note.
u	"	"	"	"	u in full.
ai, ay	"	"	"	"	oy in boy.
au	"	"	"	"	o pronounced deep in the throat.
ch	"	"	"	"	ch in church.
ḍ	"	"	"	"	hard d (in English).
g	"	"	"	"	g in god.
jn	"	"	"	"	hard gy (in English).
ś	"	"	"	"	sh in shut.
th	"	"	"	"	t-h in boat-house.

sh may be pronounced as in English.
t and d are soft as in French.

Other consonants appearing in the transliterations may be pronounced as in English.

Diacritical marks have generally not been used in proper names belonging to recent times or in modern and well-known geographical names.

VIVEKANANDA

Vivekananda in Meditation

VIVEKANANDA

S WAMI VIVEKANANDA, the great soul loved and revered in East and West alike as the rejuvenator of Hinduism in India and the preacher of its eternal truths abroad, was born at 6:49, a few minutes after sunrise, on Monday, January 12, 1863. It was the day of the great Hindu festival Makarasamkrānti, when special worship is offered to the Ganges by millions of devotees. Thus the future Vivekananda first drew breath when the air above the sacred river not far from the house was reverberating with the prayers, worship, and religious music of thousands of Hindu men and women.

While Vivekananda was still in his mother's womb, she, like many other pious Hindu mothers, had observed religious vows, fasted, and prayed so that she might be blessed with a son who would do honour to the family. She requested a relative who was living in Benares to offer special worship to the Vireśwara Śiva of that holy place and seek His blessings; for Śiva, the great god of renunciation, dominated her thought. One night she dreamt that this supreme Deity aroused Himself from His meditation and agreed to be born as her son. When she woke she was filled with joy.

The mother, Bhuvaneswari Devi, accepted the child as a boon from Vireśwara Śiva and named him Vireśwara. The family, however, gave him the name of Narendranath Datta, calling him, for short, Narendra, or more endearingly, Naren.

The Datta family of Calcutta, into which Narendranath had been born, was well known for its affluence, philanthropy, scholarship, and independent spirit. The grandfather, Durgacharan, after the birth of his first son, had renounced the world in search of God. The father, Viswanath, an attorney-at-law of the High Court of Calcutta, was versed in English and Persian literature and often entertained himself and his friends by reciting from the Bible and the poetry of Hafiz, both of which, he believed, contained truths unmatched by human thinking elsewhere. He was particularly attracted to the Islāmic culture, with which he was familiar because of his close contact with the educated Moslems of Northwestern India. Moreover, he derived a large income from his law practice and, unlike his father, thoroughly enjoyed the worldly life. An expert in cookery, he prepared rare dishes and liked to share them with his friends. Travel was another of his hobbies. Though agnostic in religion and a mocker of social conventions, he possessed a large heart and often went out of his way to support idle relatives, some of whom were given to drunkenness. Once, when Narendra protested against this lack of judgement, his father said: "How can

1

you understand the great misery of human life? When you realize the depths of men's suffering, you will sympathize with these unfortunate creatures who try to forget their sorrows, even though only for a short while, in the oblivion created by intoxicating drink." Naren's father, however, kept a sharp eye on his children and would not tolerate the slightest deviation from good manners.

Bhuvaneswari Devi, the mother, was cast in a different mould. Regal in appearance and gracious in conduct, she belonged to the old tradition of Hindu womanhood. As mistress of a large household, she devoted her spare time to sewing and singing, being particularly fond of the great Indian epics, the Rāmāyana and the Mahābhārata, large portions of which she had memorized. She became the special refuge of the poor, and commanded universal respect because of her calm resignation to God, her inner tranquillity, and her dignified detachment in the midst of her many arduous duties. Two sons were born to her besides Narendranath, and four daughters, two of whom died at an early age.

Narendra grew up to be a sweet, sunny-tempered, but very restless boy. Two nurses were necessary to keep his exuberant energy under control, and he was a great tease to his sisters. In order to quiet him, the mother often put his head under the cold-water tap, repeating Śiva's name, which always produced the desired effect. Naren felt a child's love of birds and animals, and this characteristic reappeared during the last days of his life. Among his boyhood pets were a family cow, a monkey, a goat, a peacock, and several pigeons and guinea-pigs. The coachman of the family, with his turban, whip, and bright-coloured livery, was his boyhood ideal of a magnificent person, and he often expressed the ambition to be like him when he grew up.

Narendra bore a striking resemblance to the grandfather who had renounced the world to lead a monastic life, and many thought that the latter had been reborn in him. The youngster developed a special fancy for wandering monks, whose very sight would greatly excite him. One day when such a monk appeared at the door and asked for alms, Narendra gave him his only possession, the tiny piece of new cloth that was wrapped round his waist. Thereafter, whenever a monk was seen in the neighbourhood, Narendra would be locked in a room. But even then he would throw out of the window whatever he found near at hand as an offering to the holy man. In the meantime, he was receiving his early education from his mother, who taught him the Bengali alphabet and his first English words, as well as stories from the Rāmāyana and the Mahābhārata.

During his childhood Narendra, like many other Hindu children of his age, developed a love for the Hindu deities, of whom he had learnt from his mother. Particularly attracted by the heroic story of Rāma and his faithful consort Sitā, he procured their images, bedecked them with flowers, and worshipped them in his boyish fashion. But disillusionment came when he heard someone denounce marriage vehemently as a terrible bondage. When he had thought this over he discarded Rāma and Sitā as unworthy of worship. In their place he installed the image of Śiva, the god of renunciation, who was the ideal of the yogis. Nevertheless he retained a fondness for the Rāmāyana.

At this time he daily experienced a strange vision when he was about to fall asleep. Closing his eyes, he would see between his eyebrows a ball of light of changing colours, which would slowly expand and at last burst, bathing his whole body in a white radiance. Watching this light he would gradually fall asleep. Since it was a daily occurrence, he regarded the phenomenon as common to all people, and was surprised when a friend denied ever having seen such a thing. Years later, however, Narendra's spiritual teacher, Śri Ramakrishna, said to him, "Naren, my boy, do you see a light when you go to sleep?" Ramakrishna knew that such a vision indicated a great spiritual past and an inborn habit of meditation. The vision of light remained with Narendra until the end of his life, though later it lost its regularity and intensity.

While still a child Narendra practised meditation with a friend before the image of Śiva. He had heard that the holy men of ancient India would become so absorbed in contemplation of God that their hair would grow and gradually enter into the earth, like the roots of the banyan tree. While meditating, therefore, he would open his eyes, now and then, to see if his own hair had entered into the earth. Even so, during meditation, he often became unconscious of the world. On one occasion he saw in a vision a luminous person of serene countenance who was carrying the staff and water-bowl of a monk. The apparition was about to say something when Naren became frightened and left the room. He thought later that perhaps this had been a vision of Buddha.

At the age of six he was sent to a primary school. One day, however, he repeated at home some of the vulgar words that he had learnt from his classmates, whereupon his disgusted parents took him out of the school and appointed a private tutor, who conducted classes for him and some other children of the neighbourhood in the worship hall of the house. Naren soon showed a precocious mind and developed a keen memory. Very easily he learnt by heart the whole of a Sanskrit grammar and long passages from the Rāmāyana and the Mahābhārata. Some of the friendships he made at this age lasted his whole lifetime. At school he was the undisputed leader. When playing his favourite game of "King and the Court," he would assume the rôle of the monarch and assign to his friends the parts of the ministers, commander-in-chief, and other state officials.

He was marked from birth to be a leader of men, as his name Narendra (lord of men) signified, yet even at that early age he could not tolerate caste arrogance. In his father's office separate tobacco pipes were provided for clients belonging to the different castes, as orthodox Hindu custom required, and the pipe from which the Moslems smoked was set quite apart. Narendra once smoked tobacco from all the pipes, including the one marked for the Moslems, and when reprimanded, remarked, "I cannot see what difference it makes."

During these early years, Narendra's future personality was influenced by his gifted father and his saintly mother, both of whom kept a chastening eye upon him. The father had his own manner of discipline. For example, when, in the course of an argument with his mother, the impetuous boy once uttered a few rude words and the report came to the father, Viswanath did not directly scold his son, but wrote with charcoal on the door of his room: "Narendra today said to his mother—" and added the words that had been used. He wanted Narendra's friends to know how rudely he had treated his mother.

Another time Narendra bluntly asked his father, "What have you done for me?"

Instead of being annoyed, Viswanath said, "Go and look at yourself in the mirror, and then you will know."

Still another day, Narendra said to his father, "How shall I conduct myself in the world?"

"Never show surprise at anything," his father replied.

This priceless advice enabled Narendranath, in his future chequered life, to preserve his serenity of mind whether dwelling with princes in their palaces or sharing the straw huts of beggars.

The mother, Bhuvaneswari, played her part in bringing out Narendranath's innate virtues. When he told her, one day, of having been unjustly treated in school, she said to him, in consolation: "My child, what does it matter, if you are in the right? Always follow the truth without caring about the result. Very often you may have to suffer injustice or unpleasant consequences for holding to the truth; but you must not, under any circumstances, abandon it." Many years later Narendranath proudly said to an audience, "I am indebted to my mother for whatever knowledge I have acquired."

One day, when he was fighting with his play-fellows, Narendra accidentally fell from the porch and struck his forehead against a stone. The wound bled profusely and left a permanent scar over his right eye. Years later, when Ramakrishna heard of this accident, he remarked: "In a way it was a good thing. If he had not thus lost some of his blood, he would have created havoc in the world with his excessive energy."

In 1870, at the age of seven, Narendra entered high school. His exceptional intelligence was soon recognized by his teachers and classmates. Though at first reluctant to study English because of its foreign origin, he soon took it up with avidity. But the curriculum consumed very little of his time. He used most of his inexhaustible energy in outside activities. Games of various kinds, many of which he invented or improvised, kept him occupied. He made an imitation gas-works and a factory for aerating water, these two novelties having just been introduced in Calcutta. He organized an amateur theatrical company and a gymnasium, and took lessons in fencing, wrestling, rowing, and other manly sports. He also tried his hand at the art of cooking. Intensely restless, he would soon tire of one pastime and seek a new one. With his friends he visited the museums and the zoological garden. He arbitrated the disputes of his play-fellows and was a favourite with the people of the neighbourhood. Everybody admired his courage, straightforwardness, and simplicity.

From an early age this remarkable youth had no patience with fear or superstition. One of his boyish pranks had been to climb a flowering tree belonging to a neighbour, pluck the flowers, and do other mischief. The owner of the tree, finding his remonstrances unheeded, once solemnly told Naren's friends that the tree was guarded by a white-robed ghost who would certainly wring their necks if they disturbed his peace. The boys were frightened and kept away. But Narendra persuaded them to follow him back, and he climbed the tree, enjoying his usual measure of fun, and broke some branches by way of further mischief. Turning to his friends, he then said: "What asses you all are! See, my neck is still there. The old man's story is simply not true. Don't believe what others say unless you yourselves know it to be true."

These simple but bold words were an indication of his future message to the world. Addressing large audiences in later years, he would often say: "Do not believe in a thing because you have read about it in a book. Do not believe in a thing because another man has said it was true. Do not believe in words because they are hallowed by tradition. Find out the truth for yourself. Reason it out. That is realization."

The following incident illustrates his courage and presence of mind. He one day wished to set up a heavy trapeze in the gymnasium, and so asked the help of some people who were there. Among them was an English sailor. The trapeze fell and knocked the sailor unconscious, and the crowd, thinking him dead, ran away for fear of the police. But Naren tore a piece from his cloth, bandaged the sailor's wound, washed his face with water, and gradually revived him. Then he moved the wounded man to a neighbouring schoolhouse where he nursed him for a week. When the sailor had recovered, Naren sent him away with a little purse collected from his friends.

All through this period of boyish play Narendra retained his admiration for the life of the wandering monk. Pointing to a certain line on the palm of his hand, he would say to his friends: "I shall certainly become a sannyāsin. A palmist has predicted it."

ON THE THRESHOLD OF YOUTH

As Narendra grew into adolescence, his temperament showed a marked change. He became keen about intellectual matters, read serious books on history and literature, devoured newspapers, and attended public meetings. Music was his favourite pastime. He insisted that it should express a lofty idea and arouse the feelings of the musician.

At the age of fifteen he experienced his first spiritual ecstasy. The family was journeying to Raipur in the Central Provinces, and part of the trip had to be made in a bullock cart. On that particular day the air was crisp and clear; the trees and creepers were covered with green leaves and many-coloured blossoms; birds of brilliant plumage warbled in the woods. The cart was moving along a narrow pass where the lofty peaks rising on the two sides almost touched each other. Narendra's eyes spied a large bee-hive in the cleft of a giant cliff, and suddenly his mind was filled with awe and reverence for the Divine Providence. He lost outer consciousness and lay thus in the cart for a long time. Even after returning to the sense-perceived world he radiated joy.

Another interesting mental phenomenon may be mentioned here; for it was one often experienced by Narendranath. From boyhood, on first beholding certain people or places, he would feel that he had known them before; but how long before he could never remember. One day he and some of his companions were in a room in a friend's house, where they were discussing various topics. Something was mentioned, and Narendra felt at once that he had on a previous occasion talked about the same subject with the selfsame friends in that very house. He even correctly described every nook and corner of the building, which he had not seen before. He tried at first to explain this singular phenomenon by the doctrine of reincarnation, thinking that perhaps he had lived in that house in a previous life. But he dismissed the idea as improbable. Later he concluded that before his birth he must have had previsions of the people, places, and events that he was to experience in his present incarnation; that was why, he thought, he could recognize them as soon as they presented themselves to him.

At Raipur Narendra was encouraged by his father to meet notable scholars and discuss with them various intellectual topics usually considered too abstruse for boys of his age. On such occasions he exhibited great mental power. From his father, Narendra had learnt the art of grasping the essentials of things, seeing truth from the widest and most comprehensive standpoints, and holding to the real issue under discussion.

In 1879 the family returned to Calcutta, and Narendra within a short time graduated from high school in the first division. In the meantime he had read a great many standard books of English and Bengali literature. History was his favourite subject. He also acquired at this time an unusual method of reading a book and acquiring the knowledge of its subject matter. To quote his own words: "I could understand an author without reading every line of his book. I would read the first and last lines of a paragraph and grasp its meaning. Later I found that I could understand the subject matter by reading only the first and last lines of a page. Afterwards I could follow the whole trend of a writer's argument by merely reading a few lines, though the author himself tried to explain the subject in five or more pages."

COLLEGE DAYS

Soon the excitement of his boyhood days was over, and in 1879 Narendranath entered the Presidency College of Calcutta for higher studies. After a year he joined the General Assembly's Institution, founded by the Scottish General Missionary Board and later known as the Scottish Church College. It was from Hastie, the principal of the college and the professor of English literature, that he first heard the name Śri Ramakrishna.

In college Narendra, now a handsome youth, muscular and agile, though slightly inclined to stoutness, enjoyed serious studies. During the first two years he studied Western logic. Thereafter he specialized in Western philosophy and the ancient and modern history of the different European nations. His memory was prodigious. It took him only three days to assimilate Green's *History of the English People*. Often, on the eve of an examination, he would read the whole night, keeping awake by drinking strong tea or coffee.

About this time he came in contact with Śri Ramakrishna; this event, as we shall presently see, was to become the major turning-point of his life. As a result of his association with Śri Ramakrishna, his innate spiritual yearning was stirred up, and he began to feel the transitoriness of the world and the futility of academic education. The day before his B.A. examination, he suddenly felt an all-consuming love for God and, standing before the room of a college-mate, was heard to sing with great feeling:

Sing ye, O mountains, O clouds, O great winds!
Sing ye, sing ye, sing His glory!
Sing with joy, all ye suns and moons and stars!
Sing ye, sing ye, His glory!

The friend, surprised, reminded him of the next day's examination, but Narendra was unconcerned; the shadow of the approaching monastic life was fast falling on him. He appeared for the examination, however, and easily passed.

About Narendra's scholarship, Professor Hastie once remarked: "Narendra is a real genius. I have travelled far and wide, but have not yet come across a lad of his talents and possibilities even among the philosophical students in the German universities. He is bound to make his mark in life."

Narendra's many-sided genius found its expression in music, as well. He studied both instrumental and vocal music under expert teachers. He could play on many instruments, but excelled in singing. From a Moslem teacher he learnt Hindi, Urdu, and Persian songs, most of them of devotional nature.

He also became associated with the Brāhmo Samāj, an important religious movement of the time, which influenced him during this formative period of his life.

THE BRĀHMO SAMĀJ

The introduction of English education in India following the British conquest of the country brought Hindu society in contact with the intellectual and aggressive European culture. The Hindu youths who came under the spell of the new, dynamic way of life realized the many shortcomings of their own society. Under the Moslem rule, even before the coming of the British, the dynamic aspect of the Hindu culture had been suppressed and the caste-system stratified. The priests controlled the religious life of the people for their own selfish interest. Meaningless dogmas and lifeless ceremonies supplanted the invigorating philosophical teachings of the Upanishads and the Bhagavad Gītā. The masses were exploited, moreover, by the landlords, and the lot of women was especially pitiable. Following the breakdown of the Moslem rule, chaos reigned in every field of Indian life, social, political, religious, and economic. The newly introduced English education brought into sharp focus the many drawbacks of society, and various reform movements, both liberal and orthodox, were initiated to make the national life flow once more through healthy channels.

The Brāhmo Samāj, one of these liberal movements, captured the imagination of the educated youths of Bengal. Rājā Rammohan Roy (1774-1833), the founder of this religious organization, broke away from the rituals, image worship, and priestcraft of orthodox Hinduism and exhorted his followers to dedicate themselves to the "worship and adoration of the Eternal, the Unsearchable, the Immutable Being, who is the Author and the Preserver of the universe." The Rājā, endowed with a gigantic intellect, studied the Hindu, Moslem, Christian, and Buddhist scriptures and was the first Indian to realize the importance of the Western rational method for solving the diverse problems of Hindu society. He took a prominent part in the introduction of English education in India, which, though it at first produced a deleterious effect on the newly awakened Hindu consciousness, ultimately revealed to a few Indians the glorious heritage of their own indigenous civilization.

Among the prominent leaders of the Brāhmo Samāj who succeeded Rammohan Roy were Devendranath Tagore (1817-1905), a great devotee of the Upanishads, and Keshab Chandra Sen (1838-1884), who was inclined to the rituals and doctrines of Christianity. The Brāhmo Samāj, under their leadership, discarded many of the conventions of Hinduism, such as rituals and the worship of God through images. Primarily a reformist movement, it directed its main energy to the emancipation of women, the remarriage of Hindu widows, the abolition of early marriage, and the spread of mass education. Influenced by Western culture, the Brāhmo Samāj upheld the supremacy of reason, preached against the uncritical acceptance of scriptural authority, and strongly supported the slogans of the French Revolution. The whole movement was intellectual and eclectic in character, born of the necessity of the times; unlike traditional Hinduism, it had no root in the spiritual experiences of saints and seers. Narendra, like many other contemporary young men, felt the appeal of its progressive ideas and became one of its members. But, as will be presently seen, the Brāhmo Samāj could not satisfy the deep spiritual yearning of his soul.

About this time Narendra was urged by his father to marry, and an opportunity soon presented itself. A wealthy man, whose daughter Narendra was asked to accept as his bride, offered to defray his expenses for higher studies in England so that he might qualify himself for the much coveted Indian Civil Service. Narendra refused. Other proposals of similar nature produced no different result. Apparently it was not his destiny to lead a householder's life.

From boyhood Narendra had shown a passion for purity. Whenever his warm and youthful nature tempted him to walk into a questionable adventure, he was held back by an unseen hand. His mother had taught him the value of chastity and had made him observe it as a matter of honour, in loyalty to herself and the family tradition. But purity to Narendra was not a negative virtue, a mere abstention from carnal pleasures. To be pure, he felt, was to conserve an intense spiritual force that would later manifest itself in all the noble aspirations of life. He regarded himself as a brahmachārin, a celibate student of the Hindu tradition, who worked hard, prized ascetic disciplines, held holy things in reverence, and enjoyed clean words, thoughts, and acts. For according to the Hindu scriptures, a man, by means of purity, which is the greatest of all virtues, can experience the subtlest spiritual perceptions. In Naren it accounts for the great power of concentration, memory, and insight, and for his indomitable mental energy and physical stamina.

In his youth Narendra used to see every night two visions, utterly dissimilar in nature, before falling asleep. One was that of a worldly man with an accomplished wife and children, enjoying wealth, luxuries, fame, and social position; the other, that of a sannyāsin, a wandering monk, bereft of earthly security and devoted to the contemplation of God. Narendra felt that he had the power to realize either of these ideals; but when his mind reflected on their respective virtues, he was inevitably drawn to the life of renunciation. The glamour of the world would fade and disappear. His deeper self instinctively chose the austere path.

For a time the congregational prayers and the devotional songs of the Brāhmo Samāj exhilarated Narendra's mind, but soon he found that they did not give him any real spiritual experience. He wanted to realize God, the goal of religion, and so felt the imperative need of being instructed by a man who had seen God.

In his eagerness he went to Devendranath, the venerable leader of the Brāhmo Samāj, and bluntly asked him, "Sir, have you seen God?"

Devendranath was embarrassed and replied: "My boy, you have the eyes of a yogi. You should practise meditation."

The youth was disappointed and felt that this teacher was not the man to help him in his spiritual struggle. But he received no better answer from the leaders of other religious sects. Then he remembered having heard the name of Ramakrishna Paramahamsa from Professor Hastie, who, while lecturing his class on Wordsworth's poem *The Excursion*, had spoken of trances, remarking that such religious ecstasies were the result of purity and concentration. He had said, further, that an exalted experience of this kind was a rare phenomenon, especially in modern times. "I have known," he had said, "only one person who has realized that blessed state, and he is Ramakrishna of Dakshineswar. You will understand trances if you visit the saint."

Narendra had also heard about Śri Ramakrishna from a relative, Ramchandra Datta, who was one of the foremost householder disciples of the Master. Learning of Narendra's unwillingness to marry and ascribing it to his desire to lead a spiritual life, Ramchandra had said to him, "If you really want to cultivate spirituality, then visit Ramakrishna at Dakshineswar."

Narendra met Ramakrishna for the first time in November 1881 at the house of the Master's devotee Surendranath Mitra, the young man having been invited there to entertain the visitors with his melodious music. The Paramahamsa was much impressed by his sincerity and devotion, and after a few inquiries asked him to visit him at Dakshineswar. Narendra accepted. He wished to learn if Ramakrishna was the man to help him in his spiritual quest.

RAMAKRISHNA

Ramakrishna, the God-man of modern times, was born on February 18, 1836, in the little village of Kamarpukur, in the district of Hooghly in Bengal. How different were his upbringing and the environment of his boyhood from those of Narendranath, who was to become, later, the bearer and interpreter of his message! Ramakrishna's parents, belonging to the brāhmin caste, were poor, pious, and devoted to the traditions of their ancient religion. Full of fun and innocent joys, the fair child, with flowing hair and a sweet, musical voice, grew up in a simple countryside of rice-fields, cows, and banyan and mango trees. He was apathetic about his studies and remained practically illiterate all his life, but his innate spiritual tendencies found expression through devotional songs and the company of wandering monks, who fired his boyish imagination by the stories of their spiritual adventures. At the age of six he experienced a spiritual ecstasy while watching a flight of snow-white cranes against a black sky overcast with rain-clouds. He began to go into trances as he meditated on gods and goddesses. His father's death, which left the family in straitened circumstances, deepened his spiritual mood. And so, though at the age of sixteen he joined his brother in Calcutta, he refused to go on there with his studies; for, as he remarked, he was simply not interested in an education whose sole purpose was to earn mere bread and butter. He felt a deep longing for the realization of God.

The floodgate of Ramakrishna's emotion burst all bounds when he took up the duties of a priest in the Kāli temple of Dakshineswar, where the Deity was worshipped as the Divine Mother. Ignorant of the scriptures and of the intricacies of ritual, Ramakrishna poured his whole soul into prayer, which often took the form of devotional songs. Food, sleep, and other physical needs were completely forgotten in an all-consuming passion for the vision of God. His nights were spent in contemplation in the neighbouring woods. Doubt sometimes alternated with hope; but an inner certainty and the testimony of the illumined saints sustained him in his darkest hours of despair. Formal worship or the mere sight of the image did not satisfy his inquiring mind; for he felt that a figure of stone could not be the bestower of peace and immortality. Behind the image there must be the real Spirit, which he was determined to behold. This was not an easy task. For a long time the Spirit played with him a teasing game of hide-and-seek, but at last It yielded to the demand of love on the part of the young devotee. When he felt the direct presence of the Divine Mother, Ramakrishna dropped unconscious to the floor, experiencing within himself a constant flow of bliss.

This foretaste of what was to follow made him God-intoxicated, and whetted his appetite for further experience. He wished to see God uninterruptedly, with eyes open as well as closed. He therefore abandoned himself recklessly to the practice of various extreme spiritual disciplines. To remove from his mind the least trace of the arrogance of his high brāhmin caste, he used to clean the dirty places at a pariah's house. Through a stern process of discrimination he effaced all sense of distinction between gold and clay. Purity became the very breath of his nostrils, and he could not regard a woman, even in a dream, in any other way except as his own mother or the Mother of the universe. For several years his eyelids did not touch each other in sleep. And he was finally thought to be insane.

Indeed, the stress of his spiritual practice soon told upon Ramakrishna's delicate body and he returned to Kamarpukur to recover his health. His relatives and old friends saw a marked change in his nature; for the gay boy had been transformed into a contemplative young man whose vision was directed to something on a distant horizon. His mother proposed marriage, and finding in this the will of the Divine Mother, Ramakrishna consented. He even indicated where the girl was to be found, namely, in the village of Jayrambati, only three miles away. Here lived the little Saradamani, a girl of five, who was in many respects very different from the other girls of her age. The child would pray to God to make her character as fragrant as the tuberose and purer than the full moon, which, pure as it was, showed a few dark spots. The marriage was celebrated and Ramakrishna, participating, regarded the whole affair as fun or a new excitement.

In a short while he came back to Dakshineswar and plunged again into the stormy life of religious experimentation. His mother, his newly married wife, and his relatives were forgotten. Now, however, his spiritual disciplines took a new course. He wanted to follow the time-honoured paths of the Hindu religion under the guidance of competent teachers, and they came to him one by one, nobody knew from where. One was a woman, under whom he practised the disciplines of Tantra and of the Vaishnava faith and achieved the highest result in an incredibly short time. It was she who diagnosed his physical malady as the manifestation of deep spiritual emotions and described his apparent insanity as the result of an agonizing love for God; he was immediately relieved. It was she, moreover, who first declared him to be an Incarnation of God, and she proved her statement before an assembly of theologians by scriptural evidence. Under another teacher, the monk Jatadhari, Ramakrishna delved into the mysteries of Rāma worship and experienced Rāma's visible presence. Further, he communed with God through the divine relationships of Father, Mother, Friend, and Beloved. By an austere sannyāsin named Totapuri, he was initiated into the monastic life, and in three days he realized his complete oneness with Brahman, the undifferentiated Absolute, which is the culmination of man's spiritual endeavour. Totapuri himself had had to struggle for forty years to realize this identity.

Ramakrishna turned next to Christianity and Islām, to practise their respective disciplines, and he attained the same result that he had attained through Hinduism. He was thereby convinced that these, too, were ways to the realization of God-consciousness. Finally, he worshipped his own wife—who in the meantime had grown into a young woman of seventeen—as the manifestation of the Divine Mother of the universe and surrendered at her feet the fruit of his past spiritual practices. After this he left behind all his disciplines and struggles. For according to Hindu tradition, when the normal relationship between husband and wife, which is the strongest foundation of the worldly life, has been transcended and a man sees in his wife the divine presence, he then sees God everywhere in the universe. This is the culmination of the spiritual life.

Ramakrishna himself was now convinced of his divine mission on earth and came to know that through him the Divine Mother would found a new religious order comprising those who would accept the doctrine of the Universal Religion which he had experienced. It was further revealed to him that anyone who had prayed to God sincerely, even once, as well as those who were passing through their final birth on earth, would accept him as their spiritual ideal and mould their lives according to his universal teaching.

The people around him were bewildered to see this transformation of a man whom they had ridiculed only a short while ago as insane. The young priest had become God's devotee; the devotee, an ascetic; the ascetic, a saint; the saint, a man of realization; and the man of realization, a new Prophet. Like the full-blown blossom attracting bees, Ramakrishna drew to him men and women of differing faith, intelligence, and social position. He gave generously to all from the inexhaustible storehouse of divine wisdom, and everyone felt uplifted in his presence. But the Master himself was not completely satisfied. He longed for young souls yet untouched by the world, who would renounce everything for the realization of God and the service of humanity. He was literally consumed with this longing. The talk of worldly people was tasteless to him. He

often compared such people to a mixture of milk and water with the latter pre-
ponderating, and said that he had become weary of trying to prepare thick
milk from that mixture. Evenings, when his anguish reached its limit, he would
climb the roof of a building near the temple and cry at the top of his voice:
"Come, my boys! Oh, where are you all? I cannot bear to live without you!" A
mother could not feel more intensely for her beloved children, a friend for his
dearest friend, or a lover for her sweetheart.

Shortly thereafter the young men destined to be his monastic disciples began
to arrive. And foremost among them was Narendranath.

RAMAKRISHNA AND NARENDRANATH

The first meeting at Dakshineswar between the Master and Narendra was
momentous. Śri Ramakrishna recognized instantaneously his future messenger.
Narendra, careless about his clothes and general appearance, was so unlike the
other young men who had accompanied him to the temple. His eyes were
impressive, partly indrawn, indicating a meditative mood. He sang a few songs,
and as usual poured into them his whole soul.

His first song was this:

> Let us go back once more, O mind, to our proper home!
> Here in this foreign land of earth
> Why should we wander aimlessly in stranger's guise?
> These living beings round about,
> And the five elements,
> Are strangers to you, all of them; none are your own.
> Why do you so forget yourself,
> In love with strangers, foolish mind?
> Why do you so forget your own?
>
> Mount the path of truth, O mind! Unflaggingly climb,
> With love as the lamp to light your way.
> As your provision on the journey, take with you
> The virtues, hidden carefully;
> For, like two highwaymen,
> Greed and delusion wait to rob you of your wealth.
> And keep beside you constantly,
> As guards to shelter you from harm,
> Calmness of mind and self-control.
>
> Companionship with holy men will be for you
> A welcome rest-house by the road;
> There rest your weary limbs awhile, asking your way,
> If ever you should be in doubt,
> Of him who watches there.
> If anything along the path should cause you fear,
> Then loudly shout the name of God;
> For He is ruler of that road,
> And even Death must bow to Him.

When the singing was over, Śri Ramakrishna suddenly grasped Narendra's
hand and took him into the northern porch. To Narendra's utter amazement,

the Master said with tears streaming down his cheeks: "Ah! You have come so late. How unkind of you to keep me waiting so long! My ears are almost scared listening to the cheap talk of worldly people. Oh, how I have been yearning to unburden my mind to one who will understand my thought!" Then with folded hands he said: "Lord! I know you are the ancient sage Nara—the Incarnation of Nārāyana—born on earth to remove the miseries of mankind." The rationalist Naren regarded these words as the meaningless jargon of an insane person. He was further dismayed when Śri Ramakrishna presently brought from his room some sweets and fed him with his own hands. But the Master nevertheless extracted from him a promise to visit Dakshineswar again.

They returned to the room and Naren asked the Master, "Sir, have you seen God?" Without a moment's hesitation the reply was given: "Yes, I have seen God. I see Him as I see you here, only more clearly. God can be seen. One can talk to Him. But who cares for God? People shed torrents of tears for their wives, children, wealth, and property, but who weeps for the vision of God? If one cries sincerely for God, one can surely see Him."

Narendra was astounded. For the first time, he was face to face with a man who asserted that he had seen God. For the first time, in fact, he was hearing that God could be seen. He could feel that Ramakrishna's words were uttered from the depths of an inner experience. They could not be doubted. Still he could not reconcile these words with Ramakrishna's strange conduct, which he had witnessed only a few minutes before. What puzzled Narendra further was Ramakrishna's normal behaviour in the presence of others. The young man returned to Calcutta bewildered, but yet with a feeling of inner peace.

During his second visit to the Master, Narendra had an even stranger experience. After a minute or two Śri Ramakrishna drew near him in an ecstatic mood, muttered some words, fixed his eyes on him, and placed his right foot on Naren's body. At this touch Naren saw, with eyes open, the walls, the room, the temple garden—nay, the whole world—vanishing, and even himself disappearing into a void. He felt sure that he was facing death. He cried in consternation: "What are you doing to me? I have my parents, brothers, and sisters at home."

The Master laughed and stroked Naren's chest, restoring him to his normal mood. He said, "All right, everything will happen in due time."

Narendra, completely puzzled, felt that Ramakrishna had cast a hypnotic spell upon him. But how could that have been? Did he not pride himself in the possession of an iron will? He felt disgusted that he should have been unable to resist the influence of a madman. Nonetheless he felt a great inner attraction for Śri Ramakrishna.

On his third visit Naren fared no better, though he tried his utmost to be on guard. Śri Ramakrishna took him to a neighbouring garden and, in a state of trance, touched him. Completely overwhelmed, Naren lost consciousness.

Śri Ramakrishna, referring later to this incident, said that after putting Naren into a state of unconsciousness, he had asked him many questions about his past, his mission in the world, and the duration of his present life. The answers had only confirmed what he himself had thought about these matters. Ramakrishna told his other disciples that Naren had attained perfection even before this birth; that he was an adept in meditation; and that the day Naren recognized his true self, he would give up the body by an act of will, through yoga. Often he was heard to say that Naren was a Saptarshi, one of the Seven Sages, who live in the realm of the Absolute. He narrated to them a vision he had had regarding the disciple's spiritual heritage.

Absorbed, one day, in samādhi, Ramakrishna had found that his mind was soaring high, going beyond the physical universe of the sun, moon, and stars, and passing into the subtle region of ideas. As it continued to ascend, the forms of gods and goddesses were left behind, and it crossed the luminous barrier separating the phenomenal universe from the Absolute, entering finally the transcendental realm. There Ramakrishna saw seven venerable sages absorbed in meditation. These, he thought, must have surpassed even the gods and goddesses in wisdom and holiness, and as he was admiring their unique spirituality he saw a portion of the undifferentiated Absolute become congealed, as it were, and take the form of a Divine Child. Clambering upon the lap of one of the sages and gently clasping his neck with His soft arms, the Child whispered something in his ear, and at this magic touch the sage awoke from meditation. He fixed his half-open eyes upon the wondrous Child, who said in great joy: "I am going down to earth. Won't you come with me?" With a benign look the sage expressed assent and returned into deep spiritual ecstasy. Ramakrishna was amazed to observe that a tiny portion of the sage, however, descended to earth, taking the form of light, which struck the house in Calcutta where Narendra's family lived, and when he saw Narendra for the first time, he at once recognized him as the incarnation of the sage. He also admitted that the Divine Child who brought about the descent of the rishi was none other than himself.

THE MASTER AND THE DISCIPLE

The meeting of Narendranath and Śri Ramakrishna was an important event in the lives of both. A storm had been raging in Narendra's soul when he came to Śri Ramakrishna, who himself had passed through a similar struggle but was now firmly anchored in peace as a result of his intimate communion with the Godhead and his realization of Brahman as the immutable essence of all things.

A genuine product of the Indian soil and thoroughly acquainted with the spiritual traditions of India, Śri Ramakrishna was ignorant of the modern way of thinking. But Narendra was the symbol of the modern spirit. Inquisitive, alert, and intellectually honest, he possessed an open mind and demanded rational proof before accepting any conclusion as valid. As a loyal member of the Brāhmo Samāj he was critical of image worship and the rituals of the Hindu religion. He did not feel the need of a guru, a human intermediary between God and man. He was even sceptical about the existence of such a person, who was said to be free from human limitations and to whom an aspirant was expected to surrender himself completely and offer worship as to God. Ramakrishna's visions of gods and goddesses he openly ridiculed, and called them hallucinations.

For five years Narendra closely watched the Master, never allowing himself to be influenced by blind faith, always testing the words and actions of Śri Ramakrishna in the crucible of reason. It cost him many sorrows and much anguish before he accepted Śri Ramakrishna as the guru and the ideal of his spiritual life. But when the acceptance came, it was wholehearted, final, and irrevocable. The Master, too, was overjoyed to find a disciple who doubted, and he knew that Naren was the one to carry his message to the world.

The inner process that gradually transformed the chrysalis of Narendra into a beautiful butterfly will for ever remain, like all deep spiritual mysteries, unknown to the outer world. People, however, noticed the growth of an intimate relationship between the loving, patient, and forgiving teacher and his imperious and stubborn disciple. The Master never once asked Naren to abandon reason. He met the challenge of Naren's intellect with his superior understanding, acquired through first-hand knowledge of the essence of things. When Naren's reasoning failed to solve the ultimate mystery, the teacher gave him the necessary insight. Thus, with infinite patience, love, and vigilance, he tamed the rebellious spirit, demanding complete obedience to moral and spiritual disciplines, without which the religious life cannot be built on a firm foundation.

The very presence of Narendranath would fill the Master's mind with indescribable joy and create ecstatic moods. He had already known, by many indications, of the disciple's future greatness, the manifestation of which awaited only the fullness of time. What others regarded in Naren as stubbornness or haughtiness appeared to Śri Ramakrishna as the expression of his manliness and self-reliance, born of his self-control and innate purity. He could not bear the slightest criticism of Naren and often said: "Let no one judge him hastily. People will never understand him fully."

Ramakrishna loved Narendranath because he saw him as the embodiment of Nārāyana, the Divine Spirit, undefiled by the foul breath of the world. But he was criticized for his attachment. Once a trouble-maker of twisted mind named Hazra, who lived with the Master at Dakshineswar, said to him, "If you long for Naren and the other youngsters all the time, when will you think of God?" The Master was distressed by this thought. But it was at once revealed to him that though God dwelt in all beings, He was especially manifest in a pure soul like Naren. Relieved of his worries, he then said: "Oh, what a fool Hazra is! How he unsettled my mind! But why blame the poor fellow? How could he know?"

Śri Ramakrishna was outspoken in Narendra's praise. This often embarrassed the young disciple, who would criticize the Master for what he termed a sort of infatuation. One day Ramakrishna said in the presence of Keshab Sen and the saintly Vijay Goswami, the two outstanding leaders of the Brāhmo Samāj: "If Keshab possesses one virtue which has made him world-famous, Naren is endowed with eighteen such virtues. I have seen in Keshab and Vijay the divine light burning like a candle flame, but in Naren it shines with the radiance of the sun."

Narendra, instead of feeling flattered by these compliments, became annoyed and sharply rebuked the Master for what he regarded as his foolhardiness. "I cannot help it," the Master protested. "Do you think these are my words? The Divine Mother showed me certain things about you, which I repeated. And She reveals to me nothing but the truth."

But Naren was hardly convinced. He was sure that these so-called revelations were pure illusions. He carefully explained to Śri Ramakrishna that, from the viewpoint of Western science and philosophy, very often a man is deceived by his mind, and that the chances of deception are greater when a personal attachment is involved. He said to the Master, "Since you love me and wish to see me great, these fancies naturally come to your mind."

The Master was perplexed. He prayed to the Divine Mother for light and was told: "Why do you care about what he says? In a short time he will accept your every word as true."

On another occasion, when the Master was similarly reprimanded by the disciple, he was reassured by the Divine Mother. Thereupon he said to Naren with a smile: "You are a rogue. I won't listen to you any more. Mother says that I love you because I see the Lord in you. The day I shall not see Him in you, I shall not be able to bear even the sight of you."

On account of his preoccupation with his studies, or for other reasons, Narendra could not come to Dakshineswar as often as Śri Ramakrishna wished. But the Master could hardly endure his prolonged absence. If the disciple had not visited him for a number of days, he would send someone to Calcutta to fetch him. Sometimes he went to Calcutta himself. One time, for example, Narendra remained away from Dakshineswar for several weeks; even the Master's eager importunities had failed to bring him. Śri Ramakrishna knew that he sang regularly at the prayer meetings of the Brāhmo Samāj, and so one day he made his way to the Brāhmo temple that the disciple attended. Narendra was singing as the Master entered the hall, and when he heard Narendra's voice, Śri Ramakrishna fell into a deep ecstasy. The eyes of the congregation turned to him, and soon a commotion followed. Narendra hurried to his side. One of the Brāhmo leaders, in order to stop the excitement, put out the lights. The young disciple, realizing that the Master's sudden appearance was the cause of the disturbance, sharply took him to task. The latter answered, with tears in his eyes, that he had simply not been able to keep himself away from Narendra.

On another occasion a comical incident occurred that reveals a different side of Narendra's character. That day, too, Śri Ramakrishna had been unable to bear Narendra's absence, and he had gone to Calcutta to visit the disciple at his own home. He was told that Naren was studying in an attic that could be reached only by a steep ladder. A disciple named Latu, who was a sort of caretaker of the Master, had accompanied him, and with Latu's help Śri Ramakrishna climbed a few steps of the ladder. Narendra opened the door, and at the very sight of him Śri Ramakrishna exclaimed, "Naren, my beloved!" and went into ecstasy. With considerable difficulty the two disciples helped him to finish climbing the ladder, and as he entered the room the Master fell into deep samādhi. A fellow student who was with Naren at the time and did not know anything of religious trances, asked Naren in bewilderment, "Who is this man?"

"Never mind," replied Naren. "He is an *idiot*. You had better go home now."

After a while Śri Ramakrishna regained ordinary consciousness. Latu, who was illiterate, had heard the English word *idiot* and remembered it. He now asked Naren its meaning. When the word was explained to him, he flew into a rage, asking Naren how he dared apply such an insulting word to Śri Ramakrishna. Naren tried to pacify him and declared that since his friend did not have the slightest idea about ecstasy, and since he could not possibly have explained to him the meaning of samādhi, he had thought that the easiest way of avoiding an endless discussion with his friend was simply to describe Śri Ramakrishna as an idiot.

Naren often said that the "Old Man," meaning Ramakrishna, bound the disciple for ever to him by his love. "What do worldly men," he remarked, "know about love? They only make a show of it. The Master alone loves us genuinely." Naren, in return, bore a deep love for Śri Ramakrishna, though he seldom expressed it in words. He took delight in criticizing the Master's spiritual experiences as evidences of a lack of self-control. He made fun of his worship of Kāli.

"Why do you come here," Śri Ramakrishna once asked him, "if you do not accept Kāli, my Mother?"

"Bah! Must I accept Her," Naren retorted, "simply because I come to see you? I come to you because I love you."

"All right," said the Master, "ere long you will not only accept my blessed Mother, but weep in Her name."

Turning to his other disciples, he said: "This boy has no faith in the forms of God and tells me that my visions are pure imagination. But he is a fine lad of pure mind. He does not accept anything without direct evidence. He has studied much and cultivated great discrimination. He has fine judgement."

TRAINING OF THE DISCIPLE

It is hard to say when Naren actually accepted Śri Ramakrishna as his guru. As far as the Master was concerned, the spiritual relationship was established at the first meeting at Dakshineswar, when he had touched Naren, stirring him to his inner depths. From that moment he had implicit faith in the disciple and bore him a great love. But he encouraged Naren in the independence of his thinking. The love and faith of the Master acted as a restraint upon the impetuous youth and became his strong shield against the temptations of the world. By gradual steps the disciple was then led from doubt to certainty, and from anguish of mind to the bliss of the Spirit. This, however, was not an easy attainment.

Śri Ramakrishna, perfect teacher that he was, never laid down identical disciplines for disciples of diverse temperaments. He did not insist that Narendra should follow strict rules about food, nor did he ask him to believe in the reality of the gods and goddesses of Hindu mythology. It was not necessary for Narendra's philosophic mind to pursue the disciplines of concrete worship. But a strict eye was kept on Naren's practice of discrimination, detachment, self-control, and regular meditation. Śri Ramakrishna enjoyed Naren's vehement arguments with the other devotees regarding the dogmas and creeds of religion and was delighted to hear him tear to shreds their unquestioning beliefs. But when, as often happened, Naren teased the gentle Rakhal for showing reverence to the Divine Mother Kāli, the Master would not tolerate these attempts to unsettle the brother disciple's faith in the forms of God.

As a member of the Brāhmo Samāj, Narendra accepted its doctrine of monotheism and the Personal God. He also believed in the natural depravity of man. Such doctrines of non-dualistic Vedānta as the divinity of the soul and the oneness of existence he regarded as blasphemy; the view that man is one with God appeared to him pure nonsense. When the Master warned him against thus limiting God's infinitude and asked him to pray to God to reveal to him His true nature, Narendra smiled. One day he was making fun of Śri Ramakrishna's non-dualism before a friend and said, "What can be more absurd than to say that this jug is God, this cup is God, and that we too are God?" Both roared with laughter.

Just then the Master appeared. Coming to learn the cause of their fun, he gently touched Naren and plunged into deep samādhi. The touch produced a magic effect, and Narendra entered a new realm of consciousness. He saw the whole universe permeated by the Divine Spirit and returned home in a daze. While eating his meal, he felt the presence of Brahman in everything— in the food, and in himself too. While walking in the street, he saw the carriages, the horses, the crowd, and himself as if made of the same substance. After a few days the intensity of the vision lessened to some extent, but still he could see the world only as a dream. While strolling in the public park of Calcutta, he struck his head against the iron railings, several times, to see if they were real or a mere illusion of the mind. Thus he got a glimpse of non-dualism, the fullest realization of which was to come only later, at the Cossipore garden.

Śri Ramakrishna was always pleased when his disciples put to the test his statements or behaviour before accepting his teachings. He would say: "Test me as the money-changers test their coins. You must not believe me without testing me thoroughly." The disciples often heard him say that his nervous system had undergone a complete change as a result of his spiritual experiences, and that he could not bear the touch of any metal, such as gold or silver. One day, during his absence in Calcutta, Narendra hid a coin under Ramakrishna's bed. After his return, when the Master sat on the bed, he started up in pain as if stung by an insect. The mattress was examined and the hidden coin was found.

Naren, on the other hand, was often tested by the Master. One day, when he entered the Master's room, he was completely ignored. Not a word of greeting was uttered. A week later he came back and met with the same indifference, and during the third and fourth visits saw no evidence of any thawing of the Master's frigid attitude.

At the end of a month Śri Ramakrishna said to Naren, "I have not exchanged a single word with you all this time, and still you come."

The disciple replied: "I come to Dakshineswar because I love you and want to see you. I do not come here to hear your words."

The Master was overjoyed. Embracing the disciple, he said: "I was only testing you. I wanted to see if you would stay away on account of my outward indifference. Only a man of your inner strength could put up with such indifference on my part. Anyone else would have left me long ago."

On one occasion Śri Ramakrishna proposed to transfer to Narendranath many of the spiritual powers that he had acquired as a result of his ascetic disciplines and visions of God. Naren had no doubt concerning the Master's possessing such powers. He asked if they would help him to realize God. Śri Ramakrishna replied in the negative but added that they might assist him in his future work as a spiritual teacher. "Let me realize God first," said Naren, "and then I shall perhaps know whether or not I want supernatural powers. If I accept them now, I may forget God, make selfish use of them, and thus come to grief." Śri Ramakrishna was highly pleased to see his chief disciple's single-minded devotion.

NARENDRA'S STRUGGLE

Several factors were at work to mould the personality of young Narendranath. Foremost of these were his inborn spiritual tendencies, which were beginning to show themselves under the influence of Śri Ramakrishna, but against which his rational mind put up a strenuous fight. Second was his habit of thinking highly and acting nobly, disciplines acquired from a mother steeped in the spiritual heritage of India. Third were his broadmindedness and regard for truth wherever found, and his sceptical attitude towards the religious beliefs and social conventions of the Hindu society of his time. These he had learnt from his English-educated father, and he was strengthened in them through his own contact with Western culture.

With the introduction in India of English education during the middle of the nineteenth century, as we have seen, Western science, history, and philosophy were studied in the Indian colleges and universities. The educated Hindu youths, allured by the glamour, began to mould their thought according to this new light, and Narendra could not escape the influence. He developed a great respect for the analytical scientific method and subjected many of the Master's spiritual visions to such scrutiny. The English poets stirred his feelings, especially Wordsworth and Shelley, and he took a course in Western medical science to understand the functioning of the nervous system, particularly the brain and spinal cord, in order to find out the secrets of Śri Ramakrishna's trances. But all this only deepened his inner turmoil.

John Stuart Mill's *Three Essays on Religion* upset his boyish theism and the easy optimism imbibed from the Brāhmo Samāj. The presence of evil in nature and man haunted him and he could not reconcile it at all with the goodness of an omnipotent Creator. Hume's scepticism and Herbert Spencer's doctrine of the Unknowable filled his mind with a settled philosophical agnosticism. After the wearing out of his first emotional freshness and naïveté, he was beset with a certain dryness and incapacity for the old prayers and devotions. He was filled with an ennui which he concealed, however, under his jovial nature. Music, at this difficult stage of his life, rendered him great help; for it moved him as nothing else and gave him a glimpse of unseen realities that often brought tears to his eyes.

Narendra did not have much patience with humdrum reading, nor did he care to absorb knowledge from books as much as from living communion and personal experience. He wanted life to be kindled by life, and thought kindled by thought. He studied Shelley under a college friend, Brajendranath Seal, who later became the leading Indian philosopher of his time, and deeply felt with the poet his pantheism, impersonal love, and vision of a glorified millennial humanity. The universe, no longer a mere lifeless, loveless mechanism, was seen to contain a spiritual principle of unity. Brajendranath, moreover, tried to present him with a synthesis of the Supreme Brahman of Vedānta, the Universal Reason of Hegel, and the gospel of Liberty, Equality, and Fraternity of the French Revolution. By accepting as the principle of morals the sovereignty of Universal Reason and the negation of the individual, Narendra achieved an intellectual victory over scepticism and materialism, but no peace of mind.

Narendra now had to face a new difficulty. The "ballet of bloodless categories" of Hegel and his creed of Universal Reason required of Naren a suppression of the yearning and susceptibility of his artistic nature and joyous temperament, the destruction of the cravings of his keen and acute senses, and the smothering of his free and merry conviviality. This amounted almost to killing his own true self. Further, he could not find in such a philosophy any help in the struggle of a hot-blooded youth against the cravings of the passions, which appeared to him as impure, gross, and carnal. Some of his musical associates were men of loose morals for whom he felt a bitter and undisguised contempt.

Narendra therefore asked his friend Brajendra if the latter knew the way of deliverance from the bondage of the senses, but he was told only to rely upon Pure Reason and to identify the self with it, and was promised that through this he would experience an ineffable peace. The friend was a Platonic transcendentalist and did not have faith in what he called the artificial prop of grace, or the mediation of a guru. But the problems and difficulties of Narendra were very different from those of his intellectual friend. He found that mere philosophy was impotent in the hour of temptation and in the struggle for his soul's deliverance. He felt the need of a hand to save, to uplift, to protect—a śakti or power outside his rational mind that would transform his impotence into strength and glory. He wanted a flesh-and-blood reality established in peace and certainty, in short, a living guru, who, by embodying perfection in the flesh, would compose the commotion of his soul.

The leaders of the Brāhmo Samāj, as well as those of the other religious sects, had failed. It was only Ramakrishna who spoke to him with authority, as none had spoken before, and by his power brought peace into the troubled soul and healed the wounds of the spirit. At first Naren feared that the serenity that possessed him in the presence of the Master was illusory, but his misgivings were gradually vanquished by the calm assurance transmitted to him by Ramakrishna out of his own experience of Satchidānanda Brahman—Existence, Knowledge, and Bliss Absolute.[1]

Narendra could not but recognize the contrast of the *Sturm und Drang* of

[1] This account of the struggle of Naren's collegiate days summarizes an article on Swami Vivekananda by Brajendranath Seal, published in the *Life of Swami Vivekananda* by the Advaita Āśrama, Mayavati, India.

his soul with the serene bliss in which Śri Ramakrishna was always bathed. He begged the Master to teach him meditation, and Śri Ramakrishna's reply was to him a source of comfort and strength. The Master said: "God listens to our sincere prayer. I can swear that you can see God and talk with Him as intensely as you see me and talk with me. You can hear His words and feel His touch." Further the Master declared: "You may not believe in divine forms, but if you believe in an Ultimate Reality who is the Regulator of the universe, you can pray to Him thus: 'O God, I do not know Thee. Be gracious to reveal to me Thy real nature.' He will certainly listen to you if your prayer is sincere."

Narendra, intensifying his meditation under the Master's guidance, began to lose consciousness of the body and to feel an inner peace, and this peace would linger even after the meditation was over. Frequently he felt the separation of the body from the soul. Strange perceptions came to him in dreams, producing a sense of exaltation that persisted after he awoke. The guru was performing his task in an inscrutable manner. Narendra's friends observed only his outer struggle; but the real transformation was known to the teacher alone— or perhaps to the disciple too.

BEREAVEMENT

In 1884, when Narendranath was preparing for the B.A. examination, his family was struck by a calamity. His father suddenly died, and the mother and children were plunged into great grief. For Viswanath, a man of generous nature, had lived beyond his means, and his death burdened the family with a heavy debt. Creditors, like hungry wolves, began to prowl about the door, and to make matters worse, certain relatives brought a lawsuit for the partition of the ancestral home. Though they lost it, Narendra was faced, thereafter, with poverty. As the eldest male member of the family, he had to find the wherewithal for the feeding of seven or eight mouths. He attended the law classes clad in coarse clothes, barefoot, and hungry, and often refused invitations for dinner from friends, remembering his starving mother, brothers, and sisters at home. He would skip family meals on the fictitious plea that he had already eaten at a friend's house, so that the people at home might receive a larger share of the scanty food. The Datta family was proud and would not dream of soliciting help from outsiders. With his companions Narendra was his usual gay self. His rich friends no doubt noticed his pale face, but they did nothing to help. Only one friend sent occasional anonymous aid, and Narendra remained grateful to him for life. Meanwhile, all his efforts to find employment failed. Some friends who earned money in a dishonest way asked him to join them, and a rich woman sent him an immoral proposal, promising to put an end to his financial distress. But Narendra gave to these a blunt rebuff. Sometimes he would wonder if the world were not the handiwork of the Devil—for how could one account for so much suffering in God's creation?

One day, after a futile search for a job, he sat down, weary and footsore, in the big park of Calcutta. There some friends joined him and one of them sang a song, perhaps to console him, describing God's abundant grace.

Furiously Naren said: "Will you please stop that song? Such fancies are, no doubt, pleasing to those who are born with silver spoons in their mouths.

Yes, there was a time when I, too, thought like that. But today these ideas appear to me a mockery."

The friends were bewildered.

One morning, as usual, Naren left his bed repeating God's name, and was about to go out in search of work after seeking divine blessings. His mother heard the prayer and said bitterly: "Hush, you fool! You have been crying yourself hoarse for God since your childhood. Tell me what has God done for you?" Evidently the crushing poverty at home was too much for the pious mother.

These words stung Naren to the quick. A doubt crept into his mind about God's existence and His Providence.

It was not in Naren's nature to hide his feelings. He argued before his friends and the devotees of Śri Ramakrishna about God's non-existence and the futility of prayer even if God existed. His over-zealous friends thought he had become an atheist and ascribed to him many unmentionable crimes, which he had supposedly committed to forget his misery. Some of the devotees of the Master shared these views. Narendra cried in anguish and roared with anger, mortified to think that they could believe him to have sunk so low. He became hardened and justified drinking and the other dubious pleasures resorted to by miserable people for a respite from their suffering. He said, further, that he himself would not hesitate to follow such a course if he were assured of its efficacy. Openly asserting that only cowards believed in God for fear of hell-fire, he argued the possibility of God's non-existence and quoted Western philosophers in support of his position. And when the devotees of the Master became convinced that he was hopelessly lost, he felt a sort of inner satisfaction.

A garbled report of the matter reached Śri Ramakrishna, and Narendra thought that perhaps the Master, too, doubted his moral integrity. The very idea revived his anger. "Never mind," he said to himself. "If good or bad opinion of a man rests on such flimsy grounds, I don't care."

But Narendra was mistaken. For one day Bhavanath, a devotee of the Master and an intimate friend of Narendra, cast aspersions on the latter's character, and the Master said angrily: "Stop, you fool! The Mother has told me that it is simply not true. I shan't look at your face if you speak to me again that way."

The fact was that Narendra could not, in his heart of hearts, disbelieve in God. He remembered the spiritual visions of his own boyhood and many others that he had experienced in the company of the Master. Inwardly he longed to understand God and His ways. And one day he gained this understanding. It happened in the following way:

He had been out since morning in a soaking rain in search of employment, having had neither food nor rest for the whole day. That evening he sat down on the porch of a house by the roadside, exhausted. He was in a daze. Thoughts began to flit before his mind, which he could not control. Suddenly he had a strange vision, which lasted almost the whole night. He felt that veil after veil was removed from before his soul, and he understood the reconciliation of God's justice with His mercy. He came to know—but he never told how—that misery could exist in the creation of a compassionate God without impairing His sovereign power or touching man's real self. He understood the meaning of it all and was at peace. Just before daybreak, refreshed both in body and in mind, he returned home.

This revelation profoundly impressed Narendranath. He became indifferent to people's opinion and was convinced that he was not born to lead an ordinary worldly life, enjoying the love of a wife and children and physical luxuries. He recalled how the several proposals of marriage made by his relatives had come to nothing, and he ascribed all this to God's will. The peace and freedom of the monastic life cast a spell upon him. He determined to renounce the world, and set a date for this act. Then, coming to learn that Sri Ramakrishna would visit Calcutta that very day, he was happy to think that he could embrace the life of a wandering monk with his guru's blessings.

When they met, the Master persuaded his disciple to accompany him to Dakshineswar. As they arrived in his room, Sri Ramakrishna went into an ecstatic mood and sang a song, while tears bathed his eyes. The words of the song clearly indicated that the Master knew of the disciple's secret wish. When other devotees asked him about the cause of his grief, Sri Ramakrishna said, "Oh, never mind, it is something between me and Naren, and nobody else's business." At night he called Naren to his side and said with great feeling: "I know you are born for Mother's work. I also know that you will be a monk. But stay in the world as long as I live, for my sake at least." He wept again.

Next day Naren procured a temporary job, which was sufficient to provide a hand-to-mouth living for the family.

One day Narendra asked himself why, since Kāli, the Divine Mother, listened to Sri Ramakrishna's prayers, should not the Master pray to Her to relieve his poverty. When he spoke to Sri Ramakrishna about this idea, the latter inquired why he did not pray himself to Kāli, adding that Narendranath suffered because he did not acknowledge Kāli as the Sovereign Mistress of the universe.

"Today," the Master continued, "is a Tuesday, an auspicious day for the Mother's worship. Go to Her shrine in the evening, prostrate yourself before the image, and pray to Her for any boon; it will be granted. Mother Kāli is the embodiment of Love and Compassion. She is the Power of Brahman. She gives birth to the world by Her mere wish. She fulfils every sincere prayer of Her devotees."

At nine o'clock in the evening, Narendranath went to the Kāli temple. Passing through the courtyard, he felt within himself a surge of emotion, and his heart leapt with joy in anticipation of the vision of the Divine Mother. Entering the temple, he cast his eyes upon the image and found the stone figure to be nothing else but the living Goddess, the Divine Mother Herself, ready to give him any boon he wanted—either a happy worldly life or the joy of spiritual freedom. He was in ecstasy. He prayed for the boon of wisdom, discrimination, renunciation, and Her uninterrupted vision, but forgot to ask the Deity for money. He felt great peace within as he returned to the Master's room, and when asked if he had prayed for money, was startled. He said that he had forgotten all about it. The Master told him to go to the temple again and pray to the Divine Mother to satisfy his immediate needs. Naren did as he was bidden, but again forgot his mission. The same thing happened a third time.

Then Naren suddenly realized that Śri Ramakrishna himself had made him forget to ask the Divine Mother for worldly things; perhaps he wanted Naren to lead a life of renunciation. So he now asked Śri Ramakrishna to do something for the family. The Master told the disciple that it was not Naren's destiny to enjoy a worldly life, but assured him that the family would be able to eke out a simple existence.

The above incident left a deep impression upon Naren's mind; it enriched his spiritual life, for he gained a new understanding of the Godhead and Its ways in the phenomenal universe. Naren's idea of God had hitherto been confined either to that of a vague Impersonal Reality or to that of an extra-cosmic Creator removed from the world. He now realized that the Godhead is immanent in the creation, that after projecting the universe from within Itself, It has entered into all created entities as life and consciousness, whether manifest or latent. This same immanent Spirit, or the World Soul, when regarded as a person creating, preserving, and destroying the universe, is called the Personal God, and is worshipped by different religions through such a relationship as that of father, mother, king, or beloved. These relationships, he came to understand, have their appropriate symbols, and Kāli is one of them.

Embodying in Herself creation and destruction, love and terror, life and death, Kāli is the symbol of the total universe. The eternal cycle of the manifestation and non-manifestation of the universe is the breathing-out and breathing-in of this Divine Mother. In one aspect She is death, without which there cannot be life. One of Her hands is smeared with blood, since without blood the picture of the phenomenal universe is not complete. To the wicked who have transgressed Her laws, She is the embodiment of terror, and to the virtuous, the benign Mother. Before creation She contains within Her womb the seed of the universe, which is left from the previous cycle. After the manifestation of the universe She becomes its preserver and nourisher, and at the end of the cycle She draws it back within Herself and remains as the undifferentiated Śakti, the creative power of Brahman. She is non-different from Brahman. When free from the acts of creation, preservation, and destruction, the Spirit, in Its acosmic aspect, is called Brahman; otherwise It is known as the World Soul or the Divine Mother of the universe. She is therefore the doorway to the realization of the Absolute; She is the Absolute. To the daring devotee who wants to see the transcendental Absolute, She reveals that form by withdrawing Her garment of the phenomenal universe. Brahman is Her transcendental aspect. She is the Great Fact of the universe, the totality of created beings. She is the Ruler and the Controller.

All this had previously been beyond Narendra's comprehension. He had accepted the reality of the phenomenal world and yet denied the reality of Kāli. He had been conscious of hunger and thirst, pain and pleasure, and the other characteristics of the world, and yet he had not accepted Kāli, who controlled them all. That was why he had suffered. But on that auspicious Tuesday evening the scales dropped from his eyes. He accepted Kāli as the Divine Mother of the universe. He became Her devotee.

Many years later he wrote to an American lady: "Kāli worship is my especial fad." But he did not preach Her in public, because he thought that all that modern man required was to be found in the Upanishads. Further, he realized that the Kāli symbol would not be understood by universal humanity.

IN THE COMPANY OF THE MASTER

Narendra enjoyed the company of the Master for six years, during which time his spiritual life was moulded. Śri Ramakrishna was a wonderful teacher in every sense of the word. Without imposing his ideas upon anyone, he taught more by the silent influence of his inner life than by words or even by personal example. To live near him demanded of the disciple purity of thought and concentration of mind. He often appeared to his future monastic followers as their friend and playmate. Through fun and merriment he always kept before them the shining ideal of God-realization. He would not allow any deviation from bodily and mental chastity, nor any compromise with truth and renunciation. Everything else he left to the will of the Divine Mother.

Narendra was his "marked" disciple, chosen by the Lord for a special mission. Śri Ramakrishna kept a sharp eye on him, though he appeared to give the disciple every opportunity to release his pent-up physical and mental energy. Before him, Naren often romped about like a young lion cub in the presence of a firm but indulgent parent. His spiritual radiance often startled the Master, who saw that māyā, the Great Enchantress, could not approach within "ten feet" of that blazing fire.

Narendra always came to the Master in the hours of his spiritual difficulties. One time he complained that he could not meditate in the morning on account of the shrill note of a whistle from a neighbouring mill, and was advised by the Master to concentrate on the very sound of the whistle. In a short time he overcame the distraction. Another time he found it difficult to forget the body at the time of meditation. Śri Ramakrishna sharply pressed the space between Naren's eyebrows and asked him to concentrate on that sensation. The disciple found this method effective.

Witnessing the religious ecstasy of several devotees, Narendra one day said to the Master that he too wanted to experience it. "My child," he was told, "when a huge elephant enters a small pond, a great commotion is set up, but when it plunges into the Ganges, the river shows very little agitation. These devotees are like small ponds; a little experience makes their feelings flow over the brim. But you are a huge river."

Another day the thought of excessive spiritual fervour frightened Naren. The Master reassured him by saying: "God is like an ocean of sweetness; wouldn't you dive into it? Suppose there is a bottle, with a wide mouth, filled with syrup, and that you are a fly, hungry for the sweet liquid. How would you like to drink it?" Narendra said that he would sit on the edge of the bottle, otherwise he might be drowned in the syrup and lose his life. "But," the Master said, "you must not forget that I am talking of the Ocean of Satchidānanda, the Ocean of Immortality. Here one need not be afraid of death. Only fools say that one should not have too much of divine ecstasy. Can anybody carry to excess the love of God? You must dive deep in the Ocean of God."

On one occasion Narendra and some of his brother disciples were vehemently arguing about God's nature—whether He was personal or impersonal, whether

Divine Incarnation was fact or myth, and so forth and so on. Narendra silenced his opponents by his sharp power of reasoning and felt jubilant at his triumph. Śri Ramakrishna enjoyed the discussion and after it was over sang in an ecstatic mood:

> How are you trying, O my mind, to know the nature of God?
> You are groping like a madman locked in a dark room.
> He is grasped through ecstatic love; how can you fathom Him without it?
> Only through affirmation, never negation, can you know Him;
> Neither through Veda nor through Tantra nor the six darśanas.

All fell silent, and Narendra realized the inability of the intellect to fathom God's mystery.

In his heart of hearts Naren was a lover of God. Pointing to his eyes, Ramakrishna said that only a bhakta possessed such a tender look; the eyes of the jnāni were generally dry. Many a time, in his later years, Narendra said, comparing his own spiritual attitude with that of the Master: "He was a jnāni within, but a bhakta without; but I am a bhakta within, and a jnāni without." He meant that Ramakrishna's gigantic intellect was hidden under a thin layer of devotion, and Narendra's devotional nature was covered by a cloak of knowledge.

We have already referred to the great depth of Śri Ramakrishna's love for his beloved disciple. He was worried about the distress of Naren's family and one day asked a wealthy devotee if he could not help Naren financially. Naren's pride was wounded and he mildly scolded the Master. The latter said with tears in his eyes: "O my Naren! I can do anything for you, even beg from door to door." Narendra was deeply moved but said nothing. Many days after, he remarked, "The Master made me his slave by his love for me."

This great love of Śri Ramakrishna enabled Naren to face calmly the hardships of life. Instead of hardening into a cynic, he developed a mellowness of heart. But, as will be seen later, Naren to the end of his life was often misunderstood by his friends. A bold thinker, he was far ahead of his time. Once he said: "Why should I expect to be understood? It is enough that they love me. After all, who am I? The Mother knows best. She can do Her own work. Why should I think myself to be indispensable?"

The poverty at home was not an altogether unmitigated evil. It drew out another side of Naren's character. He began to feel intensely for the needy and afflicted. Had he been nurtured in luxury, the Master used to say, he would perhaps have become a different person—a statesman, a lawyer, an orator, or a social reformer. But instead, he dedicated his life to the service of humanity.

Śri Ramakrishna had had the prevision of Naren's future life of renunciation. Therefore he was quite alarmed when he came to know of the various plans made by Naren's relatives for his marriage. Prostrating himself in the shrine of Kāli, he prayed repeatedly: "O Mother! Do break up these plans. Do not let him sink in the quagmire of the world." He closely watched Naren and warned him whenever he discovered the trace of an impure thought in his mind.

Naren's keen mind understood the subtle implications of Śri Ramakrishna's teachings. One day the Master said that the three salient disciplines of Vaishnavism were love of God's name, service to the devotees, and compassion for all living beings. But he did not like the word compassion and said to the devotees: "How foolish to speak of compassion! Man is an insignificant worm crawling on the earth—and he to show compassion to others! This is absurd. It must not be compassion, but service to all. Recognize them as God's manifestations and serve them."

The other devotees heard the words of the Master but could hardly understand their significance. Naren, however, fathomed the meaning. Taking his young friends aside, he said that Śri Ramakrishna's remarks had thrown wonderful light on the philosophy of non-dualism with its discipline of non-attachment, and on that of dualism with its discipline of love. The two were not really in conflict. A non-dualist did not have to make his heart dry as sand, nor did he have to run away from the world. As Brahman alone existed in all men, a non-dualist must love all and serve all. Love, in the true sense of the word, is not possible unless one sees God in others. Naren said that the Master's words also reconciled the paths of knowledge and action. An illumined person did not have to remain inactive; he could commune with Brahman through service to other embodied beings, who also are embodiments of Brahman.

"If it be the will of God," Naren concluded, "I shall one day proclaim this noble truth before the world at large. I shall make it the common property of all—the wise and the fool, the rich and the poor, the brāhmin and the pariah."

Years later he expressed these sentiments in a noble poem which concluded with the following words:

> Thy God is here before thee now,
> Revealed in all these myriad forms:
> Rejecting them, where seekest thou
> His presence? He who freely shares
> His love with every living thing
> Proffers true service unto God.

It was Śri Ramakrishna who re-educated Narendranath in the essentials of Hinduism. He, the fulfilment of the spiritual aspirations of the three hundred millions of Hindus for the past three thousand years, was the embodiment of the Hindu faith. The beliefs Narendra had learnt on his mother's lap had been shattered by a collegiate education, but the young man now came to know that Hinduism does not consist of dogmas or creeds; it is an inner experience, deep and inclusive, which respects all faiths, all thoughts, all efforts, and all realizations. Unity in diversity is its ideal.

Narendra further learnt that religion is a vision which, at the end, transcends all barriers of caste and race and breaks down the limitations of time and space. He learnt from the Master that the Personal God and worship through symbols ultimately lead the devotee to the realization of complete oneness with the Deity. The Master taught him the divinity of the soul, the non-duality of the Godhead, the unity of existence, and the harmony of religions. He showed Naren by his own example how a man in this very life could reach perfection, and the disciple found that the Master had realized the same God-consciousness by following the diverse disciplines of Hinduism, Christianity, and Islam.

One day the Master, in an ecstatic mood, said to the devotees: "There are many opinions and many ways. I have seen them all and do not like them any more. The devotees of different faiths quarrel among themselves. Let me tell you something. You are my own people. There are no strangers around. I clearly see that God is the whole and I am a part of Him. He is the Lord and I am His servant. And sometimes I think He is I and I am He."

Narendra regarded Śri Ramakrishna as the embodiment of the spirit of religion and did not bother to know whether or not he was an Incarnation of God. He was reluctant to cast the Master in any theological mould. It was enough for Naren if he could see through the vista of Ramakrishna's spiritual experiences all the aspects of the Godhead.

How did Narendra impress the other devotees of the Master, especially the youngsters? He was their idol. They were awed by his intellect and fascinated by his personality. In appearance he was a dynamic youth, overflowing with vigour and vitality, having a physical frame slightly over middle height and somewhat thickset in the shoulders. He was graceful without being feminine. He had a strong jaw, suggesting his staunch will and fixed determination. The chest was expansive, and the breadth of the head towards the front signified high mental power and development. But the most remarkable thing about him was his eyes, which Śri Ramakrishna compared to lotus petals. They were prominent but not protruding, and part of the time their gaze was indrawn, suggesting the habit of deep meditation; their colour varied according to the feeling of the moment. Sometimes they would be luminous in profundity, and sometimes they sparkled in merriment. Endowed with the native grace of an animal, he was free in his movements. He walked sometimes with a slow gait and sometimes with rapidity, always a part of his mind absorbed in deep thought. And it was a delight to hear his resonant voice, either in conversation or in music.

But when Naren was serious his face often frightened his friends. In a heated discussion his eyes glowed. If immersed in his own thoughts, he created such an air of aloofness that no one dared to approach him. Subject to various moods, sometimes he showed utter impatience with his environment, and sometimes a tenderness that melted everybody's heart. His smile was bright and infectious. To some he was a happy dreamer, to some he lived in a real world rich with love and beauty, but to all he unfailingly appeared a scion of an aristocratic home.

And how did the Master regard his beloved disciple? To quote his own words:

"Narendra belongs to a very high plane—the realm of the Absolute. He has a manly nature. So many devotees come here, but there is no one like him.

"Every now and then I take stock of the devotees. I find that some are like lotuses with ten petals, some like lotuses with a hundred petals. But among lotuses Narendra is a thousand-petalled one.

"Other devotees may be like pots or pitchers; but Narendra is a huge water-barrel.

"Others may be like pools or tanks; but Narendra is a huge reservoir like the Hāldārpukur.

"Among fish, Narendra is a huge red-eyed carp; others are like minnows or smelts or sardines.

THE TEMPLE OF KĀLI AT DAKSHINESWAR

Śri Ramakrishna

THE HOLY MOTHER

The Cossipore Garden House

"Narendra is a 'very big receptacle,' one that can hold many things. He is like a bamboo with a big hollow space inside.

"Narendra is not under the control of anything. He is not under the control of attachment or sense pleasures. He is like a male pigeon. If you hold a male pigeon by its beak, it breaks away from you; but the female pigeon keeps still. I feel great strength when Narendra is with me in a gathering."

RAMAKRISHNA'S ILLNESS AND DEATH

Sometime about the middle of 1885 Śri Ramakrishna showed the first symptoms of a throat ailment that later was diagnosed as cancer. Against the advice of the physicians, he continued to give instruction to spiritual seekers, and to fall into frequent trances. Both of these practices aggravated the illness. For the convenience of the physicians and the devotees, he was at first removed to a house in the northern section of Calcutta and then to a garden house at Cossipore, a suburb of the city. Narendra and the other young disciples took charge of nursing him. Disregarding the wishes of their guardians, the boys gave up their studies or neglected their duties at home, at least temporarily, in order to devote themselves heart and soul to the service of the Master. His wife, known among the devotees as the Holy Mother, looked after the cooking; the older devotees met the expenses. All regarded this service to the guru as a blessing and privilege.

Narendra time and again showed his keen insight and mature judgement during Śri Ramakrishna's illness. Many of the devotees, who looked upon the Master as God's Incarnation and therefore refused to see in him any human frailty, began to give a supernatural interpretation of his illness. They believed that it had been brought about by the will of the Divine Mother or the Master himself to fulfil an inscrutable purpose, and that it would be cured without any human effort after the purpose was fulfilled. Narendra said, however, that since Śri Ramakrishna was a combination of God and man the physical element in him was subject to such laws of nature as birth, growth, decay, and destruction. He refused to give the Master's disease, a natural phenomenon, any supernatural explanation. Nonetheless, he was willing to shed his last drop of blood in the service of Śri Ramakrishna.

Emotion plays an important part in the development of the spiritual life. While intellect removes the obstacles, it is emotion that gives the urge to the seeker to move forward. But mere emotionalism without the disciplines of discrimination and renunciation often leads him astray. He often uses it as a short-cut to trance or ecstasy. Śri Ramakrishna, no doubt, danced and wept while singing God's name and experienced frequent trances; but behind his emotion there was the long practice of austerities and renunciation. His devotees had not witnessed the practice of his spiritual disciplines. Some of them, especially the elderly householders, began to display ecstasies accompanied by tears and physical contortions, which in many cases, as later appeared, were the result of careful rehearsal at home or mere imitation of Śri Ramakrishna's genuine trances. Some of the devotees, who looked upon the Master as a Divine Incarnation, thought that he had assumed their responsibilities, and therefore they relaxed their own efforts. Others began to speculate about the part each of them was destined to play in the new dispensation of Śri Ramakrishna. In short, those who showed the highest emotionalism posed as the most spiritually advanced.

Narendra's alert mind soon saw this dangerous trend in their lives. He began to make fun of the elders and warned his young brother disciples about the harmful effect of indulging in such outbursts. Real spirituality, he told them over and over again, was the eradication of worldly tendencies and the development of man's higher nature. He derided their tears and trances as symptoms of nervous disorder, which should be corrected by the power of the will, and, if necessary, by nourishing food and proper medical treatment. Very often, he said, unwary devotees of God fall victims to mental and physical breakdown. "Of one hundred persons who take up the spiritual life," he grimly warned, "eighty turn out to be charlatans, fifteen insane, and only five, maybe, get a glimpse of the real truth. Therefore, beware." He appealed to their inner strength and admonished them to keep away from all sentimental nonsense. He described to the young disciples Śri Ramakrishna's uncompromising self-control, passionate yearning for God, and utter renunciation of attachment to the world, and he insisted that those who loved the Master should apply his teachings in their lives. Śri Ramakrishna, too, coming to realize the approaching end of his mortal existence, impressed it upon the devotees that the realization of God depended upon the giving up of lust and greed. The young disciples became grateful to Narendranath for thus guiding them during the formative period of their spiritual career. They spent their leisure hours together in meditation, study, devotional music, and healthy spiritual discussions.

The illness of Śri Ramakrishna showed no sign of abatement; the boys redoubled their efforts to nurse him, and Narendra was constantly by their side, cheering them whenever they felt depressed. One day he found them hesitant about approaching the Master. They had been told that the illness was infectious. Narendra dragged them to the Master's room. Lying in a corner was a cup containing part of the gruel which Śri Ramakrishna could not swallow. It was mixed with his saliva. Narendra seized the cup and swallowed its contents. This set at rest the boys' misgivings.

Narendra, understanding the fatal nature of Śri Ramakrishna's illness and realizing that the beloved teacher would not live long, intensified his own spiritual practices. His longing for the vision of God knew no limit. One day he asked the Master for the boon of remaining merged in samādhi three or four days at a stretch, interrupting his meditation now and then for a bite of food. "You are a fool," said the Master. "There is a state higher than that. It is you who sing: 'O Lord! Thou art all that exists.'" Śri Ramakrishna wanted the disciple to see God in all beings and to serve them in a spirit of worship. He often said that to see the world alone, without God, is ignorance, ajñāna; to see God alone, without the world, is a kind of philosophical knowledge, jñāna; but to see all beings permeated by the spirit of God is supreme wisdom, vijñāna. Only a few blessed souls could see God dwelling in all. He wanted Naren to attain this supreme wisdom. So the Master said to him, "Settle your family affairs first, then you shall know a state even higher than samādhi."

On another occasion, in response to a similar request, Śri Ramakrishna said to

Naren: "Shame on you! You are asking for such an insignificant thing. I thought that you would be like a big banyan tree, and that thousands of people would rest in your shade. But now I see that you are seeking your own liberation." Thus scolded, Narendra shed profuse tears. He realized the greatness of Śri Ramakrishna's heart.

An intense fire was raging within Narendra's soul. He could hardly touch his college books; he felt it was a dreadful thing to waste time in that way. One morning he went home but suddenly experienced an inner fear. He wept for not having made much spiritual progress, and hurried to Cossipore almost unconscious of the outside world. His shoes slipped off somewhere, and as he ran past a rick of straw some of it stuck to his clothes. Only after entering the Master's room did he feel some inner peace.

Śri Ramakrishna said to the other disciples present: "Look at Naren's state of mind. Previously he did not believe in the Personal God or divine forms. Now he is dying for God's vision." The Master then gave Naren certain spiritual instructions about meditation.

Naren was being literally consumed by a passion for God. The world appeared to him to be utterly distasteful. When the Master reminded him of his college studies, the disciple said, "I would feel relieved if I could swallow a drug and forget all I have learnt." He spent night after night in meditation under the trees in the Panchavati at Dakshineswar, where Śri Ramakrishna, during the days of his spiritual discipline, had contemplated God. He felt the awakening of the Kundalini[2] and had other spiritual visions.

One day at Cossipore Narendra was meditating under a tree with Girish, another disciple. The place was infested with mosquitoes. Girish tried in vain to concentrate his mind. Casting his eyes on Naren, he saw him absorbed in meditation, though his body appeared to be covered by a blanket of the insects.

A few days later Narendra's longing seemed to have reached the breaking-point. He spent an entire night walking around the garden house at Cossipore and repeating Rāma's name in a heart-rending manner. In the early hours of the morning Śri Ramakrishna heard his voice, called him to his side, and said affectionately: "Listen, my child, why are you acting that way? What will you achieve by such impatience?" He stopped for a minute and then continued: "See, Naren. What you have been doing now, I did for twelve long years. A storm raged in my head during that period. What will you realize in one night?"

But the master was pleased with Naren's spiritual struggle and made no secret of his wish to make him his spiritual heir. He wanted Naren to look after the young disciples. "I leave them in your care," he said to him. "Love them intensely and see that they practise spiritual disciplines even after my death, and that they do not return home." He asked the young disciples to regard Naren as their leader. It was an easy task for them. Then, one day, Śri Ramakrishna initiated several of the young disciples into the monastic life, and thus himself laid the foundation of the future Ramakrishna Order of monks.

Attendance on the Master during his sickness revealed to Narendra the true import of Śri Ramakrishna's spiritual experiences. He was amazed to find that

---

[2] The spiritual energy, usually dormant in man, but aroused by the practice of spiritual disciplines. See glossary.

the Master could dissociate himself from all consciousness of the body by a mere wish, at which time he was not aware of the least pain from his ailment. Constantly he enjoyed an inner bliss, in spite of the suffering of the body, and he could transmit that bliss to the disciples by a mere touch or look. To Narendra, Śri Ramakrishna was the vivid demonstration of the reality of the Spirit and the unsubstantiality of matter.

One day the Master was told by a scholar that he could instantly cure himself of his illness by concentrating his mind on his throat. This Śri Ramakrishna refused to do since he could never withdraw his mind from God. But at Naren's repeated request, the Master agreed to speak to the Divine Mother about his illness. A little later he said to the disciple in a sad voice: "Yes, I told Her that I could not swallow any food on account of the sore in my throat, and asked Her to do something about it. But the Mother said, pointing to you all, 'Why, are you not eating enough through all these mouths?' I felt so humiliated that I could not utter another word." Narendra realized how Śri Ramakrishna applied in life the Vedāntic idea of the oneness of existence and also came to know that only through such realization could one rise above the pain and suffering of the individual life.

To live with Śri Ramakrishna during his illness was in itself a spiritual experience. It was wonderful to witness how he bore with his pain. In one mood he would see that the Divine Mother alone was the dispenser of pleasure and pain and that his own will was one with the Mother's will, and in another mood he would clearly behold the utter absence of diversity, God alone becoming men, animals, gardens, houses, roads, "the executioner, the victim, and the slaughter-post," to use the Master's own words.

Narendra saw in the Master the living explanation of the scriptures regarding the divine nature of the soul and the illusoriness of the body. Further, he came to know that Śri Ramakrishna had attained to that state by the total renunciation of "woman" and "gold," which, indeed, was the gist of his teaching. Another idea was creeping into Naren's mind. He began to see how the transcendental Reality, the Godhead, could embody Itself as the Personal God, and the Absolute become a Divine Incarnation. He was having a glimpse of the greatest of all divine mysteries: the incarnation of the Father as the Son for the redemption of the world. He began to believe that God becomes man so that man may become God. Śri Ramakrishna thus appeared to him in a new light.

Under the intellectual leadership of Narendranath, the Cossipore garden house became a miniature university. During the few moments' leisure snatched from nursing and meditation, Narendra would discuss with his brother disciples religions and philosophies, both Eastern and Western. Along with the teachings of Śankara, Krishna, and Chaitanya, those of Buddha and Christ were searchingly examined.

Narendra had a special affection for Buddha, and one day suddenly felt a strong desire to visit Bodh-Gayā, where the great Prophet had attained enlightenment. With Kali and Tarak, two of the brother disciples, he left, unbeknown to the others, for that sacred place and meditated for long hours under the sacred Bo-tree. Once while thus absorbed he was overwhelmed with emotion and, weeping profusely, embraced Tarak. Explaining the incident, he said afterwards that during the meditation he keenly felt the presence of Buddha and saw vividly how the history of India had been changed by his noble teachings; pondering all this he could not control his emotion.

Back in Cossipore, Narendra described enthusiastically to the Master and the brother disciples Buddha's life, experiences, and teachings. Sri Ramakrishna in turn related some of his own experiences. Narendra had to admit that the Master, after the attainment of the highest spiritual realization, had of his own will kept his mind on the plane of simplicity.

He further understood that a coin, however valuable, which belonged to an older period of history, could not be used as currency at a later date. God assumes different forms in different ages to serve the special needs of the time.

Narendra practised spiritual disciplines with unabating intensity. Sometimes he felt an awakening of a spiritual power that he could transmit to others. One night in March 1886, he asked his brother disciple Kali to touch his right knee, and then entered into deep meditation. Kali's hand began to tremble; he felt a kind of electric shock. Afterwards Narendra was rebuked by the Master for frittering away spiritual powers before accumulating them in sufficient measure. He was further told that he had injured Kali's spiritual growth, which had been following the path of dualistic devotion, by forcing upon the latter some of his own non-dualistic ideas. The Master added, however, that the damage was not serious.

Narendra had had enough of visions and manifestations of spiritual powers, and he now wearied of them. His mind longed for the highest experience of non-dualistic Vedānta, the nirvikalpa samādhi, in which the names and forms of the phenomenal world disappear and the aspirant realizes total non-difference between the individual soul, the universe, and Brahman, or the Absolute. He told Sri Ramakrishna about it, but the master remained silent. And yet one evening the experience came to him quite unexpectedly.

He was absorbed in his usual meditation when he suddenly felt as if a lamp were burning at the back of his head. The light glowed more and more intensely and finally burst. Narendra was overwhelmed by that light and fell unconscious. After some time, as he began to regain his normal mood, he could feel only his head and not the rest of his body.

In an agitated voice he said to Gopal, a brother disciple who was meditating in the same room, "Where is my body?"

Gopal answered: "Why, Naren, it is there. Don't you feel it?"

Gopal was afraid that Narendra was dying, and ran to Sri Ramakrishna's room. He found the Master in a calm but serious mood, evidently aware of what had happened in the room downstairs. After listening to Gopal the Master said, "Let him stay in that state for a while; he has teased me long enough for it."

For a long time Narendra remained unconscious, and when he regained his normal state of mind he was bathed in an ineffable peace. As he entered Sri Ramakrishna's room the latter said: "Now the Mother has shown you everything. But this realization, like the jewel locked in a box, will be hidden away from you and kept in my custody. I will keep the key with me. Only after you have fulfilled your mission on this earth will the box be unlocked, and you will know everything as you have known now."

The experience of this kind of samādhi usually has a most devastating effect upon the body; Incarnations and special messengers of God alone can survive its impact. By way of advice, Śri Ramakrishna asked Naren to use great discrimination about his food and companions, only accepting the purest.

Later the Master said to the other disciples: "Narendra will give up his body of his own will. When he realizes his true nature, he will refuse to stay on this earth. Very soon he will shake the world by his intellectual and spiritual powers. I have prayed to the Divine Mother to keep away from him the Knowledge of the Absolute and cover his eyes with a veil of māyā. There is much work to be done by him. But the veil, I see, is so thin that it may be rent at any time."

Śri Ramakrishna, the Avatār of the modern age, was too gentle and tender to labour, himself, for humanity's welfare. He needed some sturdy souls to carry on his work. Narendra was foremost among those around him; therefore Śri Ramakrishna did not want him to remain immersed in nirvikalpa samādhi before his task in this world was finished.

The disciples sadly watched the gradual wasting away of Śri Ramakrishna's physical frame. His body became a mere skeleton covered with skin; the suffering was intense. But he devoted his remaining energies to the training of the disciples, especially Narendra. He had been relieved of his worries about Narendra; for the disciple now admitted the divinity of Kāli, whose will controls all things in the universe. Naren said later on: "From the time he gave me over to the Divine Mother, he retained the vigour of his body only for six months. The rest of the time—and that was two long years—he suffered."

One day the Master, unable to speak even in a whisper, wrote on a piece of paper: "Narendra will teach others." The disciple demurred. Śri Ramakrishna replied: "But you must. Your very bones will do it." He further said that all the supernatural powers he had acquired would work through his beloved disciple.

A short while before the curtain finally fell on Śri Ramakrishna's earthly life, the Master one day called Naren to his bedside. Gazing intently upon him, he passed into deep meditation. Naren felt that a subtle force, resembling an electric current, was entering his body. He gradually lost outer consciousness. After some time he regained knowledge of the physical world and found the Master weeping. Śri Ramakrishna said to him: "O Naren, today I have given you everything I possess—now I am no more than a fakir, a penniless beggar. By the powers I have transmitted to you, you will accomplish great things in the world, and not until then will you return to the source whence you have come."

Narendra from that day became the channel of Śri Ramakrishna's powers and the spokesman of his message.

Two days before the dissolution of the Master's body, Narendra was standing by the latter's bedside when a strange thought flashed into his mind: Was the Master truly an Incarnation of God? He said to himself that he would accept Śri Ramakrishna's divinity if the Master, on the threshold of death, declared himself to be an Incarnation. But this was only a passing thought. He stood looking intently at the Master's face. Slowly Śri Ramakrishna's lips parted and he said in a clear voice: "O my Naren, are you still not convinced? He who in the past was born as Rāma and Krishna is now living in this very body as Ramakrishna—but not from the standpoint of your Vedānta." Thus Śri Ramakrishna, in answer to Narendra's mental query, put himself in the category of Rāma and Krishna, who are recognized by orthodox Hindus as two of the Avatārs, or Incarnations of God.

A few words may be said here about the meaning of the Incarnation in the Hindu religious tradition. One of the main doctrines of Vedānta is the divinity of the soul: every soul, in reality, is Brahman. Thus it may be presumed that there is no difference between an Incarnation and an ordinary man. To be sure, from the standpoint of the Absolute, or Brahman, no such difference exists. But from the relative standpoint, where multiplicity is perceived, a difference must be admitted. Embodied human beings reflect godliness in varying measure. In an Incarnation this godliness is fully manifest. Therefore an Incarnation is unlike an ordinary mortal or even an illumined saint. To give an illustration: There is no difference between a clay lion and a clay mouse, from the standpoint of the clay. Both become the same substance when dissolved into clay. But the difference between the lion and the mouse, from the standpoint of form, is clearly seen. Likewise, as Brahman, an ordinary man is identical with an Incarnation. Both become the same Brahman when they attain final illumination. But in the relative state of name and form, which is admitted by Vedānta, the difference between them is accepted. According to the Bhagavad Gitā (IV. 6-8), Brahman in times of spiritual crisis assumes a human body through Its own inscrutable power, called māyā. Though birthless, immutable, and the Lord of all beings, yet in every age Brahman appears to be incarnated in a human body for the protection of the good and the destruction of the wicked.

As noted above, the Incarnation is quite different from an ordinary man, even from a saint. Among the many vital differences may be mentioned the fact that the birth of an ordinary mortal is governed by the law of karma, whereas that of an Incarnation is a voluntary act undertaken for the spiritual redemption of the world. Further, though māyā is the cause of the embodiment of both an ordinary mortal and an Incarnation, yet the former is fully under māyā's control, whereas the latter always remains its master. A man, though potentially Brahman, is not conscious of his divinity; but an Incarnation is fully aware of the true nature of His birth and mission. The spiritual disciplines practised by an Incarnation are not for His own liberation, but for the welfare of humanity; as far as He is concerned, such terms as bondage and liberation have no meaning, He being ever free, ever pure, and ever illumined. Lastly, an Incarnation can bestow upon others the boon of liberation, whereas even an illumined saint is devoid of such power.

Thus the Master, on his death-bed, proclaimed himself through his own words as the Incarnation or God-man of modern times.

On August 15, 1886, the Master's suffering became almost unbearable. At midnight he summoned Naren to his bedside and gave him the last instructions, almost in a whisper. The disciples stood around him. At two minutes past one in the early morning, Śri Ramakrishna uttered three times in a ringing voice the name of his beloved Kāli and entered into the final samādhi, from which his mind never again returned to the physical world.

The body was given to the fire in the neighbouring cremation ground on the bank of the Ganges. But to the Holy Mother, as she was putting on the signs of a Hindu widow, there came these words of faith and reassurance: "I am not dead. I have just moved from one room to another."

As the disciples returned from the cremation ground to the garden house, they felt great desolation. Sri Ramakrishna had been more than their earthly father. His teachings and companionship still inspired them. They felt his presence in his room. His words rang in their ears. But they could no longer see his physical body or enjoy his seraphic smile. They all yearned to commune with him.

Within a week of the Master's passing away, Narendra one night was strolling in the garden with a brother disciple, when he saw in front of him a luminous figure. There was no mistaking: it was Śri Ramakrishna himself. Narendra remained silent, regarding the phenomenon as an illusion. But his brother disciple exclaimed in wonder, "See, Naren! See!" There was no room for further doubt. Narendra was convinced that it was Śri Ramakrishna who had appeared in a luminous body. As he called to the other brother disciples to behold the Master, the figure disappeared.

THE BARANAGORE MONASTERY

Among the Master's disciples, Tarak, Latu, and the elder Gopal had already cut off their relationship with their families. The young disciples whom Śri Ramakrishna had destined for the monastic life were in need of a shelter. The Master had asked Naren to see to it that they should not become householders. Naren vividly remembered the Master's dying words: "Naren, take care of the boys." The householder devotees, moreover, wanted to meet, from time to time, at a place where they could talk about the Master. They longed for the company of the young disciples who had renounced the world and totally dedicated their lives to the realization of God. But who would bear the expenses of a house where the young disciples could live? How would they be provided with food and the basic necessaries of life?

All these problems were solved by the generosity of Surendranath Mitra, the beloved householder disciple of Śri Ramakrishna. He came forward to pay the expenses of new quarters for the Master's homeless disciples. A house was rented at Baranagore, midway between Calcutta and Dakshineswar. Dreary and dilapidated, it was a building that had the reputation of being haunted by evil spirits. The young disciples were happy to take refuge in it from the turmoil of Calcutta. This Baranagore Math, as the new monastery was called, became the first headquarters of the monks of the Ramakrishna Order.[3] Its centre was

---

[3] The monastery remained at Baranagore from 1886 to 1892; then it was shifted to Alambazar, in the neighbourhood of Dakshineswar, where it functioned till 1897. Next it was removed to the garden house of Nilambar Mukherjee, on the bank of the Ganges across from Baranagore. Finally, the permanent monastery was dedicated in 1898 at the Belur Math, adjacent to Nilambar Mukherjee's garden house.

NARENDRANATH AT THE COSSIPORE GARDEN (1886)

VIVEKANANDA AS A WANDERING MONK

the shrine room, where the copper vessel containing the sacred ashes of the Master was daily worshipped as his visible presence.[4]

Narendranath devoted himself heart and soul to the training of the young brother disciples. He spent the daytime at home, supervising a lawsuit that was pending in the court and looking after certain other family affairs; but during the evenings and nights he was always with his brothers at the monastery, exhorting them to practise spiritual disciplines. His presence was a source of unfailing delight and inspiration to all.

The future career of the youths began to take shape during these early days at Baranagore. The following incident hastened the process. At the invitation of the mother of Baburam, one of the disciples, they all went to the village of Antpur to spend a few days away from the austerities of Baranagore. Here they realized, more intensely than ever before, a common goal of life, a sense of brotherhood and unity integrating their minds and hearts. Their consecrated souls were like pearls in a necklace held together by the thread of Ramakrishna's teachings. They saw in one another a reservoir of spiritual power, and the vision intensified their mutual love and respect. Narendra, describing to them the glories of the monastic life, asked them to give up the glamour of academic studies and the physical world, and all felt in their hearts the ground-swell of the spirit of renunciation. This reached its height one night when they were sitting for meditation around a fire, in the fashion of Hindu monks. The stars sparkled overhead and the stillness was unbroken except for the crackling of the firewood. Suddenly Naren opened his eyes and began, with an apostolic fervour, to narrate to the brother disciples the life of Christ. He exhorted them to live like Christ, who had had no place "to lay his head." Inflamed by a new passion, the youths, making God and the sacred fire their witness, vowed to become monks.[5] When they had returned to their rooms in a happy mood,

---

[4] Some of the ashes were later buried at Kankurgachi, a suburb of Calcutta, where a temple was built by the Master's disciple Ramchandra Datta. The place had been hallowed by Śri Ramakrishna's visit during his lifetime. But most of the ashes are now preserved in the shrine at the Belur Math.

[5] Some time after, these chosen disciples of the Master performed the formal sacrifice called virajā and took the monastic vows of celibacy and poverty. Further, they dedicated their lives to the realization of God and the service of men. They assumed new names to signify their utter severance from the world. Narendra, who later became world-famous as Swami Vivekananda, did not take that name till his departure for America in 1893. Prior to that he assumed the names of Vividishananda and Satchidananda in order to conceal his identity from the public. The monastic names of the Master's disciples who renounced the world soon after his death were as follows:

Narendra	Swami Vivekananda	Hari	Swami Turiyananda
Rakhal	Swami Brahmananda	Sarat	Swami Saradananda
Jogin	Swami Jogananda	Sashi	Swami Ramakrishnananda
Niranjan	Swami Niranjanananda	Kali	Swami Abhedananda
Latu	Swami Adbhutananda	Gangadhar	Swami Akhandananda
Baburam	Swami Premananda	Gopal (elder)	Swami Advaitananda
Tarak	Swami Shivananda	Sarada Prasanna	Swami Trigunatitananda
		Subodh	Swami Subodhananda

someone found out that it was Christmas Eve, and all felt doubly blest. It is no wonder that the monks of the Ramakrishna Order have always cherished a high veneration for Jesus of Nazareth.

The young disciples, after their return to Baranagore, finally renounced home and became permanent inmates of the monastery. And what a life of austerity they lived there! They forgot their food when absorbed in meditation, worship, study, or devotional music. At such times Sashi, who had constituted himself their caretaker, literally dragged them to the dining-room. The privations they suffered during this period form a wonderful saga of spiritual discipline. Often there would be no food at all, and on such occasions they spent day and night in prayer and meditation. Sometimes there would be only rice, with no salt for flavouring; but nobody cared. They lived for months on boiled rice, salt, and bitter herbs. Not even demons could have stood such hardship. Each had two pieces of loin-cloth, and there were some regular clothes that were worn, by turns, when anyone had to go out. They slept on straw mats spread on the hard floor. A few pictures of saints, gods, and goddesses hung on the walls, and some musical instruments lay here and there. The library contained about a hundred books.

But Narendra did not want the brother disciples to be pain-hugging, cross-grained ascetics. They should broaden their outlook by assimilating the thought-currents of the world. He examined with them the histories of different countries and various philosophical systems. Aristotle and Plato, Kant and Hegel, together with Śankarāchārya and Buddha, Rāmānuja and Madhva, Chaitanya and Nimbārka, were thoroughly discussed. The Hindu philosophical systems of Jnāna, Bhakti, Yoga, and Karma, each received a due share of attention, and their apparent contradictions were reconciled in the light of Śri Ramakrishna's teachings and experiences. The dryness of discussion was relieved by devotional music. There were many moments, too, when the inmates indulged in light-hearted and witty talk, and Narendra's bons mots on such occasions always convulsed them with laughter. But he would never let them forget the goal of the monastic life: the complete control of the lower nature, and the realization of God. "During those days," one of the inmates of the monastery said, "he worked like a madman. Early in the morning, while it was still dark, he would rise from bed and wake up the others, singing, 'Awake, arise, all who would drink of the Divine Nectar!' And long after midnight he and his brother disciples would still be sitting on the roof of the monastery building, absorbed in religious songs. The neighbours protested, but to no avail. Pandits came and argued. He was never for one moment idle, never dull." Yet the brothers complained that they could not realize even a fraction of what Ramakrishna had taught.

Some of the householder devotees of the Master, however, did not approve of the austerities of the young men, and one of them teasingly inquired if they had realized God by giving up the world. "What do you mean?" Narendra said furiously. "Suppose we have not realized God; must we then return to the life of the senses and deprave our higher nature?"

Soon the youths of the Baranagore monastery became restless for the life of the wandering monk with no other possessions except staff and begging-bowl. Thus they would learn self-surrender to God, detachment, and inner serenity.

They remembered the Hindu proverb that the monk who constantly moves on remains pure, like water that flows. They wanted to visit the holy places and thus give an impetus to their spiritual life.

Narendra, too, wished to enjoy the peace of solitude. He wanted to test his own inner strength as well as teach the others not to depend upon him always. Some of the brother disciples had already gone away from the monastery when he began his wanderings. The first were in the nature of temporary excursions; he had to return to Baranagore in response to the appeal of the inmates of the monastery. But finally in 1891, when he struck out again—without a companion, without a name, with only a staff and begging-bowl—he was swallowed in the immensity of India and the dust of the vast sub-continent completely engulfed him. When rediscovered he was no longer the unknown Naren, but the Swami Vivekananda who had made history in Chicago in 1893.

IN NORTHERN INDIA

In order to satisfy his wanderlust, Narendra went to Benares, considered the holiest place in India—a city sanctified from time out of mind by the association of monks and devotees. Here have come prophets like Buddha, Śankarāchārya, and Chaitanya, to receive, as it were, the commandment of God to preach their messages. The Ganges charges the atmosphere with a rare holiness. Narendra felt uplifted by the spirit of renunciation and devotion that pervades this sacred place. He visited the temples and paid his respects to such holy men as Trailanga Swami, who lived on the bank of the Ganges constantly absorbed in meditation, and Swami Bhaskarananda, who annoyed Naren by expressing doubt as to the possibility of a man's total conquest of the temptation of "woman" and "gold."[6] With his own eyes Naren had seen the life of Śri Ramakrishna, who had completely subdued his lower nature.

In Benares, one day, hotly pursued by a troop of monkeys, he was running away when a monk called to him: "Face the brutes." He stopped and looked defiantly at the ugly beasts. They quickly disappeared. Later, as a preacher, he sometimes used this experience to exhort people to face the dangers and vicissitudes of life and not run away from them.

After a few days Naren returned to Baranagore and plunged into meditation, study, and religious discourses. From this time he began to feel a vague premonition of his future mission. He often asked himself if such truths of the Vedānta philosophy as the divinity of the soul and the unity of existence should remain imprisoned in the worm-eaten pages of the scriptures to furnish a pastime for erudite scholars or to be enjoyed only by solitary monks in caves and the depths of the wilderness; did they not have any significance for the average

[6] The words woman and gold occur again and again in the teachings cf Śri Ramakrishna to designate the two chief impediments to spiritual progress. By these words he really meant lust and greed, the baneful influence of which retards the aspirant's spiritual growth. He used the word woman as a concrete term for the sex instinct when addressing his men devotees; while speaking to women, however, he warned them against man. The word gold symbolizes greed, which is the other obstacle. Śri Ramakrishna never taught his disciples to hate any woman, or womankind in general. He regarded women as so many images of the Divine Mother of the universe.

man struggling with life's problems? Must the common man, because of his ignorance of the scriptures, be shut out from the light of Vedānta?

Narendra spoke to his brother disciples about the necessity of preaching the strength-giving message of the Vedānta philosophy to one and all, and especially to the down-trodden masses. But these monks were eager for their own salvation, and protested. Naren said to them angrily: "All are preaching. What they do unconsciously, I will do consciously. Ay, even if you, my brother monks, stand in my way, I will go to the pariahs and preach in the lowest slums."

After remaining at Baranagore a short while, Naren set out again for Benares, where he met the Sanskrit scholar Pramadadas Mitra. These two felt for each other a mutual respect and affection, and they discussed, both orally and through letters, the social customs of the Hindus and abstruse passages of the scriptures. Next he visited Ayodhyā, the ancient capital of Rāma, the hero of the Rāmāyana. Lucknow, a city of gardens and palaces created by the Moslem Nawabs, filled his mind with the glorious memories of Islāmic rule, and the sight of the Tāj Mahal in Agra brought tears to his eyes. In Vrindāvan he recalled the many incidents of Krishna's life and was deeply moved.

While on his way to Vrindāvan, trudging barefoot and penniless, Naren saw a man seated by the roadside enjoying a smoke. He asked the stranger to give him a puff from his tobacco bowl, but the man was an untouchable and shrank from such an act; for it was considered sacrilegious by Hindu society. Naren continued on his way, but said to himself suddenly: "What a shame! The whole of my life I have contemplated the non-duality of the soul, and now I am thrown into the whirlpool of the caste-system. How difficult it is to get over innate tendencies!" He returned to the untouchable, begged him to lend him his smoking-pipe, and in spite of the remonstrances of the low-caste man, enjoyed a hearty smoke and went on to Vrindāvan.

Next we find Naren at the railroad station of Hathras, on his way to the sacred pilgrimage centre of Hardwar in the foothills of the Himālayas. The stationmaster, Sarat Chandra Gupta, was fascinated at the very first sight of him. "I followed the two diabolical eyes," he said later. Narendra accepted Sarat as a disciple and called him "the child of my spirit." At Hathras he discussed with visitors the doctrines of Hinduism and entertained them with music, and then one day confided to Sarat that he must move on.

"My son," he said, "I have a great mission to fulfil and I am in despair at the smallness of my power. My guru asked me to dedicate my life to the regeneration of my motherland. Spirituality has fallen to a low ebb and starvation stalks the land. India must become dynamic again and earn the respect of the world through her spiritual power."

Sarat immediately renounced the world and accompanied Narendra from Hathras to Hardwar. The two then went on to Hrishikesh, on the bank of the Ganges several miles north of Hardwar, where they found themselves among monks of various sects, who were practising meditation and austerities. Presently Sarat fell ill and his companion took him back to Hathras for treatment. But Naren, too, had been attacked with malarial fever at Hrishikesh. He now made his way to the Baranagore monastery.

Naren had now seen northern India, the Āryāvarta, the sacred land of the

Āryans, where the spiritual culture of India had originated and developed. The main stream of this ancient Indian culture, issuing from the Vedas and the Upanishads and branching off into the Purānas and the Tantras, was subsequently enriched by contributions from the Śaks, the Huns, the Greeks, the Pathans, the Moghuls, and numerous other foreign peoples. Thus India developed a unique civilization based upon the ideal of unity in diversity. Some of the foreign elements were entirely absorbed into the traditional Hindu consciousness; others, though flavoured by the ancient thought of the land, retained their individuality. Realizing the spiritual unity of India and Asia, Narendra discovered the distinctive characteristics of Oriental civilization: renunciation of the finite and communion with the Infinite.

But the stagnant life of the Indian masses, for which he chiefly blamed the priests and the landlords, saddened his heart. Naren found that his country's downfall had not been caused by religion. On the contrary, as long as India had clung to her religious ideals, the country had overflowed with material prosperity. But the enjoyment of power for a long time had corrupted the priests. The people at large were debarred from true knowledge of religion, and the Vedas, the source of the Hindu culture, were completely forgotten, especially in Bengal. Moreover, the caste-system, which had originally been devised to emphasize the organic unity of Hindu society, was now petrified. Its real purpose had been to protect the weak from the ruthless competition of the strong and to vindicate the supremacy of spiritual knowledge over the power of military weapons, wealth, and organized labour; but now it was sapping the vitality of the masses. Narendra wanted to throw open the man-making wisdom of the Vedas to all, and thus bring about the regeneration of his motherland. He therefore encouraged his brothers at the Baranagore monastery to study the grammar of Pānini, without which one could not acquire first-hand knowledge of the Vedas.

The spirit of democracy and equality in Islām appealed to Naren's mind and he wanted to create a new India with Vedāntic brain and Moslem body. Further, the idea began to dawn in his mind that the material conditions of the masses could not be improved without the knowledge of science and technology as developed in the West. He was already dreaming of building a bridge to join the East and the West. But the true leadership of India would have to spring from the soil of the country. Again and again he recalled that Śri Ramakrishna had been a genuine product of the Indian soil, and he realized that India would regain her unity and solidarity through the understanding of the Master's spiritual experiences.

Naren again became restless to "do something," but what, he did not know. He wanted to run away from his relatives since he could not bear the sight of their poverty. He was eager to forget the world through meditation. During the last part of December 1889, therefore, he again struck out from the Baranagore monastery and turned his face towards Benares. "My idea," he wrote to a friend, "is to live in Benares for some time and to watch how Viśwanāth and Annapurnā deal out my lot. I have resolved either to realize my ideal or to lay down my life in the effort—so help me Lord of Benares!"

On his way to Benares he heard that Swami Jogananda, one of his brother disciples, was lying ill in Allahabad and decided to proceed there immediately. In Allahabad he met a Moslem saint, "every line and curve of whose face showed that he was a paramahamsa." Next he went to Ghazipur and there he came to know the saint Pavhari Baba, the "air-eating holy man."

Pavhari Baba was born near Benares of brāhmin parents. In his youth he had mastered many branches of Hindu philosophy. Later he renounced the world, led an austere life, practised the disciplines of Yoga and Vedānta, and travelled over the whole of India. At last he settled in Ghazipur, where he built an underground hermitage on the bank of the Ganges and spent most of his time in meditation. He lived on practically nothing and so was given by the people the sobriquet of the "air-eating holy man"; all were impressed by his humility and spirit of service. Once he was bitten by a cobra and said while suffering terrible pain, "Oh, he was a messenger from my Beloved!" Another day, a dog ran off with his bread and he followed, praying humbly, "Please wait, my Lord; let me butter the bread for you." Often he would give away his meagre food to beggars or wandering monks, and starve. Pavhari Baba had heard of Sri Ramakrishna, held him in high respect as a Divine Incarnation, and kept in his room a photograph of the Master. People from far and near visited the Baba, and when not engaged in meditation he would talk to them from behind a wall. For several days before his death he remained indoors. Then, one day, people noticed smoke issuing from his underground cell with the smell of burning flesh. It was discovered that the saint, having come to realize the approaching end of his earthly life, had offered his body as the last oblation to the Lord, in an act of supreme sacrifice.

Narendra, at the time of his meeting Pavhari Baba, was suffering from the severe pain of lumbago, and this had made it almost impossible for him either to move about or to sit in meditation. Further, he was mentally distressed, for he had heard of the illness of Abhedananda, another of his brother disciples, who was living at Hrishikesh. "You know not, sir," he wrote to a friend, "that I am a very soft-natured man in spite of the stern Vedāntic views I hold. And this proves to be my undoing. For however I may try to think only of my own good, I begin, in spite of myself, to think of other people's interests." Narendra wished to forget the world and his own body through the practice of Yoga, and went for instruction to Pavhari Baba, intending to make the saint his guru. But the Baba, with characteristic humility, put him off from day to day.

One night when Naren was lying in bed thinking of Pavhari Baba, Sri Ramakrishna appeared to him and stood silently near the door, looking intently into his eyes. The vision was repeated for twenty-one days. Narendra understood. He reproached himself bitterly for his lack of complete faith in Sri Ramakrishna. Now, at last, he was convinced. He wrote to a friend: "Ramakrishna has no peer. Nowhere else in the world exists such unprecedented perfection, such wonderful kindness to all, such intense sympathy for men in bondage." Tearfully he recalled how Sri Ramakrishna had never left unfulfilled a single prayer of his, how he had forgiven his offenses by the million and removed his afflictions.

But as long as Naren lived he cherished sincere affection and reverence for Pavhari Baba, and he remembered particularly two of his instructions. One of these was: "Live in the house of your teacher like a cow," which emphasizes the spirit of service and humility in the relationship between the teacher and the disciple. The second instruction of the Baba was: "Regard spiritual discipline in the same way as you regard the goal," which means that an aspirant should not differentiate between cause and effect.

Narendranath again breathed peace and plunged into meditation. After a few days he went to Benares, where he learnt of the serious illness of Balaram Bose, one of the foremost lay disciples of Śri Ramakrishna. At Ghazipur he had heard that Surendranath Mitra, another lay disciple of the Master, was dying. He was overwhelmed with grief, and to Pramadadas, who expressed his surprise at the sight of a sannyāsin indulging in a human emotion, he said: "Please do not talk that way. We are not dry monks. Do you think that because a man has renounced the world he is devoid of all feeling?"

He came to Calcutta to be at the bedside of Balaram, who passed away on May 13. Surendra Mitra died on May 25. But Naren steadied his nerves, and in addition to the practice of his own prayer and meditation, devoted himself again to the guidance of his brother disciples. Sometime during this period he conceived the idea of building a permanent temple to preserve the relics of Śri Ramakrishna.

From his letters and conversations one can gain some idea of the great storm that was raging in Naren's soul during this period. He clearly saw to what an extent the educated Hindus had come under the spell of the materialistic ideas of the West. He despised sterile imitation. But he was also aware of the great ideals that formed the basis of European civilization. He told his friends that in India the salvation of the individual was the accepted goal, whereas in the West it was the uplift of the people, without distinction of caste or creed. Whatever was achieved there was shared by the common man; freedom of spirit manifested itself in the common good and in the advancement of all men by the united efforts of all. He wanted to introduce this healthy factor into the Indian consciousness.

Yet he was consumed by his own soul's hunger to remain absorbed in samādhi. He felt at this time a spiritual unrest like that which he had experienced at the Cossipore garden house during the last days of Śri Ramakrishna's earthly existence. The outside world had no attraction for him. But another factor, perhaps unknown to him, was working within him. Perfect from his birth, he did not need spiritual disciplines for his own liberation. Whatever disciplines he practised were for the purpose of removing the veil that concealed, for the time being, his true divine nature and mission in the world. Even before his birth, the Lord had chosen him as His instrument to help Him in the spiritual redemption of humanity.

Now Naren began to be aware that his life was to be quite different from that of a religious recluse: he was to work for the good of the people. Every time he wanted to taste for himself the bliss of samādhi, he would hear the piteous moans of the teeming millions of India, victims of poverty and ignorance. Must they, Naren asked himself, for ever grovel in the dust and live like brutes? Who would be their saviour?

He began, also, to feel the inner agony of the outwardly happy people of the West, whose spiritual vitality was being undermined by the mechanistic and materialistic conception of life encouraged by the sudden development of the physical sciences. Europe, he saw, was sitting on the crater of a smouldering volcano, and any moment Western culture might be shattered by its fiery eruption. The suffering of man, whether in the East or in the West, hurt his tender soul. The message of Vedānta, which proclaimed the divinity of the soul and the oneness of existence, he began to realize, could alone bind up and heal the wounds of India and the world. But what could he, a lad of twenty-five, do? The task was gigantic. He talked about it with his brother disciples, but received scant encouragement. He was determined to work alone if no other help was forthcoming.

Narendra felt cramped in the monastery at Baranagore and lost interest in its petty responsibilities. The whole world now beckoned him to work. Hence, one day in 1890, he left the monastery again with the same old determination never to return. He would go to the Himālayas and bury himself in the depths of his own thought. To a brother disciple he declared, "I shall not return until I gain such realization that my very touch will transform a man." He prayed to the Holy Mother that he might not return before attaining the highest Knowledge, and she blessed him in the name of Śri Ramakrishna. Then she asked whether he would not like to take leave of his earthly mother. "Mother," Naren replied, "you are my only mother."

WANDERINGS IN THE HIMĀLAYAS

Accompanied by Swami Akhandananda, Naren left Calcutta and set out for Northern India. The two followed the course of the Ganges, their first halting-place being Bhagalpur. To one of the people who came to visit him there Naren said that whatever of the ancient Āryan knowledge, intellect, and genius remained could be found mostly in those parts of the country that lay near the banks of the Ganges. The farther one departed from the river, the less one saw of that culture. This fact, he believed, explained the greatness of the Ganges as sung in the Hindu scriptures. He further observed: "The epithet 'mild Hindu,' instead of being a word of reproach, ought really to point to our glory, as expressing greatness of character. For see how much moral and spiritual advancement and how much development of the qualities of love and compassion have to be acquired before one can get rid of the brutish force of one's nature, which impels a man to slaughter his brother men for self-aggrandizement."

He spent a few days in Benares and left the city with the prophetic words: "When I return here the next time, I shall burst upon society like a bomb-shell, and it will follow me like a dog."

After visiting one or two places, Naren and Akhandananda arrived at Nainital, their destination being the sacred Badarikāśrama, in the heart of the Himālayas. They decided to travel the whole way on foot, and also not to touch money. Under an old peepul tree by the side of a stream they spent many hours in meditation. Naren had a deep spiritual experience, which he thus jotted down in his note-book:

In the beginning was the Word, etc.

The microcosm and the macrocosm are built on the same plan. Just as the individual soul is encased in a living body, so is the Universal Soul, in the living prakriti (nature), the objective universe. Kāli is embracing Śiva. This is not a fancy. This covering of the one (Soul) by the other (nature) is analogous to the relation between an idea and the word expressing it. They are one and the same, and it is only by a mental abstraction that one can distinguish them. Thought is impossible without words. Therefore in the beginning was the Word, etc.

This dual aspect of the Universal Soul is eternal. So what we perceive or feel is the combination of the eternally formed and the eternally formless.

Thus Naren realized, in the depths of meditation, the oneness of the universe and man, who is a universe in miniature. He realized that all that exists in the universe also exists in the body, and further, that the whole universe exists in the atom.

Several other brother disciples joined Naren. But they could not go to Badarikāśrama since the road was closed by Government order on account of famine. They visited different holy places, lived on alms, studied the scriptures, and meditated. At this time, the sad news arrived of the suicide of one of Naren's sisters under tragic conditions, and reflecting on the plight of Hindu women in the cruel present-day society, he thought that he would be a criminal if he remained an indifferent spectator of such social injustice.

Naren proceeded to Hrishikesh, a beautiful valley at the foot of the Himālayas, which is surrounded by hills and almost encircled by the Ganges. From an immemorial past this sacred spot has been frequented by monks and ascetics. After a few days, however, Naren fell seriously ill and his friends despaired of his life. When he was convalescent he was removed to Meerut. There he met a number of his brother disciples and together they pursued the study of the scriptures, practised prayer and meditation, and sang devotional songs, creating in Meerut a miniature Baranagore monastery.

After a stay of five months Naren became restless, hankering again for his wandering life; but he desired to be alone this time and break the chain of attachment to his brother disciples. He wanted to reflect deeply about his future course of action, of which now and then he was getting glimpses. From his wanderings in the Himālayas he had become convinced that the Divine Spirit would not allow him to seal himself within the four walls of a cave. Every time he had thought to do so, he had been thrown out, as it were, by a powerful force. The degradation of the Indian masses and the spiritual sickness of people everywhere were summoning him to a new line of action, whose outer shape was not yet quite clear to him.

In the later part of January 1891, Naren bade farewell to his brother disciples and set out for Delhi, assuming the name of Swami Vividishananda. He wished to travel without being recognized. He wanted the dust of India to cover up his footprints. It was his desire to remain an unknown sannyāsin, among the thousands of others seen in the country's thoroughfares, market-places, deserts, forests, and caves. But the fires of the Spirit that burnt in his eyes, and his aristocratic bearing, marked him as a prince among men despite all his disguises.

In Delhi, Naren visited the palaces, mosques, and tombs. All around the modern city he saw a vast ruin of extinct empires dating from the prehistoric days of the *Mahābhārata*, revealing the transitoriness of material achievements. But gay and lively Delhi also revealed to him the deathless nature of the Hindu spirit.

Some of his brother disciples from Meerut came to the city and accidentally discovered their beloved leader. Naren was angry. He said to them: "Brethren! I told you that I desired to be left alone. I asked you not to follow me. This I repeat once more. I must not be followed. I shall presently leave Delhi. No one must try to know my whereabouts. I shall sever all old associations. Wherever the Spirit leads, there I shall wander. It matters not whether I wander about in a forest or in a desert, on a lonely mountain or in a populous city. I am off. Let everyone strive to realize his goal according to his lights."

Narendra proceeded towards historic Rajputana, repeating the words of the Dhammapāda:

> Go forward without a path,
> Fearing nothing, caring for nothing,
> Wandering alone, like the rhinoceros!
> Even as a lion, not trembling at noises,
> Even as the wind, not caught in a net,
> Even as the lotus leaf, untainted by water,
> Do thou wander alone, like the rhinoceros!

Several factors have been pointed out as influencing Naren's life and giving shape to his future message: the holy association of Śri Ramakrishna, his own knowledge of Eastern and Western cultures, and his spiritual experiences. To these another must be added: the understanding of India gained through his wanderings. This new understanding constituted a unique education for Naren. Here, the great book of life taught him more than the printed words of the libraries.

He mixed with all—today sleeping with pariahs in their huts and tomorrow conversing on equal terms with Mahārājās, Prime Ministers, orthodox pandits, and liberal college professors. Thus he was brought into contact with their joys and sorrows, hopes and frustrations. He witnessed the tragedy of present-day India and also reflected on its remedy. The cry of the people of India, the God struggling in humanity, and the anxiety of men everywhere to grasp a hand for aid, moved him deeply. In the course of his travels Naren came to know how he could make himself a channel of the Divine Spirit in the service of mankind.

During these wandering days he both learnt and taught. The Hindus he asked to go back to the eternal truths of their religion, hearken to the message of the Upanishads, respect temples and religious symbols, and take pride in their birth in the holy land of India. He wanted them to avoid both the outmoded orthodoxy still advocated by fanatical leaders, and the misguided rationalism of the Westernized reformers. He was struck by the essential cultural unity of India in spite of the endless diversity of form. And the people who came to know him saw in him the conscience of India, her unity, and her destiny.

TRAVELS IN RAJPUTANA

As already noted, Narendranath while travelling in India often changed his name to avoid recognition. It will not be improper to call him, from this point of his life, by the monastic title of "Swami," or the more affectionate and respectful appellation of "Swamiji."

In Alwar, where Swamiji arrived one morning in the beginning of February 1891, he was cordially received by Hindus and Moslems alike. To a Moslem scholar he said: "There is one thing very remarkable about the Koran. Even to this day it exists as it was recorded eleven hundred years ago. The book has retained its original purity and is free from interpolation."

He had a sharp exchange of words with the Mahārājā, who was Westernized in his outlook. To the latter's question as to why the Swami, an able-bodied young man and evidently a scholar, was leading a vagabond's life, the Swami retorted, "Tell me why you constantly spend your time in the company of Westerners and go out on shooting excursions, neglecting your royal duties." The Mahārājā said, "I cannot say why, but, no doubt, because I like to." "Well," the Swami exclaimed, "for that very reason I wander about as a monk."

Next, the Mahārājā ridiculed the worship of images, which to him were nothing but figures of stone, clay, or metal. The Swami tried in vain to explain to him that Hindus worshipped God alone, using the images as symbols. The Prince was not convinced. Thereupon the Swami asked the Prime Minister to take down a picture of the Mahārājā, hanging on the wall, and spit on it. Everyone present was horror-struck at this effrontery. The Swami turned to the Prince and said that though the picture was not the Mahārājā himself, in flesh and blood, yet it reminded everyone of his person and thus was held in high respect; likewise the image brought to the devotee's mind the presence of the Deity and was therefore helpful for concentration, especially at the beginning of his spiritual life. The Mahārājā apologized to Swamiji for his rudeness.

The Swami exhorted the people of Alwar to study the eternal truths of Hinduism, especially to cultivate the knowledge of Sanskrit, side by side with Western science. He also encouraged them to read Indian history, which he remarked should be written by Indians following the scientific method of the West. European historians dwelt mainly on the decadent period of Indian culture.

In Jeypore the Swami devoted himself to the study of Sanskrit grammar, and in Ajmere he recalled the magnificence of the Hindu and Moslem rules. At Mount Abu he gazed in wonder at the Jain temples of Dilwara, which, it has been said, were begun by titans and finished by jewellers. There he accepted the hospitality of a Moslem official. To his scandalized Hindu friends the Swami said that he was, as a sannyāsin belonging to the highest order of paramahamsas, above all rules of caste. His conduct in dining with Moslems, he further said, was not in conflict with the teachings of the scriptures, though it might be frowned upon by the narrow-minded leaders of Hindu society.

At Mount Abu the Swami met the Mahārājā of Khetri, who later became one of his devoted disciples. The latter asked the Swami for the boon of a male heir and obtained his blessing.

Next we see the Swami travelling in Gujrat and Kathiawar in Western India.

In Ahmedabad he refreshed his knowledge of Jainism. Kathiawar, containing a large number of places sacred both to the Hindus and to the Jains, was mostly ruled by Hindu Mahārājās, who received the Swami with respect. To Babu Haridas Beharidas, the Prime Minister of the Moslem state of Junagad, he emphasized the need of preaching the message of Hinduism throughout the world. He spent eleven months in Porebandar and especially enjoyed the company of the Prime Minister, Pandit Sankar Pandurang, a great Sanskrit scholar who was engaged in the translation of the Vedas. Impressed by the Swami's intellectuality and originality, the pandit said: "Swamiji, I am afraid you cannot do much in this country. Few will appreciate you here. You ought to go the West, where people will understand you and your work. Surely you can give to the Western people your enlightening interpretation of Hinduism."

The Swami was pleased to hear these words, which coincided with something he had been feeling within. The Prime Minister encouraged the Swami to continue his study of the French language since it might be useful to him in his future work.

During this period the Swami was extremely restless. He felt within him a boundless energy seeking channels for expression. The regeneration of India was uppermost in his mind. A reawakened India could, in her turn, help the world at large. The sight of the pettiness, jealousy, disunion, ignorance, and poverty among the Hindus filled his mind with great anguish. But he had no patience with the Westernized reformers, who had lost their contact with the soul of the country. He thoroughly disapproved of their method of social, religious, and political reform through imitation of the West. He wanted the Hindus to cultivate self-confidence. Appreciation of India's spiritual culture by the prosperous and powerful West, he thought, might give the Hindus confidence in their own heritage. He prayed to the Lord for guidance. He became friendly with the Hindu Mahārājās who ruled over one-fifth of the country and whose influence was great over millions of people. Through them he wanted to introduce social reforms, improved methods of education, and other measures for the physical and cultural benefit of the people. The Swami felt that in this way his dream of India's regeneration would be realized with comparative ease.

After spending a few days in Baroda, the Swami came to Khandwa in Central India. Here he dropped the first hint of his willingness to participate in the Parliament of Religions to be held shortly in Chicago. He had heard of this Parliament either in Junagad or Porebandar.

After visiting Bombay, Poona, and Kolhapur, the Swami arrived at Belgaum. In Bombay he had accidentally met Swami Abhedananda and in the course of a talk had said to him, "Brother, such a great power has grown within me that sometimes I feel that my whole body will burst."

All through this wandering life he exchanged ideas with people in all stations and stages of life and impressed everyone with his earnestness, eloquence, gentleness, and vast knowledge of Indian and Western culture. Many of the ideas he expressed at this time were later repeated in his public lectures in America and India. But the thought nearest to his heart concerned the poor and ignorant villagers, victims of social injustice: how to improve the sanitary

condition of the villages, introduce scientific methods of agriculture, and procure pure water for daily drinking; how to free the peasants from their illiteracy
and ignorance, how to give back to them their lost confidence. Problems like
these tormented him day and night. He remembered vividly the words of Śri
Ramakrishna that religion was not meant for "empty bellies."

To his hypochondriac disciple Haripada he gave the following sound advice:
"What is the use of thinking always of disease? Keep cheerful, lead a religious
life, cherish elevating thoughts, be merry, but never indulge in pleasures which
tax the body or for which you will feel remorse afterwards; then all will be well.
And as regards death, what does it matter if people like you and me die? That
will not make the earth deviate from its axis! We should not consider ourselves
so important as to think that the world cannot move on without us."

When he mentioned to Haripada his desire to proceed to America, the
disciple was delighted and wanted to raise money for the purpose, but the
Swami said to him that he would not think about it until after making his
pilgrimage to Rameswaram and worshipping the Deity there.

SOUTH INDIA

From Belgaum the Swami went to Bangalore in the State of Mysore, which
was ruled by a Hindu Mahārājā. The Mahārājā's Prime Minister described the
young monk as "a majestic personality and a divine force destined to leave his
mark on the history of his country." The Mahārājā, too, was impressed by his
"brilliancy of thought, charm of character, wide learning, and penetrating
religious insight." He kept the Swami as his guest in the palace.

One day, in front of his high officials, the Mahārājā asked the Swami,
"Swamiji, what do you think of my courtiers?"

"Well," came the bold reply, "I think Your Highness has a very good heart,
but you are unfortunately surrounded by courtiers who are generally flatterers.
Courtiers are the same everywhere."

"But," the Mahārājā protested, "my Prime Minister is not such. He is
intelligent and trustworthy."

"But, Your Highness, a Prime Minister is 'one who robs the Mahārājā and
pays the Political Agent.' "

The Prince changed the subject and afterwards warned the Swami to be
more discreet in expressing his opinion of the officials in a Native State; otherwise those unscrupulous people might even poison him. But the Swami burst
out: "What! Do you think an honest sannyāsin is afraid of speaking the truth,
even though it may cost him his very life? Suppose your own son asks me about
my opinion of yourself; do you think I shall attribute to you all sorts of virtues
which I am quite sure you do not possess? I can never tell a lie."

The Swami addressed a meeting of Sanskrit scholars and gained their applause
for his knowledge of Vedānta. He surprised an Austrian musician at the Prince's
court with his knowledge of Western music. He discussed with the Mahārājā
his plan of going to America, but when the latter came forward with an offer
to pay his expenses for the trip, he declined to make a final decision before
visiting Rameswaram. Perhaps he was not yet quite sure of God's will in the

matter. When pressed by the Mahārājā and the Prime Minister to accept some gifts, the costlier the better, the Swami took a tobacco pipe from the one and a cigar from the other.

Now the Swami turned his steps towards picturesque Malabar. At Trivandrum, the capital of Travancore, he moved in the company of college professors, state officials, and in general among the educated people of the city. They found him equally at ease whether discussing Spencer or Śankarāchārya, Shakespeare or Kālidāsa, Darwin or Patanjali, Jewish history or Āryan civilization. He pointed out to them the limitations of the physical sciences and the failure of Western psychology to understand the superconscious aspect of human nature.

Orthodox brāhmins regarded with abhorrence his habit of eating animal food. The Swami courageously told them about the eating of beef by the brāhmins in Vedic times. One day, asked about what he considered the most glorious period of Indian history, the Swami mentioned the Vedic period, when "five brāhmins used to polish off one cow." He advocated animal food for the Hindus if they were to cope at all with the rest of the world in the present reign of power and find a place among the other great nations, whether within or outside the British Empire.

An educated person of Travancore said about him: "Sublimity and simplicity were written boldly on his features. A clean heart, a pure and austere life, an open mind, a liberal spirit, wide outlook, and broad sympathy were the outstanding characteristics of the Swami."

At Rameswaram the Swami met Bhaskara Setupati, the Rājā of Ramnad, who later became one of his ardent disciples. He discussed with the Prince many of his ideas regarding the education of the Indian masses and the improvement of their agricultural conditions. The Rājā urged the Swami to represent India at the Parliament of Religions in Chicago and promised to help him in his venture. From Rameswaram the Swami went to Kanyākumāri (Cape Comorin), which is the southernmost tip of India.

THE GREAT VISION

At Cape Comorin the Swami became as excited as a child. He rushed to the temple to worship the Divine Mother. He prostrated himself before the Virgin Goddess.[7] As he came out and looked at the sea his eyes fell on a rock. Swimming to the islet through shark-infested waters, he sat on a stone. His heart thumped with emotion. His great journey from the snow-capped Himālayas to the "Land's End" was completed. He had travelled the whole length of the Indian subcontinent, his beloved motherland, which, together with his earthly mother, was "superior to heaven itself."

Sitting on the stone, he recalled what he had seen with his own eyes: the pitiable condition of the Indian masses, victims of the unscrupulous whims of their rulers, landlords, and priests. The tyranny of caste had sapped their last drop of blood. In most of the so-called leaders who shouted from the housetops for the liberation of the people, he had seen selfishness personified. And now

[7] The Deity worshipped in the temple is known as Kanyākumāri, the Virgin Goddess, the Jungfrau.

he asked himself what his duty was in this situation. Should he regard the world as a dream and go into solitude to commune with God? He had tried this several times, but without success. He remembered that, as a sannyāsin, he had taken the vow to dedicate himself to the service of God; but this God, he was convinced, was revealed through humanity. And his own service to this God must begin, therefore, with the humanity of India. "May I be born and reborn," he exclaimed, "and suffer a thousand miseries, if only I may worship the only God in whom I believe, the sum total of all souls, and above all, my God the wicked, my God the afflicted, my God the poor of all races!"

Through austerity and self-control the Swami had conserved great spiritual power. His mind had been filled with the wisdom of the East and the West. He had received in abundance Śri Ramakrishna's blessings. He also had had many spiritual experiences of his own. He must use all of these assets, he concluded, for the service of God in man.

But what was to be the way?

The clear-eyed prophet saw that religion was the backbone of the Indian nation. India would rise through a renewal and restoration of that highest spiritual consciousness which had made her, at all times, the cradle of nations and the cradle of faith. He totally disagreed with foreign critics and their Indian disciples who held that religion was the cause of India's downfall. The Swami blamed, rather, the falsehood, superstition, and hypocrisy that were practised in the name of religion. He himself had discovered that the knowledge of God's presence in man was the source of man's strength and wisdom. He was determined to awaken this sleeping divinity. He knew that the Indian culture had been created and sustained by the twin ideals of renunciation and service, which formed the core of Hinduism. And he believed that if the national life could be intensified through these channels, everything else would take care of itself. The workers for India's regeneration must renounce selfishness, jealousy, greed, and lust for power; and they must dedicate themselves to the service of the poor, the illiterate, the hungry, and the sick, seeing in them the tangible manifestations of the Godhead. People required education, food, health, and the knowledge of science and technology to raise their standard of living. The attempt to teach metaphysics to empty stomachs was sheer madness. The masses everywhere were leading the life of animals on account of ignorance and poverty; therefore these conditions should be removed.

But where would the Swami find the fellow workers to help him in this gigantic task?

He wanted whole-time servants of God, workers without worldly ties or vested interests. And he wanted them by thousands. His eyes fell upon the numerous monks who had renounced the world in search of God. But alas, in present-day India most of these led unproductive lives. He would have to infuse a new spirit into them, and they in their turn would have to dedicate themselves to the service of the people. He hit upon a plan, which he revealed later in a letter to a friend. "Suppose," the Swami wrote, "some disinterested sannyāsins, bent on doing good to others, went from village to village, disseminating education and seeking in various ways to better the condition of all down to the untouchable, through oral teaching and by means of maps, magic lanterns, globes, and other accessories—would that not bring forth good in time? All these plans I cannot write out in this brief letter. The long and short of it is that if the mountain does not come to Mahomet, Mahomet must go to the mountain. The poor are too poor to go to schools; they will gain nothing by reading poetry and all that sort of thing. We, as a nation, have lost our individuality. We have to give back to the nation its lost individuality and raise the masses."

Verily, the Swami, at Kanyākumāri, was the patriot and prophet in one. There he became, as he declared later to a Western disciple, "a condensed India."

But where were the resources to come from, to help him realize his great vision?

He himself was a sannyāsin, a penniless beggar. The rich of the country talked big and did nothing. His admirers were poor. Suddenly a heroic thought entered his mind: he must approach the outside world and appeal to its conscience. But he was too proud to act like a beggar. He wanted to tell the West that the health of India and the sickness of India were the concern of the whole world. If India sank, the whole world would sink with her. For the outside world, in turn, needed India, her knowledge of the Soul and of God, her spiritual heritage, her ideal of genuine freedom through detachment and renunciation; it needed these in order to extricate itself from the sharp claws of the monster of materialism.

Then to the Swami, brooding alone and in silence on that point of rock off the tip of India, the vision came; there flashed before his mind the new continent of America, a land of optimism, great wealth, and unstinted generosity. He saw America as a country of unlimited opportunities, where people's minds were free from the encumbrance of castes or classes. He would give the receptive Americans the ancient wisdom of India and bring back to his motherland, in exchange, the knowledge of science and technology. If he succeeded in his mission to America, he would not only enhance India's prestige in the Occident, but create a new confidence among his own people. He recalled the earnest requests of his friends to represent India in the forthcoming Parliament of Religions in Chicago. And in particular, he remembered the words of the friend in Kathiawar who had been the first to encourage him to go to the West: "Go and take it by storm, and then return!"

He swam back to the continent of India and started northwards again, by the eastern coast.

It may be mentioned here that during the Swami's trip across the country, just described, there had taken place many incidents that strengthened his faith in God, intensified his sympathy for the so-called lower classes, and broadened his general outlook on life and social conventions.

Several times, when he had had nothing to eat, food had come to him unsought, from unexpected quarters. The benefactors had told him that they were directed by God. Then, one day, it had occurred to the Swami that he had no right to lead the life of a wandering monk, begging his food from door to door, and thus depriving the poor of a few morsels which they could otherwise share with their families. Forthwith he entered a deep forest and walked the whole day without eating a grain of food. At nightfall he sat down under a tree, footsore and hungry, and waited to see what would happen next.

Presently he saw a tiger approaching. "Oh," he said, "this is right; both of us are hungry. As this body of mine could not be of any service to my fellow men, let it at least give some satisfaction to this hungry animal." He sat there calmly, but the tiger for some reason or other changed its mind and went off in another direction. The Swami spent the whole night in the forest, meditating on God's inscrutable ways. In the morning he felt a new surge of power.

During his wanderings in the Himālayas, he was once the guest of a Tibetan family and was scandalized to see that polyandry was practised by its members, six brothers sharing a common wife. To the Swami's protest, the eldest brother replied that a Tibetan would consider it selfishness to enjoy a good thing all by himself and not share it with his brothers. After deep thought the Swami realized the relativity of virtue. He saw that many so-called good and evil practices had their roots in the traditions of society. One might argue for or against almost anything. The conventions of a particular society should be judged by its own standards. After that experience, the Swami was reluctant to condemn hastily the traditions of any social group.

One day Swamiji was sharing a railway compartment with two Englishmen, who took him for an illiterate beggar and began to crack jokes in English at his expense. At the next station they were astonished to hear him talking with the station master in perfect English. Embarrassed, they asked him why he had not protested against their rude words. With a smile, the Swami replied, "Friends, this is not the first time that I have seen fools." The Englishmen became angry and wanted a fight. But looking at the Swami's strong body, they thought that discretion was the better part of valour, and apologized.

In a certain place in Rajputana, the Swami was kept busy for three days and nights by people seeking religious instruction. Nobody cared about his food or rest. After they left, a poor man belonging to a low caste offered him, with great hesitation, some uncooked food, since he, being an untouchable, was afraid to give him a prepared meal. The Swami, however, persuaded the kind-hearted man to prepare the meal for him and ate it with relish. Shedding tears of gratitude, the Swami said to himself, "Thousands of such good people live in huts, and we despise them as untouchables!"

In Central India he had to pass many hard days without food or shelter, and it was during this time that he lived with a family of outcaste sweepers and discovered the many priceless spiritual virtues of those people, who cowered at the feet of society. Their misery choked him and he sobbed: "Oh, my country! Oh, my country!"

To resume the story of Swamiji's wandering life: From Cape Comorin he walked most of the way to Madras, stopping at Ramnad and Pondicherry. His fame had already spread to the premier city of South India, and he was greeted by a group of enthusiastic young men. In Madras he publicly announced his intention of going to America. His devotees here collected funds for the trip, and it was through them that he later started his Indian work in an organized form.

Here, in Madras, he poured his whole soul into the discussion of religion, philosophy, science, literature, and history. He would blaze up at people who, for lack of time or zeal, did not practise meditation. "What!" he thundered at a listener. "Those giants of old, the ancient rishis, who never walked but strode, standing by whose side you would shrivel into a moth—they, sir, had time for meditation and devotions, and you have none!"

To a scoffer he said: "How dare you criticize your venerable forefathers in such a fashion? A little learning has muddled your brain. Have you tested the wisdom of the rishis? Have you even as much as read the Vedas? There is a challenge thrown by the rishis. If you dare oppose them, take it up."

At Hyderabad, the capital of the Nizam's State, he gave his first public lecture, the subject being "My Mission to the West." The audience was impressed and the Swami was pleased to see that he could hold his own in this new field of activity.

When the devotees in Madras brought him the money for his voyage to America, he refused to accept it and asked them to distribute it among the poor. How was he to know that the Lord wanted him to go to America? Perhaps he was being carried away by his own ambition. He began to pray intensely for divine guidance. Again money was offered to him by some of his wealthy friends, and again he refused. He said to his disciples: "If it is the Mother's wish that I should go to the West, then let us collect money from the people. It is for them that I am going to the West—for the people and the poor!"

The Swami one day had a symbolic dream, in which he saw Śri Ramakrishna walking into the water of the ocean and beckoning him to follow. He also heard the authoritative word "Go!" In response to a letter that he had written to Sarada Devi, the Holy Mother, she gave him her blessings for the fulfilment of his desire, knowing that it was Ramakrishna's wish that he should undertake the journey to America. And now, at last, he felt sure of his call.

When everything was arranged for the departure, there suddenly arrived in Madras the private secretary of Swamiji's disciple the Mahārājā of Khetri, bearing the happy news of the birth of a royal son. The Swami was earnestly desired to bless the heir apparent. He consented, and the Mahārājā was overjoyed to see him.

The Swami assumed at the Mahārājā's request the name of Vivekananda, and the Mahārājā accompanied him as far as Jeypore when he departed for Bombay.

Here in Jeypore an incident occurred that the Swami remembered all his life. He was invited by the Mahārājā to a musical entertainment in which a nautch-girl was to sing, and he refused to come, since he was a monk and not permitted to enjoy secular pleasures. The singer was hurt and sang in a strain of lamentation. Her words reached the Swami's ears:

> Look not, O Lord, upon my sins!
> Is not Same-sightedness Thy name?
> One piece of iron is used
> Inside the holy shrine,
> Another for the knife
> Held in the butcher's hand;
> Yet both of these are turned to gold
> When touched by the philosophers' stone.

Sacred the Jumnā's water,
Foul the water in the ditch;
Yet both alike are sanctified
Once they have joined the Ganges' stream.
So, Lord, look not upon my sins!
Is not Same-sightedness Thy name?

The Swami was deeply moved. This girl, whom society condemned as impure, had taught him a great lesson: Brahman, the Ever Pure, Ever Free, and Ever Illumined, is the essence of all beings. Before God there is no distinction of good and evil, pure and impure. Such pairs of opposites become manifest only when the light of Brahman is obscured by māyā. A sannyāsin ought to look at all things from the standpoint of Brahman. He should not condemn anything, even a so-called impure person.

The Swami then joined the party and with tears in his eyes said to the girl: "Mother, I am guilty. I was about to show you disrespect by refusing to come to this room. But your song awakened my consciousness."

On his way to Bombay the Swami stopped at the Abu Road station and met Brahmananda and Turiyananda. He told them about his going to America. The two brother disciples were greatly excited. He explained to them the reason for his going: it was India's suffering. "I travelled," he said, "all over India. But alas, it was agony to me, my brothers, to see with my own eyes the terrible poverty of the masses, and I could not restrain my tears! It is now my firm conviction that to preach religion amongst them, without first trying to remove their poverty and suffering, is futile. It is for this reason—to find means for the salvation of the poor of India—that I am going to America."

Addressing Turiyananda, he said, "Brother, I cannot understand your so-called religion." His face was red with his rising blood. Shaking with emotion, he placed his hand on his heart, and said: "But my heart has grown much, much larger, and I have learnt to feel. Believe me, I feel it very sadly." He was choked, and then fell silent. Tears rolled down his cheeks.

Many years later Turiyananda said, while describing the incident: "You can imagine what went through my mind when I heard these pathetic words and saw the majestic sadness of Swamiji. 'Were not these,' I thought, 'the very words and feelings of Buddha?'" And he remembered that long ago Naren had visited Bodh-Gayā and in deep meditation had felt the presence of Buddha.

Another scene of the same nature, though it occurred much later, may be recounted here. Swami Turiyananda called on his illustrious brother disciple, after the latter's triumphant return from America, at the Calcutta home of Balaram Bose, and found him pacing the veranda alone. Deep in thought, he did not notice Turiyananda's presence. He began to hum under his breath a celebrated song of Mirābāi, and tears welled up in his eyes. He stopped and leaned against the balustrade, and hid his face in his palms. He sang in an anguished voice, repeating several times: "Oh, nobody understands my sorrow!" And again: "Only he who suffers knows the depth of my sorrow!" The whole atmosphere became heavy with sadness. The voice pierced Swami Turiyananda's heart like an arrow; but he could not understand the cause of Vivekananda's suffering. Then he suddenly realized that it was a tremendous universal sympathy with the suffering and oppressed everywhere that often made him shed tears of burning blood; and of these the world would never know.

The Swami arrived in Bombay accompanied by the private secretary to the Mahārājā of Khetri, the Prince having provided him with a robe of orange silk, an ochre turban, a handsome purse, and a first-class ticket on the S.S. "Peninsular" of the Peninsular and Orient Company, which would be sailing on May 31, 1893. The Mahārājā had also bestowed on him the name by which he was to become famous and which was destined to raise India in the estimation of the world.

The ship steamed out of the harbour on the appointed day, and one can visualize the Swami standing on its deck, leaning against the rail and gazing at the fast fading landscape of his beloved motherland. What a multitude of pictures must have raced, at that time, through his mind: the image of Śri Ramakrishna, the Holy Mother, and the brother disciples, either living at the Baranagore monastery or wandering through the plains and hills of India! What a burden of memories this lad of twenty-nine was carrying! The legacy of his noble parents, the blessings of his Master, the wisdom learnt from the Hindu scriptures, the knowledge of the West, his own spiritual experiences, India's past greatness, her present sorrow, and the dream of her future glory, the hopes and aspirations of the millions of India's brown men toiling in their brown fields under the scorching tropical sun, the devotional stories of the Purānas, the dizzy heights of Buddhist philosophy, the transcendental truths of Vedānta, the subtleties of the Indian philosophical systems, the soul-stirring songs of the Indian poets and mystics, the stone-carvings and the frescoes of the Ellora and Ajanta caves, the heroic tales of the Rajput and Marhatta fighters, the hymns of the South Indian Alwars, the snow peaks of the towering Himālayas, the murmuring music of the Ganges—all these and many such thoughts fused together to create in the Swami's mind the image of Mother India, a universe in miniature, whose history and society were the vivid demonstration of her philosophical doctrine of unity in diversity. And could India have sent a son worthier than Vivekananda to represent her in the Parliament of Religions—a son who had learnt his spiritual lessons at the feet of a man whose very life was a Parliament of Religions—a son whose heart was big enough to embrace the whole of humanity and to feel for all in its universal compassion?

Soon the Swami adjusted himself to the new life on board the ship—a life completely different from that of a wandering monk. He found it a great nuisance to look after his suitcases, trunk, valise, and wardrobe. His orange robe aroused the curiosity of many fellow passengers, who, however, were soon impressed by his serious nature and deep scholarship. The vessel ploughed through the blue sea, pausing at various ports on the way, and the Swami enjoyed the voyage with the happy excitement of a child, devouring eagerly all he saw.

In Colombo he visited the monasteries of the Hinayāna Buddhists. On the way to Singapore he was shown the favourite haunts of the Malay pirates, whose descendants now, as the Swami wrote to an Indian friend, under the "leviathan guns of modern turreted battleships, have been forced to look about for more peaceful pursuits." He had his first glimpse of China in the busy port of Hongkong, where hundreds of junks and dinghies moved about, each with the wife of its boatman at the helm, for a whole family lived in each floating craft. The traveller was amused to notice the Chinese babies, most of whom were tied to the backs of their mothers, while the latter were busy either pushing heavy loads or jumping with agility from one craft to another. And there was a rush of boats and steam launches coming in and going out.

"Baby John," the Swami wrote humorously to the same friend, "is every moment in danger of having his little head pulverized, pigtail and all, but he does not care a fig. The busy life seems to have no charm for him, and he is quite content to learn the anatomy of a bit of rice-cake given to him by the madly busy mother. The Chinese child is quite a little philosopher and calmly goes to work at the age when your Indian boy can hardly crawl on all fours. He has learnt the philosophy of necessity too well, from his extreme poverty."

At Canton, in a Buddhist monastery, the Swami was received with respect as a great yogi from India. He saw in China, and later in Japan, many temples with manuscripts written in the ancient Bengali script. This made him realize the extent of the influence of India outside her own borders and strengthened his conviction about the spiritual unity of Asia.

Next the boat reached Japan, and the Swami visited Yokohama, Osaka, Kyoto, and Tokyo. The broad streets, the cage-like little houses, the pine-covered hills, and the gardens with shrubs, grass-plots, artificial pools, and small bridges impressed him with the innate artistic nature of the Japanese people. On the other hand, the thoroughly organized Japanese army equipped with guns made in Japan, the expanding navy, the merchant marine, and the industrial factories revealed to him the scientific skill of a newly awakened Asiatic nation. But he was told that the Japanese regarded India as the "dreamland of everything noble and great."

His thoughts always returned to India and her people. He wrote to a disciple in Madras: "Come out and be men! India wants the sacrifice of at least a thousand of her young men—men, mind you, and not brutes. How many men, unselfish and thoroughgoing men, is Madras ready to supply, who will struggle unto death to bring about a new state of things—sympathy for the poor, bread for hungry mouths, enlightenment for the people at large, who have been brought to the level of beasts by the tyranny of your forefathers?"

From Yokohama he crossed the Pacific Ocean and arrived in Vancouver, British Columbia. Next he travelled by train to Chicago, the destination of his journey and the meeting-place of the Parliament of Religions.

THE NEW WORLD

The first sight of Chicago, the third largest city of the New Continent, the great civic queen of the Middle West, enthroned on the shore of Lake Michigan, with its teeming population and strange way of life—a mixture of the refinement of the Eastern coast and the crudities of the backwoods—must have bewildered, excited, and terrified the young visitor from India. Swami Vivekananda walked through the spacious grounds of the World's Fair and was speechless with amazement. He marvelled at what the Americans had achieved through hard work, friendly co-operation with one another, and the application of scientific knowledge. Not too many years before, Chicago had consisted of only a few fishermen's huts, and now at the magic touch of human ingenuity, it was turned into a fairyland. Never before had the Swami seen such an accumulation of wealth, power, and inventive genius in a nation. In the fair-grounds he attracted people's notice. Lads ran after him, fascinated by his orange robe and turban. Shopkeepers and porters regarded him as a Mahārājā from India and tried to impose upon him. On the Swami's part, his first feeling was one of unbounded admiration. But a bitter disillusionment was to come.

Soon after his arrival in Chicago, he went one day to the information bureau of the Exposition to ask about the forthcoming Parliament of Religions. He was told that it had been put off until the first week of September (it was then only the middle of July) and that no one without credentials from a bona fide organization would be accepted as a delegate. He was told also that it was then too late for him to be registered as a delegate. All this had been unexpected by the Swami; for not one of his friends in India—the enthusiastic devotees of Madras, the Mahārājās of Khetri, Ramnad, and Mysore, the Ministers of the native states, and the disciples who had arranged his trip to America—had taken the trouble to make any inquiries concerning the details of the Parliament. No one had known what were to be the dates of the meetings or the conditions of admission. Nor had the Swami brought with him any letter of authority from a religious organization. All had felt that the young monk would need no letter of authorization, his personality being testimonial enough.

"The Swami himself," as his Irish disciple, Sister Nivedita, wrote some years later, "was as simple in the ways of the world as these his disciples, and when he was once sure that he was divinely called to make this attempt, he could see no difficulties in the way. Nothing could have been more typical of the lack of organizedness of Hinduism itself than this going forth of its representative unannounced, and without formal credentials, to enter the strongly guarded door of the world's wealth and power."

In the meantime, the purse that the Swami had carried from India was dwindling; for things were much more expensive in America than he or his friends had thought. He did not have enough to maintain him in Chicago until September. In a frantic mood he asked help from the Theosophical Society, which professed warm friendship for India. He was told that he would have to subscribe to the creed of the Society; but this he refused to do because he did not believe in most of the Theosophical doctrines. Thereupon the leader declined to give him any help. The Swami became desperate and cabled to his friends in Madras for money.

Finally, however, someone advised him to go to Boston, where the cost of living was cheaper, and in the train his picturesque dress, no less than his regal appearance, attracted a wealthy lady who resided in the suburbs of the city. She cordially invited him to be her guest, and he accepted, to save his dwindling purse. He was lodged at "Breezy Meadows," in Metcalf, Massachusetts, and the lady was delighted to display to her inquisitive friends this strange curiosity from the Far East. The Swami met a number of people, most of whom annoyed him by asking queer questions regarding Hinduism and the social customs of India, about which they had read in the tracts of Christian missionaries and sensational writers. However, there came to him a few serious-minded people, and among these were Mrs. Johnson, the lady superintendent of a women's prison, and J. H. Wright, a professor of Greek at Harvard University. On the invitation of the superintendent, he visited the prison and was impressed by the humanitarian attitude of its workers towards the inmates. At once there came to his mind the sad plight of the masses of India and he wrote to a friend on August 20, 1893:

> How benevolently the inmates are treated, how they are reformed and sent back as useful members of society—how grand, how beautiful, you must see to believe! And oh, how my heart ached to think of what we think of the poor, the low, in India. They have no chance, no escape, no way to climb up. They sink lower and lower every day, they feel the blows showered upon them by a cruel society, and they do not know whence the blows come. They have forgotten that they too are men. And the result is slavery. . . . Ah, tyrants! You do not know that the obverse is tyranny and the reverse, slavery.

Swami Vivekananda had no friends in this foreign land, yet he did not lose faith. For had not a kind Providence looked after him during the uncertain days of his wandering life? He wrote in the same letter: "I am here amongst the children of the Son of Mary, and the Lord Jesus will help me."

The Swami was encouraged by Professor Wright to represent Hinduism in the Parliament of Religions, since that was the only way he could be introduced to the nation at large. When he announced, however, that he had no credentials, the professor replied, "To ask you, Swami, for your credentials is like asking the sun about its right to shine." He wrote about the Swami to a number of important people connected with the Parliament, especially to the chairman of the committee on selection of delegates, who was one of his friends, and said, "Here is a man more learned than all our learned professors put together." Professor Wright bought the Swami's railroad ticket for Chicago.

The train bearing Vivekananda to Chicago arrived late in the evening, and he had mislaid, unfortunately, the address of the committee in charge of the delegates. He did not know where to turn for help, and no one bothered to give information to this foreigner of strange appearance. Moreover the station was located in a part of the city inhabited mostly by Germans, who could hardly understand his language. He knew he was stranded there, and looking around saw a huge empty wagon in the railroad freight-yard. In this he spent the night, without food or a bed.

In the morning he woke up "smelling fresh water," to quote his own words, and he walked along the fashionable Lake Shore Drive, which was lined with the mansions of the wealthy, asking people the way to the Parliament grounds. But he was met with indifference. Hungry and weary, he knocked at several doors for food and was rudely treated by the servants. His soiled clothes and unshaven face gave him the appearance of a tramp. Besides, he had forgotten that he was in a land that knew thousands of ways of earning the "almighty dollar," but was unfamiliar with Franciscan poverty or the ways of religious vagabonds. He sat down exhausted on the sidewalk and was noticed from an opposite window. The mistress of the house sent for him and asked the Swami if he was a delegate to the Parliament of Religions. He told her of his difficulties. The lady, Mrs. George W. Hale, a society woman of Chicago, gave him breakfast and looked after his needs. When he had rested, she accompanied him to the offices of the Parliament and presented him to Dr. J. H. Barrows, the President of the Parliament, who was one of her personal friends. The Swami was thereupon cordially accepted as a representative of Hinduism and lodged with the other Oriental delegates. Mr. and Mrs. Hale and their children became his life-long friends. Once again the Swami had been strengthened in his conviction that the Lord was guiding his footsteps, and he prayed incessantly to be a worthy instrument of His will.

THE PARLIAMENT OF RELIGIONS

On Monday, September 11, 1893, the Parliament of Religions opened its deliberations with due solemnity. This great meeting was an adjunct of the World's Columbian Exposition, which had been organized to celebrate the four hundredth anniversary of the discovery of America by Christopher Columbus. One of the main goals of the Exposition was to disseminate knowledge of the progress and enlightenment brought about in the world by Western savants and especially through physical science and technology; but as religion forms a vital factor in human culture, it had been decided to organize a Parliament of Religions in conjunction with the Exposition.

Dr. Barrows, in his history of the Parliament of Religions, writes:

Since faith in a Divine Power to whom men believe they owe service and worship has been, like the sun, a life-giving and fructifying potency in man's intellectual and moral development; since Religion lies back of Hindu literature with its marvellous and mystic developments; of the European Art, whether in the form of Grecian statues or Gothic cathedrals; and of American liberty and the recent uprisings of men in behalf of a juster social condition; and since it is as clear as the light that the Religion of Christ has led to many of the chief and noblest developments of our modern civilization, it did not appear that Religion, any more than Education, Art, or Electricity, should be excluded from the Columbian Exposition.

It is not altogether improbable that some of the more enthusiastic Christian theologians, among the promoters of the Parliament, thought that the Parliament would give them an opportunity to prove the superiority of Christianity, professed by the vast majority of the people of the progressive West, over the other faiths of the world. Much later Swami Vivekananda said, in one of his jocular moods, that the Divine Mother Herself willed the Parliament in order to give him an opportunity to present the Eternal Religion of the Hindus before the world at large, and that the stage was set for him to play his important rôle, everything else being incidental. The appropriateness of this remark can be appreciated now, half a century after the great event, from the fact that whereas all else that was said and discussed at the Parliament has been forgotten, what Vivekananda preached is still cherished in America, and the movement inaugurated by him has endeared itself to American hearts.

"One of the chief advantages," to quote the words of the Hon. Mr. Merwin-Marie Snell, president of the Scientific Section of the Parliament, "has been in the great lessons which it has taught the Christian world, especially the people of the United States, namely, that there are other religions more venerable than Christianity, which surpass it in philosophical depth, in spiritual intensity, in independent vigour of thought, and in breadth and sincerity of human sympathy, while not yielding to it a single hair's breadth in ethical beauty and efficiency."

At 10 a.m. the Parliament opened. In it every form of organized religious belief, as professed among twelve hundred millions of people, was represented. Among the non-Christian groups could be counted Hinduism, Jainism, Buddhism, Confucianism, Shintoism, Mohammedanism, and Mazdaism.

The spacious hall and the huge gallery of the Art Palace were packed with seven thousand people—men and women representing the culture of the United States. The official delegates marched in a grand procession to the platform, and in the centre, in his scarlet robe, sat Cardinal Gibbons, the highest prelate of the Roman Catholic Church in the Western hemisphere. He occupied a chair of state and opened the meeting with a prayer. On his left and right were grouped the Oriental delegates: Pratap Chandra Mazoomdar of the Calcutta Brāhmo Samāj, and Nagarkar of Bombay; Dharmapala, representing the Ceylon Buddhists; Gandhi, representing the Jains; Chakravarti and Annie Besant of the Theosophical Society. With them sat Swami Vivekananda, who represented no particular sect, but the Universal Religion of the Vedas, and who spoke, as will presently be seen, for the religious aspiration of all humanity. His gorgeous robe, large yellow turban, bronze complexion, and fine features stood out prominently on the platform and drew everybody's notice. In numerical order the Swami's position was number thirty-one.

The delegates arose, one by one, and read prepared speeches, but the Hindu sannyāsin was totally unprepared. He had never before addressed such an assembly. When he was asked to give his message he was seized with stage-fright, and requested the chairman to call on him a little later. Several times he postponed the summons. As he admitted later: "Of course my heart was fluttering and my tongue nearly dried up. I was so nervous that I could not venture to speak in the morning session."

At last he came to the rostrum and Dr. Barrows introduced him. Bowing to Sarasvati, the Goddess of Wisdom, he addressed the audience as "Sisters and Brothers of America." Instantly, thousands arose in their seats and gave him loud applause. They were deeply moved to see, at last, a man who discarded formal words and spoke to them with the natural and candid warmth of a brother.

It took a full two minutes before the tumult subsided, and the Swami began his speech by thanking the youngest of the nations in the name of the most ancient monastic order in the world, the Vedic order of sannyāsins. The keynote of his address was universal toleration and acceptance. He told the audience how India, even in olden times, had given shelter to the religious refugees of other lands—for instance, the Israelites and the Zoroastrians—and he quoted from the scriptures the following two passages revealing the Hindu spirit of toleration:

"As different streams, having their sources in different places, all mingle their water in the sea, so, O Lord, the different paths which men take through different tendencies, various though they appear, crooked or straight, all lead to Thee."

"Whosoever comes to Me, through whatsoever form, I reach him. All men are struggling through paths which in the end lead to Me."

In conclusion he pleaded for the quick termination of sectarianism, bigotry, and fanaticism.

The response was deafening applause. It appeared that the whole audience had been patiently awaiting this message of religious harmony. A Jewish intellectual remarked to the present writer, years later, that after hearing Vivekananda he realized for the first time that his own religion, Judaism, was true, and that the Swami had addressed his words on behalf of not only his religion, but all religions of the world. Whereas every one of the other delegates had spoken for his own ideal or his own sect, the Swami had spoken about God, who, as the ultimate goal of all faiths, is their inmost essence. And he had learnt that truth at the feet of Śri Ramakrishna, who had taught incessantly, from his direct experience, that all religions are but so many paths to reach the same goal. The Swami gave utterance to the yearning of the modern world to break down the barriers of caste, colour, and creed and to fuse all people into one humanity.

Not a word of condemnation for any faith, however crude or irrational, fell from his lips. He did not believe that this religion or that religion was true in this or that respect; to him all religions were equally effective paths to lead their respective devotees, with diverse tastes and temperaments, to the same goal of perfection. Years before, young Narendra had condemned before his Master, in his neophyte zeal, a questionable sect that indulged in immoral practices in the name of religion, and Ramakrishna had mildly rebuked him, saying: "Why should you criticize those people? Their way, too, ultimately leads to God. There are many doors to enter a mansion. The scavenger comes in by the back door. You need not use it."

How prophetic were the Master's words that his Naren would one day shake the world! Mrs. S. K. Blodgett, who later became the Swami's hostess in Los Angeles, said about her impressions of the Parliament: "I was at the Parliament of Religions in Chicago in 1893. When that young man got up and said, 'Sisters and Brothers of America,' seven thousand people rose to their feet as a tribute to something they knew not what. When it was over I saw scores of women walking over the benches to get near him, and I said to myself, 'Well, my lad, if you can resist that onslaught you are indeed a God!'"

Swami Vivekananda addressed the Parliament about a dozen times. His outstanding address was a paper on Hinduism in which he discussed Hindu metaphysics, psychology, and theology. The divinity of the soul, the oneness of existence, the non-duality of the Godhead, and the harmony of religions were the recurring themes of his message. He taught that the final goal of man is to become divine by realizing the Divine and that human beings are the children of "Immortal Bliss."

In the final session of the Parliament, Swami Vivekananda said in the conclusion of his speech: "The Christian is not to become a Hindu or a Buddhist, nor is a Hindu or a Buddhist to become a Christian. But each must assimilate the spirit of the others and yet preserve his individuality and grow according to his own law of growth. If the Parliament of Religions has shown anything to the world, it is this: It has proved to the world that holiness, purity, and charity are not the exclusive possessions of any church in the world, and that every system has produced men and women of the most exalted character. In the face of this evidence, if anybody dreams of the exclusive survival of his own religion and the destruction of the others, I pity him from the bottom of my heart and point out to him that upon the banner of every religion will soon be written, in spite of resistance: 'Help and not Fight,' 'Assimilation and not Destruction,' 'Harmony and Peace and not Dissension.' "

The Parliament of Religions offered Swami Vivekananda the long desired opportunity to present before the Western world the eternal and universal truths of his Āryan ancestors. And he rose to the occasion. As he stood on the platform to give his message, he formed, as it were, the confluence of two great streams of thought, the two ideals that had moulded human culture. The vast audience before him represented exclusively the Occidental mind—young, alert, restless, inquisitive, tremendously honest, well disciplined, and at ease with the physical universe, but sceptical about the profundities of the supersensuous world and unwilling to accept spiritual truths without rational proof. And behind him lay the ancient world of India, with its diverse religious and philosophical discoveries, with its saints and prophets who investigated Reality through self-control and contemplation, unruffled by the passing events of the transitory life and absorbed in contemplation of the Eternal Verities. Vivekananda's education, upbringing, personal experiences, and contact with the God-man of modern India had pre-eminently fitted him to represent both ideals and to remove their apparent conflict.

To Vivekananda the religion of the Hindus, based upon the teachings of the Vedas, appeared adequate to create the necessary synthesis. By the Vedas he did not mean any particular book containing the words of a prophet or deriving sanction from a supernatural authority, but the accumulated treasure of spiritual laws discovered by various Indian seers in different times. Just as the law of gravitation existed before its discovery, and would continue to exist even if all humanity forgot it, so do the laws that govern the spiritual world exist independently of our knowledge of them. The moral, ethical, and spiritual relations between soul and soul, and between individual spirits and the Father of all spirits, were in existence before their discovery, and will remain even if we forget them. Regarding the universal character of the Hindu faith the Swami said: "From the high spiritual flights of the Vedānta philosophy, of which the latest discoveries of science seem like echoes, to the low ideas of idolatry with its multifarious mythology, the agnosticism of the Buddhists, and the atheism of the Jains, each and all have a place in Hindu religion."

The young, unknown monk of India was transformed overnight into an outstanding figure of the religious world. From obscurity he leapt to fame. His life-size portraits were posted in the streets of Chicago, with the words "The Monk Vivekananda" written beneath them, and many passers-by would stop to do reverence with bowed heads.

Dr. J. H. Barrows, the President of the Parliament of Religions, said: "Swami Vivekananda exercised a wonderful influence over his auditors," and Mr. Merwin-Marie Snell stated, more enthusiastically: "By far the most important and typical representative of Hinduism was Swami Vivekananda, who, in fact, was beyond question the most popular and influential man in the Parliament. . . . He was received with greater enthusiasm than any other speaker, Christian or pagan. The people thronged about him wherever he went and hung with eagerness on his every word. The most rigid of orthodox Christians say of him, 'He is indeed a prince among men!' "

Newspapers published his speeches and they were read with warm interest all over the country. The *New York Herald* said: "He is undoubtedly the greatest figure in the Parliament of Religions. After hearing him we feel how foolish it is to send missionaries to this learned nation." The *Boston Evening Post* said: "He is a great favourite at the Parliament from the grandeur of his sentiments and his appearance as well. If he merely crosses the platform he is applauded; and this marked approval of thousands he accepts in a childlike spirit of gratification without a trace of conceit. . . . At the Parliament of Religions they used to keep Vivekananda until the end of the programme to make people stay till the end of the session. . . . The four thousand fanning people in the Hall of Columbus would sit smiling and expectant, waiting for an hour or two to listen to Vivekananda for fifteen minutes. The chairman knew the old rule of keeping the best until the last."

It is one of the outstanding traits of Americans to draw out the latent greatness of other people. America discovered Vivekananda and made a gift of him to India and the world.

The reports of the Parliament of Religions were published in the Indian magazines and newspapers. The Swami's vindication of the Hindu faith filled with pride the hearts of his countrymen from Colombo to Almora, from Calcutta to Bombay. Naturally Calcutta, his birthplace, and Madras, which had taken the initiative for his adventurous trip to Chicago, felt the greatest jubilation. Meetings were held in the principal cities to congratulate him on his triumph. The brother monks at the Baranagore monastery were not, at first, clear about the identity of Vivekananda. A letter from the Swami, six months after the Parliament, removed all doubts, however, and how proud they felt at the achievement of their beloved Naren!

But how did Vivekananda himself react to this triumph, which had been the fulfilment of his long cherished desire? He knew that his solitary life as a monk in constant communion with God was at an end; he could no longer live in obscurity with his dreams and visions. Instead of dwelling in peace and serenity, he was thrown into the vortex of a public career with its ceaseless turmoil and demands. When he returned to his hotel the night after the first meeting of the Parliament, he wept like a child.

AFTER THE PARLIAMENT

After he had delivered his message in the Parliament, the Swami suffered no longer from material wants. The doors of the wealthy were thrown open. Their lavish hospitality made him sick at heart when he remembered the crushing poverty of his own people. His anguish became so intense one night that he rolled on the floor, groaning: "O Mother, what do I care for name and fame when my motherland remains sunk in utmost poverty? To what a sad pass have we poor Indians come when millions of us die for want of a handful of rice, and here they spend millions of rupees upon their personal comfort! Who will raise the masses of India? Who will give them bread? Show me, O Mother, how I can help them." While addressing one session of the Parliament, the Swami had said that what India needed was not religion, but bread. Now he began to study American life in its various aspects, especially the secret of the country's high standard of living, and he communicated to his disciples in India his views on the promotion of her material welfare.

Swami Vivekananda was invited by a lecture bureau to tour the United States, and he accepted the offer. He wanted money in order to free himself from obligation to his wealthy friends and also to help his various philanthropic and religious projects in India. Further, he thought that through a lecture bureau he could effectively broadcast his ideas all over the American continent and thus remove from people's minds erroneous notions regarding Hindu religion and society. Soon he was engaged in a whirlwind tour covering the larger cities of the East and the Middle West. People called him the "cyclonic Hindu." He visited, among other places, Iowa City, Des Moines, St. Louis, Indianapolis, Minneapolis, Detroit, Buffalo, Hartford, Boston, Cambridge, New York, Baltimore, and Washington. Cherishing a deep affection for the members of the Hale family, he made his headquarters with George W. Hale in Chicago.

But his path was not always strewn with rose petals. Vivekananda was an outspoken man. Whenever he found in American society signs of brutality, inhumanity, pettiness, arrogance, and ignorance concerning cultures other than its own, he mercilessly criticized them. Often small-minded people asked him irritating questions about India, based upon malicious and erroneous reports, and the Swami fell upon them like a thunderbolt. "But woe to the man," wrote the *Iowa State Register*, "who undertook to combat the monk on his own ground, and that was where they all tried it who tried it at all. His replies came like flashes of lightning and the venturesome questioner was sure to be impaled on the Indian's shining intellectual lance. . . . Vivekananda and his cause found a place in the hearts of all true Christians."

Many Christian ministers became his warm friends and invited him to speak in their churches.

Swami Vivekananda was especially bitter about false Christianity and the religious hypocrisy of many Christian leaders. In a lecture given in Detroit he came out in one of his angriest moods, and declared in the course of his speech:

You train and educate and clothe and pay men to do what?—to come over to my country and curse and abuse all my forefathers, my religion, my everything. They walk near a temple and say, "You idolaters, you will go to hell." But the Hindu is mild; he smiles and passes on, saying, "Let the fools talk." And then you who train men to abuse and criticize, if I just touch you with the least bit of criticism, but with the kindest purpose, you shrink and cry: "Do not touch us! We are Americans; we criticize, curse, and abuse all the heathens of the world, but do not touch us, we are sensitive plants." And whenever your missionaries criticize us, let them remember this: If all India stands up and takes all the mud that lies at the bottom of the Indian Ocean and throws it up against the Western countries, it will not be doing an infinitesimal part of what you are doing to us.

Continuing, the Swami said that the military conquests of the Western nations and the activities of the Christian missionaries, strangely enough, often proceeded side by side. Most people were converted for worldly reasons. But the Swami warned:

Such things tumble down; they are built upon sand; they cannot remain long. Everything that has selfishness for its basis, competition for its right hand, and enjoyment as its goal, must die sooner or later.

If you want to live, go back to Christ. You are not Christians. No, as a nation you are not. Go back to Christ. Go back to him who had nowhere to lay his head. Yours is a religion preached in the name of luxury. What an irony of fate! Reverse this if you want to live; reverse this. You cannot serve God and Mammon at the same time. All this prosperity—all this from Christ? Christ would have denied all such heresies. If you can join these two, this wonderful prosperity with the ideal of Christ, it is well; but if you cannot, better go back to him and give up these vain pursuits. Better be ready to live in rags with Christ than to live in palaces without him.

On one occasion the Swami was asked to speak in Boston on Ramakrishna, a subject dear to his heart. When he looked at the audience—the artificial and worldly crowd of people—and contrasted it with his Master's purity and renunciation, he practically dropped the subject and mercilessly inveighed against the materialistic culture of the West. The audience was resentful and many left the meeting in an angry mood. But Vivekananda, too, had his lesson. On returning home he recalled what he had said, and wept. His Master had never uttered a word of condemnation against anybody, even the most wicked person; yet he, while talking about Ramakrishna, had criticized these good-hearted people who were eager to learn about the Master. He felt that he was unworthy of Śri Ramakrishna and resolved not to discuss him in public or even to write about him again.

Swami Vivekananda's outspoken words aroused the bitter enmity of a large section of the Christian missionaries and their American patrons, and also of Christian fanatics. Filled with rancour and hatred, these began to vilify him both openly and in private. They tried to injure his reputation by writing false stories traducing his character. Some of the Indian delegates to the Parliament, jealous of the Swami's popularity and fame, joined in the vilification. Missionaries working in India and some of the Hindu organizations started an infamous campaign against the Swami's work. The Theosophists were particularly vindictive. They declared that the Swami was violating the laws of monastic life in America by eating forbidden food and breaking caste laws.

His friends and disciples in India were frightened and sent him cuttings from Indian papers containing these malicious reports. One article stated that one of the Swami's American hostesses had had to dismiss a servant girl on account of the Swami's presence in the house. But the lady published a vehement denial and said that the Swami was an honoured guest in her home and would always be treated with affection and respect. The Swami wrote to his timorous devotees in India concerning a particular American paper that had criticized him, telling them that it was generally known in America as the "blue-nosed Presbyterian paper," that no educated American took it seriously, and that, following the well-known Yankee trick, it had tried to gain notoriety by attacking a man lionized by society. He assured them that the American people as a whole, and many enlightened Christian clergymen, were among his admiring friends, and he asked them not to send him any more of such newspaper trash with articles from his vilifiers. He told them, furthermore, that he had never deviated from the two basic vows of the monastic life, namely, chastity and poverty, and that as regards other things, he was trying to adjust himself to the customs of the people among whom he lived.

To the accusation from some orthodox Hindus that the Swami was eating beef and other forbidden food at the table of infidels, he retorted:

Do you mean to say I am born to live and die as one of those caste-ridden, super-stitious, merciless, hypocritical, atheistic cowards that you only find among the educated Hindus? I hate cowardice. I will have nothing to do with cowards. I belong to the world as much as to India, no humbug about that. What country has a special claim on me? Am I a nation's slave? . . . I see a greater power than man or God or Devil at my back. I require nobody's help. I have been all my life helping others.

To another Indian devotee he wrote in similar vein:

I am surprised that you take the missionaries' nonsense so seriously. . . . If the people of India want me to keep strictly to my Hindu diet, please tell them to send me a cook and money enough to keep him. . . . On the other hand, if the missionaries tell you that I have ever broken the two great vows of the sannyāsin—chastity and poverty—tell them that they are big liars. As for me, mind you, I stand at nobody's dictation, and no chauvinism about me. . . . I hate cowardice; I will have nothing to do with cowards or political nonsense. I do not believe in any politics. God and truth are the only politics in the world; everything else is trash.

Swami Vivekananda remained unperturbed by opposition. His lectures, intensely religious and philosophical, were attended everywhere by eminent people. Many came to him for private instruction. His aim was to preach the eternal truths of religion and to help sincere people in moulding their spiritual life. Very soon his dauntless spirit, innate purity, lofty idealism, spiritual personality, and spotless character attracted to him a band of sincere and loyal American disciples, whom he began to train as future Vedānta workers in America.

AMERICA AT THE TIME OF VIVEKANANDA

It must be said to the credit of America that she was not altogether unprepared to receive the message of Vivekananda. Certain spiritual ideas, which were congenial for the reception of the Vedāntic ideals presented by the Swami, had already begun to ferment underneath the robust, picturesque, gay, and dynamic surface of American life. Freedom, equality, and justice had always been the cherished treasures of American hearts. To these principles, which the Americans applied in politics and society for the material and ethical welfare of men, Swami Vivekananda gave a spiritual basis and interpretation.

Religion had played an important part from the very beginning of American

Colonial history. The pilgrims who crossed the Atlantic in the "Mayflower" and landed on the barren coast of Cape Cod in November 1620, were English people who had first left England and gone to Holland for freedom of worship. Later they were joined by other dissenters who could not submit to the restrictions placed upon their religious beliefs by the English rulers of the time. These were the forbears of the sturdy, religious-minded New Englanders who, two centuries later, became the leaders of the intellectual and spiritual culture of America. Swami Vivekananda found among their descendants many of his loyal and enthusiastic followers.

Both the Holy Bible and the philosophy of Locke influenced the Bill of Rights and the American Constitution. Leaders imbued with the Christian ideal of the Fatherhood of God and the brotherhood of men penned the second paragraph of the Declaration of Independence, which clearly set forth its political philosophy, namely, the equality of men before God, the state, and society. Thomas Paine, one of the high priests of the American Revolution, was an uncompromising foe of tyranny, and an upholder of human freedom. The same passion for equality, freedom, justice, enduring peace, and righteousness was later to permeate the utterances of the great Lincoln.

The political structure of America shows the sagacity and lofty idealism of her statesmen, who built up the country after the War of Independence. The original thirteen colonies, which had wrested freedom from England, gradually became the United States of America. The architects of the American Government might have created, following the imperialistic pattern of England, an American Empire, with the original thirteen states as a sort of mother country and the rest as her colonies. But instead, the newly acquired territories received complete equality of status. It may also be mentioned that, with the exception of the Mexican War of 1845, America has never started a war.

Within a hundred years of her gaining independence, America showed unprecedented material prosperity. The country's vast hidden wealth was tapped by European immigrants, who brought with them not only the flavour of an older civilization, but technical skill, indomitable courage, and the spirit of adventure. Scientists and technologists flooded the country with new inventions. Steamboats, a network of railroads, and various mechanical appliances aided in the creation of new wealth. Towns grew into cities. As big business concerns expanded, workmen and mechanics formed protective organizations. Ambition stirred everywhere, and men's very manners changed with the new haste and energy that swept them on.

Material prosperity was accompanied by a new awakening of men's minds and consciousness. Jails were converted into penitentiary systems, based upon humanitarian principles, and anti-slavery societies were inaugurated. During the five years between 1850 and 1855 were published some of the greatest books in American literature, hardly surpassed in imaginative vitality. Democracy was in full swing and it was the people's day everywhere. The crude frontier days were fast disappearing.

The Transcendentalist Movement, of which Emerson was the leader, with Thoreau and Alcott as his associates, brought spiritual India into the swift current of American life. The old and new continents had not been altogether strangers. Columbus had set out to find the short route to India, known far and wide for her fabulous wealth, and had stumbled upon America instead. The chests of tea of the Boston Tea Party, which set off the War of Independence, had come from India. Moreover, the victory of the English over the French in the eighteenth-century colonial wars in India contributed to the success of the American colonists in their struggle for freedom begun in 1775. And finally, Commodore Perry in 1853 made it possible for American merchant ships to trade with the Far East and thus visit Indian coastal towns on their long journeys.

The development of Emerson's innate idealism had been aided by the philosophy of Greece, the ethics of China, the poetry of the Sufis, and the mysticism of India. Emerson, a keen student of the Bhagavad Gītā, was familiar with the Upanishadic doctrines and published translations of religious and philosophical tracts from the Oriental languages. His beautiful poem "Brahma" and his essay "The Over-Soul" show clearly his indebtedness to Hindu spiritual thought. But Emerson's spirit, pre-eminently ethical and intellectual, could not grasp the highest flights of Hindu mysticism; it accepted only what was in harmony with a somewhat shallow optimism. Emerson's writings later influenced the New Thought movement and Mary Baker Eddy's Christian Science.

Thoreau, Emerson's neighbour for twenty-five years, read and discussed with him in great detail the Hindu religious classics. Thoreau wrote: "I bathe my intellect in the stupendous and cosmogonal philosophy of the Upanishads and the Bhagavad Gītā, in comparison with which our modern world and literature seem puny and trivial." He wanted to write a joint Bible, gathering material from the Asiatic scriptures, and took for his motto *Ex Oriente Lux*.

Alcott was a genuine friend of Indian culture. He was instrumental in bringing out the American edition of Sir Edwin Arnold's *The Light of Asia*, and this made the life and teachings of Buddha accessible, for the first time, to American readers.

The Transcendental Club, founded in Concord, near Boston, reached its height by 1840. The American Oriental Society was formed in 1842, with aims similar to those of the European Oriental societies.

Walt Whitman (1819-1892), a contemporary of the Concord philosophers, seems to have come very near to Vedāntic idealism. There is no reliable evidence to show that Whitman was directly influenced by Hindu thought. He is reputed to have denied it himself. A great religious individualist, he was free from all church conventions and creeds. To him, religion consisted entirely of inner illumination, "the secret silent ecstasy." It is not known if he practised any definite religious disciplines; most probably he did not. Yet Swami Vivekananda once called Whitman "the sannyāsin of America." *Leaves of Grass*, which Swami Vivekananda read, breathes the spirit of identity with all forms of life, and Whitman's "Song of the Open Road" is full of the sentiments that were nearest to the heart of Vivekananda. Here, for example, are three stanzas:

I inhale great draughts of space;
The east and the west are mine, and the north and the south are mine.

I am larger, better than I thought;
I did not know I held so much goodness.

*   *   *

Allons! We must not stop here!
However sweet these laid-up stores—however convenient this dwelling, we cannot remain here;
However shelter'd this port, and however calm these waters, we must not anchor here;
However welcome the hospitality that surrounds us, we are permitted to receive it but a little while.

*   *   *

Allons! Be not detain'd!
Let the paper remain on the desk unwritten, and the book on the shelf unopen'd!
Let the tools remain in the workshop! let the money remain unearn'd!
Let the school stand! mind not the cry of the teacher!
Let the preacher preach in the pulpit! let the lawyer plead in the court, and the judge expound the law.

The marriage of East and West dreamt of by Emerson and Thoreau was not consummated for several reasons. The Gold Rush of 1849, to California, had turned people's attention in other directions. Then had come the Civil War, in which brother had fought brother and men's worst passions had been let loose. Lastly, the development of science and technology had brought about a great change in people's outlook, intensifying their desire for material prosperity.

The publication of Darwin's *Origin of Species* in 1859 changed the *Weltanschauung* of the Western world, and its repercussions were felt more in the New World than in Europe. Within a decade, intellectual people gave up their belief in the Biblical story of creation and did not hesitate to trace man's origin back to an apelike ancestor, and beyond that to a primordial protoplasmic atomic globule. The implications of evolution were incorporated into every field of thought—law, history, economics, sociology, philosophy, religion, and art; transcendentalism was replaced by empiricism, instrumentalism, and pragmatism. The American life-current thus was turned into a new channel. When America had been comparatively poor she had cherished her spiritual heritage. In the midst of her struggle for existence she had preserved her spiritual sensitivity. But in the wake of the Civil War the desire to possess "bigger and better things" cast its spell everywhere. Big utilities and corporations came into existence; the spiritual and romantic glow of the frontier days degenerated into the sordidness of competitive materialistic life, while the unceasing flow of crude immigrants from Europe made difficult the stabilization of American culture.

Emerson was disillusioned by the aftermath of the Civil War. He had hoped "that in the peace after such a war, a great expansion would follow in the mind of the country, grand views in every direction—true freedom in politics, in religion, in social science, in thought. But the energy of the nation seems to have expended itself in the war."

Walt Whitman was even more caustic. He wrote bitterly:

Society in the States is cramped, crude, superstitious, and rotten. . . . Never was there, perhaps, more hollowness of heart than at present, and here in the United States. Genuine belief seems to have left us. . . . The great cities reek with respectable, as much as non-respectable, robbery and scoundrelism. In fashionable life, flippancy, tepid amours, weak infidelism, small aims, or no aims at all, only to kill time. . . . I say that our New World Democracy, however great a success in uplifting the masses out of their sloughs in materialistic development, and in a certain highly deceptive superficial popular intellectuality, is so far an almost complete failure in its social aspects. In vain do we march with unprecedented strides to empire so colossal, outvying the antique, beyond Alexander's, beyond the proudest sway of Rome. In vain we annexed Texas, California, Alaska, and reach north for Canada or south for Cuba. It is as if we were somehow being endowed with a vast and thoroughly appointed body, and left with little or no soul.

But the material prosperity or the triumph of science could not destroy the innate idealism of the American mind. It remained hidden like embers under ashes. Thoughtful Americans longed for a philosophy which, without going counter to the scientific method, would show the way to a larger vision of life, harmonizing the diverse claims of science, the humanities, and mystical experience. Now the time was ripe for the fulfilment of Thoreau's dream of the marriage of East and West, a real synthesis of science and religion. And to bring this about, no worthier person could have been found than Swami Vivekananda of India. This accounts for the spontaneous welcome received by this representative of Hinduism, who brought to America an ancient and yet dynamic philosophy of life.

VEDĀNTA IN AMERICA

After the meetings of the Parliament of Religions were concluded, Swami Vivekananda, as already noted, undertook a series of apostolic campaigns in order to sow the seed of the Vedāntic truths in the ready soil of America. Soon he discovered that the lecture bureau was exploiting him. Further, he did not like its method of advertisement. He was treated as if he were the chief attraction of a circus. The prospectus included his portrait, with the inscription, proclaiming his cardinal virtues: "An Orator by Divine Right; a Model Representative of his Race; a Perfect Master of the English Language; the Sensation of the World's Fair Parliament." It also described his physical bearing, his height, the colour of his skin, and his clothing. The Swami felt disgusted at being treated like a patent medicine or an elephant in a show. So he severed his relationship with the bureau and arranged his own lectures himself. He accepted invitations from churches, clubs, and private gatherings, and travelled extensively through the Eastern and Midwestern states of America, delivering twelve to fourteen or more lectures a week.

People came in hundreds and in thousands. And what an assorted audience he had to face! There came to his meetings professors from universities, ladies of fine breeding, seekers of truth, and devotees of God with childlike faith. But mixed with these were charlatans, curiosity-seekers, idlers, and vagabonds. It is not true that he met everywhere with favourable conditions. Leon Landsberg, one of the Swami's American disciples, thus described Vivekananda's tribulations of those days:

The Americans are a receptive nation. That is why the country is a hotbed of all kinds of religious and irreligious monstrosities. There is no theory so absurd, no doctrine so irrational, no claim so extravagant, no fraud so transparent, but can find their numerous believers and a ready market. To satisfy this craving, to feed the credulity of the people, hundreds of societies and sects are born for the salvation of the world, and to enable the prophets to pocket $25 to $100 initiation fees. Hobgoblins, spooks, mahātmās, and new prophets were rising every day. In this bedlam of religious cranks, the Swami appeared to teach the lofty religion of the Vedas, the profound philosophy of Vedānta, the sublime wisdom of the ancient rishis. The most unfavourable environment for such a task!

The Swami met with all kinds of obstacles. The opposition of fanatical Christian missionaries was, of course, one of these. They promised him help if he only would preach their brand of Christianity. When the Swami refused, they circulated all sorts of filthy stories about him, and even succeeded in persuading some of the Americans who had previously invited him to be their guest, to cancel the invitations. But Vivekananda continued to preach the religion of love, renunciation, and truth as taught by Christ, and to show him the highest veneration as a Saviour of mankind. How significant were his words: "It is well to be born in a church, but it is terrible to die there!" Needless to say, he meant by the word church all organized religious institutions. How like a thunderbolt the words fell upon the ears of his audience when one day he exclaimed: "Christ, Buddha, and Krishna are but waves in the Ocean of Infinite Consciousness that *I am!*"

Then there were the leaders of the cranky, selfish, and fraudulent organizations, who tried to induce the Swami to embrace their cause, first by promises of support, and then by threats of injuring him if he refused to ally himself with them. But he could be neither bought nor frightened—"the sickle had hit on a stone," as the Polish proverb says. To all these propositions his only answer was: "I stand for Truth. Truth will never ally itself with falsehood. Even if all the world should be against me, Truth must prevail in the end."

But the more powerful enemies he had to face were among the so-called free-thinkers, embracing the atheists, materialists, agnostics, rationalists, and others of similar breed who opposed anything associated with God or religion. Thinking that they would easily crush his ancient faith by arguments drawn from Western philosophy and science, they organized a meeting in New York and invited the Swami to present his views.

"I shall never forget that memorable evening," wrote an American disciple, "when the Swami appeared single-handed to face the forces of materialism, arrayed in the heaviest armour of law, and reason, and logic, and common sense, of matter, and force, and heredity, and all the stock phrases calculated to awe and terrify the ignorant. Imagine their surprise when they found that, far from being intimidated by these big words, he proved himself a master in wielding their own weapons, and as familiar with the arguments of materialism as with those of Advaita philosophy. He showed them that their much vaunted Western science could not answer the most vital questions of life and being, that their immutable laws, so much talked of, had no outside existence apart from the human mind, that the very idea of matter was a metaphysical conception, and that it was much despised metaphysics upon which ultimately rested the very basis of their materialism. With an irresistible logic he demonstrated that their knowledge proved itself incorrect, not by comparison with that which was true, but by the very laws upon which it depended for its basis; that pure reason could not help admitting its own limitations and pointed to something beyond reason; and that rationalism, when carried to its last consequences, must ultimately land us at something which is above matter, above force, above sense, above thought, and even consciousness, and of which all these are but manifestations."

As a result of his explaining the limitations of science, a number of people from the group of free-thinkers attended the Swami's meeting the next day and listened to his uplifting utterances on God and religion.

What an uphill work it was for Swami Vivekananda to remove the ignorance, superstition, and perverted ideas about religion in general and Hinduism in particular! No wonder he sometimes felt depressed. In one of these moods he wrote from Detroit, on March 15, 1894, to the Hale sisters in Chicago:

But I do not know—I have become very sad in my heart since I am here. I do not know why. I am wearied of lecturing and all that nonsense. This mixing with hundreds of human animals, male and female, has disturbed me. I will tell you what is to my taste. I cannot write—cannot speak—but I can think deep, and when I am heated can speak fire. But it should be to a select few—a very select few. And let them carry and sow my ideas broadcast if they will—not I. It is only a just division of labour. The same man never succeeded in thinking and in casting his thoughts all around. Such thoughts are not worth a penny. . . . I am really not "cyclonic" at all—far from it. What I want is not here—nor can I longer bear this cyclonic atmosphere. Calm, cool, nice, deep, penetrating, independent, searching thought—a few noble, pure mirrors which will reflect it back, catch it until all of them sound in unison. Let others throw it to the outside world if they will. This is the way to perfection—to be perfect, to make perfect a few men and women. My idea of doing good is this—to evolve a few giants, and not to strew pearls to the swine and lose time, breath, and energy. . . . Well, I do not care for lecturing any more. It is too disgusting to bring me to suit anybody's or any audience's fad.

Swami Vivekananda became sick of what he termed "the nonsense of public life and newspaper blazoning."

The Swami had sincere admirers and devotees among the Americans, who looked after his comforts, gave him money when he lacked it, and followed his instruction. He was particularly grateful to American women, and wrote many letters to his friends in India paying high praise to their virtues.

In one letter he wrote: "Nowhere in the world are women like those of this country. How pure, independent, self-relying, and kind-hearted! It is the women who are the life and soul of this country. All learning and culture are centred in them."

In another letter: "[Americans] look with veneration upon women, who play a most prominent part in their lives. Here this form of worship has attained its perfection—this is the long and short of it. I am almost at my wit's end to see the women of this country. They are Lakshmi, the Goddess of Fortune, in beauty, and Sarasvati, the Goddess of Learning, in virtues—they are the Divine Mother incarnate. If I can raise a thousand such Madonnas—incarnations of the Divine Mother—in our country before I die, I shall die in peace. Then only will our countrymen become worthy of their name."

Perhaps his admiration reached its highest pitch in a letter to the Mahārājā of Khetri, which he wrote in 1894:

American women! A hundred lives would not be sufficient to pay my deep debt of gratitude to you! Last year I came to this country in summer, a wandering preacher of a far distant country, without name, fame, wealth, or learning to recommend me—friendless, helpless, almost in a state of destitution; and American women befriended me, gave me shelter and food, took me to their homes, and treated me as their own son, their own brother. They stood as my friends even when their own priests were trying to persuade them to give up the "dangerous heathen"—even when, day after day, their best friends had told them not to stand by this "unknown foreigner, maybe of dangerous character." But they are better judges of character and soul—for it is the pure mirror that catches the reflection.

And how many beautiful homes I have seen, how many mothers whose purity of character, whose unselfish love for their children, are beyond expression, how many daughters and pure maidens, "pure as the icicle on Diana's temple"—and withal much culture, education, and spirituality in the highest sense! Is America, then, only full of wingless angels in the shape of women? There are good and bad everywhere, true—but a nation is not to be judged by its weaklings, called the wicked, for they are only the weeds which lag behind, but by the good, the noble, and the pure, who indicate the national life-current to be flowing clear and vigorous.

And how bitter the Swami felt when he remembered the sad plight of the women of India! He particularly recalled the tragic circumstances under which one of his own sisters had committed suicide. He often thought that the misery of India was largely due to the ill-treatment the Hindus meted out to their womenfolk. Part of the money earned by his lectures was sent to a foundation for Hindu widows at Baranagore. He also conceived the idea of sending to India women teachers from the West for the intellectual regeneration of Hindu women.

Swami Vivekananda showed great respect for the fundamentals of American culture. He studied the country's economic policy, industrial organizations, public instruction, and its museums and art galleries, and wrote to India enthusiastically about them. He praised highly the progress of science, hygiene, institutions, and social welfare work. He realized that such noble concepts as the divinity of the soul and the brotherhood of men were mere academic theories in present-day India, whereas America showed how to apply them in life. He felt indignant when he compared the generosity and liberality of the wealthy men of America in the cause of social service, with the apathy of the Indians as far as their own people were concerned.

"No religion on earth," he wrote angrily, "preaches the dignity of humanity in such a lofty strain as Hinduism, and no religion on earth treads upon the necks of the poor and the low in such a fashion as Hinduism. Religion is not at fault, but it is the Pharisees and Sadducees."

How poignant must have been his feelings when he remembered the iniquities of the caste-system! "India's doom was sealed," he wrote, "the very day they invented the word mlechcha[8] and stopped from communion with others." When he saw in New York a millionaire woman sitting side by side in a tram-

---

[8] The non-Hindu, with whom all social intercourse is forbidden.

car with a negress with a wash-basket on her lap, he was impressed with the democratic spirit of the Americans. He wanted in India "an organization that will teach the Hindus mutual help and appreciation" after the pattern of Western democracies.

Incessantly he wrote to his Indian devotees about the regeneration of the masses. In a letter dated 1894 he said:

Let each one of us pray, day and night, for the downtrodden millions in India, who are held fast by poverty, priestcraft, and tyranny—pray day and night for them. I care more to preach religion to them than to the high and the rich. I am no metaphysician, no philosopher, nay, no saint. But I am poor, I love the poor. . . . Who feels in India for the three hundred millions of men and women sunken for ever in poverty and ignorance? Where is the way out? Who feels for them? Let these people be your God— think of them, work for them, pray for them incessantly—the Lord will show you the way. Him I call a mahātmā, a noble soul, whose heart bleeds for the poor; otherwise he is a durātmā, a wicked soul. . . . So long as the millions live in hunger and ignorance, I hold every man a traitor who, having been educated at their expense, pays not the least heed to them. . . . We are poor, my brothers, we are nobodies, but such have always been the instruments of the Most High.

Never did he forget, in the midst of the comforts and luxuries of America, even when he was borne on the wings of triumph from one city to another, the cause of the Indian masses, whose miseries he had witnessed while wandering as an unknown monk from the Himālayas to Cape Comorin. The prosperity of the new continent only stirred up in his soul deeper commiseration for his own people. He saw with his own eyes what human efforts, intelligence, and earnestness could accomplish to banish from society poverty, superstition, squalor, disease, and other handicaps of human well-being. On August 20, 1893, he wrote to instil courage into the depressed hearts of his devotees in India:

Gird up your loins, my boys! I am called by the Lord for this. . . . The hope lies in you—in the meek, the lowly, but the faithful. Feel for the miserable and look up for help—it shall come. I have travelled twelve years with this load in my heart and this idea in my head. I have gone from door to door of the so-called "rich and great." With a bleeding heart I have crossed half the world to this strange land, seeking help. The Lord is great. I know He will help me. I may perish of cold and hunger in this land, but I bequeath to you young men this sympathy, this struggle for the poor, the ignorant, the oppressed. . . . Go down on your faces before Him and make a great sacrifice, the sacrifice of a whole life for them, for whom He comes from time to time, whom He loves above all—the poor, the lowly, the oppressed. Vow, then, to devote your whole lives to the cause of these three hundred millions, going down and down every day. Glory unto the Lord! We will succeed. Hundreds will fall in the struggle—hundreds will be ready to take it up. Faith—sympathy, fiery faith and fiery sympathy! Life is nothing, death is nothing—hunger nothing, cold nothing. Glory unto the Lord! March on, the Lord is our General. Do not look back to see who falls—forward—onward!

Swami Vivekananda was thoroughly convinced by his intimate knowledge of the Indian people that the life-current of the nation, far from being extinct, was only submerged under the dead weight of ignorance and poverty. India still produced great saints whose message of the Spirit was sorely needed by the Western world. But the precious jewels of spirituality discovered by them were hidden, in the absence of a jewel-box, in a heap of filth. The West had created the jewel-box, in the form of a healthy society, but it did not have the jewels. Further, it took him no long time to understand that a materialistic culture contained within it the seeds of its own destruction. Again and again he warned the West of its impending danger. The bright glow on the Western horizon might not be the harbinger of a new dawn; it might very well be the red flames of a huge funeral pyre. The Western world was caught in the maze of its incessant activity—interminable movement without any goal. The hankering for material comforts, without a higher spiritual goal and a feeling of universal sympathy, might flare up among the nations of the West into jealousy and hatred, which in the end would bring about their own destruction.

Swami Vivekananda was a lover of humanity. Man is the highest manifestation of God, and this God was being crucified in different ways in the East and the West. Thus he had a double mission to perform in America. He wanted to obtain from the Americans money, scientific knowledge, and technical help for the regeneration of the Indian masses, and, in turn, to give to the Americans the knowledge of the Eternal Spirit to endow their material progress with significance. No false pride could prevent him from learning from America the many features of her social superiority; he also exhorted the Americans not to allow racial arrogance to prevent them from accepting the gift of spirituality from India. Through this policy of acceptance and mutual respect he dreamt of creating a healthy human society for the ultimate welfare of man's body and soul.

VARIOUS EXPERIENCES AS A TEACHER

The year following the Parliament of Religions the Swami devoted to addressing meetings in the vast area spreading from the Mississippi to the Atlantic. In Detroit he spent six weeks, first as a guest of Mrs. John Bagley, widow of the former Governor of Michigan, and then of Thomas W. Palmer, President of the World's Fair Commission, formerly a United States Senator and American Minister to Spain. Mrs. Bagley spoke of the Swami's presence at her house as a "continual benediction." It was in Detroit that Miss Greenstidel first heard him speak. She later became, under the name of Sister Christine, one of the most devoted disciples of the Swami and a collaborator of Sister Nivedita in her work in Calcutta for the educational advancement of Indian women.

After Detroit, he divided his time between Chicago, New York, and Boston, and during the summer of 1894 addressed, by invitation, several meetings of the "Humane Conference" held at Greenacre, Massachusetts. Christian Scientists, spiritualists, faith-healers, and groups representing similar views participated in the Conference.

The Swami, in the course of a letter to the Hale sisters of Chicago, wrote on July 31, 1894, with his usual humour about the people who attended the meetings:

They have a lively time and sometimes all of them wear what you call your scientific dress the whole day. They have lectures almost every day. One Mr. Colville from Boston is here. He speaks every day, it is said, under spirit control. The editor of the Universal Truth from the top floor of Jimmy Mills has settled herself down here. She is conducting religious services and holding classes to heal all manner of diseases, and very soon I expect them to be giving eyes to the blind, etc., etc. After all, it is a queer gathering. They do not care much about social laws and are quite free and happy. . . .

There is a Mr. Wood of Boston here, who is one of the great lights of your sect. But he objects to belonging to the sect of Mrs. Whirlpool.[9] So he calls himself a mental healer of metaphysical, chemico, physical-religioso, what-not, etc.

Yesterday there was a tremendous cyclone which gave a good "treatment" to the tents. The big tent under which they held the lectures developed so much spirituality under the treatment that it entirely disappeared from mortal gaze, and about two hundred chairs were dancing about the grounds under spiritual ecstasy. Mrs. Figs of Mills Company gives a class every morning, and Mrs. Mills is jumping all about the place. They are all in high spirits. I am especially glad for Cora, for she suffered a good deal last winter and a little hilarity would do her good. You would be astounded with the liberty they enjoy in the camps, but they are very good and pure people—a little erratic, that is all.

Regarding his own work at Greenacre, the Swami wrote in the same letter:

The other night the camp people all went to sleep under a pine tree under which I sit every morning à la India and talk to them. Of course I went with them and we had a nice night under the stars, sleeping on the lap of Mother Earth, and I enjoyed every bit of it. I cannot describe to you that night's glories—after the year of brutal life that I have led, to sleep on the ground, to meditate under the tree in the forest! The inn people are more or less well-to-do, and the camp people are healthy, young, sincere, and holy men and women. I teach them all Śivoham, Śivoham—"I am Śiva, I am Śiva"— and they all repeat it, innocent and pure as they are, and brave beyond all bounds, and I am so happy and glorified.

Thank God for making me poor! Thank God for making these children in the tents poor! The dudes and dudines are in the hotel, but iron-bound nerves, souls of triple steel, and spirits of fire are in the camp. If you had seen them yesterday, when the rain was falling in torrents and the cyclone was overturning everything—hanging on to their tent-strings to keep them from being blown off, and standing on the majesty of their souls, these brave ones—it would have done your hearts good. I would go a hundred miles to see the like of them. Lord bless them! . . .

Never be anxious for me for a moment. I will be taken care of, and if not, I shall know my time has come—and pass out. . . . Now good dreams, good thoughts for you. You are good and noble. Instead of materializing the spirit, i.e. dragging the spiritual to the material plane as these fellers do, convert matter into spirit—catch a glimpse at least, every day, of that world of infinite beauty and peace and purity, the spiritual, and try to live in it day and night. Seek not, touch not with your toes, anything which is uncanny. Let your souls ascend day and night like an unbroken string unto the feet of the Beloved, whose throne is in your own heart, and let the rest take care of themselves, i.e. the body and everything else. Life is an evanescent, floating dream; youth and beauty fade. Say day and night: "Thou art my father, my mother, my husband, my love, my Lord, my God—I want nothing but Thee, nothing but Thee, nothing but Thee. Thou in me, I in Thee—I am Thee, Thou art me." Wealth goes, beauty vanishes, life flies, powers fly—but the Lord abideth for ever, love abideth for ever. If there is glory in keeping the machine in good trim, it is more glorious to withhold the soul from suffering with the body. That is the only demonstration of your being "not matter"— by letting matter alone.

Stick to God. Who cares what comes, in the body or anywhere? Through the terrors

[9] A reference to Mrs. Mary Baker Eddy, the founder of Christian Science.

of evil, say, "My God, my Love!" Through the pangs of death, say, "My God, my Love!" Through all the evils under the sun, say: "My God, my Love! Thou art here, I see Thee. Thou art with me, I feel Thee. I am Thine, take me. I am not the world's, but Thine—leave Thou not me." Do not go for glass beads, leaving the mine of diamonds. This life is a great chance. What! Seekest thou the pleasures of this world? He is the fountain of all bliss. Seek the highest, aim for the highest, and you *shall* reach the highest.

At Greenacre the Swami became a friend of Dr. Lewis G. Janes, Director of the School of Comparative Religions organized by the Greenacre Conference, and President of the Brooklyn Ethical Association. The following autumn he lectured in Baltimore and Washington.

During the Swami's visit in New York he was the guest of friends, mostly rich ladies of the metropolitan city. He had not yet started any serious work there. Soon he began to feel a sort of restraint put upon his movements. Very few of his wealthy friends understood the true import of his message; they were interested in him as a novelty from India. Also to them he was the man of the hour. They wanted him to mix with only the exclusive society of "the right people." He chafed under their domination and one day cried: "Śiva! Śiva! Has it ever come to pass that a great work has been grown by the rich? It is brain and heart that create, and not purse." He wanted to break away from their power and devote himself to the training of some serious students in the spiritual life. He was fed up with public lectures; now he became eager to mould silently the characters of individuals. He could no longer bear the yoke of money and all the botheration that came in its train. He would live simply and give freely, like the holy men of India. Soon an opportunity presented itself.

Dr. Lewis Janes invited the Swami to give a series of lectures on the Hindu religion before the Brooklyn Ethical Association. On the evening of December 31, 1894, he gave his first lecture, and according to the report of the Brooklyn Standard, the enthusiastic audience, consisting of doctors and lawyers and judges and teachers, remained spellbound by his eloquent defence of the religion of India. They all acknowledged that Vivekananda was even greater than his fame. At the end of the meeting they made an insistent demand for regular classes in Brooklyn, to which the Swami agreed. A series of class meetings was held and several public lectures were given at the Pouch Mansion, where the Ethical Association held its meetings. These lectures constituted the beginning of the permanent work in America which the Swami secretly desired.

Soon after, several poor but earnest students rented for the Swami some unfurnished rooms in a poor section of New York City. He lived in one of them. An ordinary room on the second floor of the lodging-house was used for the lectures and classes. The Swami when conducting the meetings sat on the floor, while the ever more numerous auditors seated themselves as best they could, utilizing the marble-topped dresser, the arms of the sofa, and even the corner wash-stand. The door was left open and the overflow filled the hall and sat on the stairs. The Swami, like a typical religious teacher in India, felt himself in his own element. The students, forgetting all the inconveniences, hung upon every word uttered from the teacher's deep personal experiences or his wide range of knowledge.

The lectures, given every morning and several evenings a week, were free. The rent was paid by the voluntary subscriptions of the students, and the deficit was met by the Swami himself, through the money he earned by giving secular lectures on India. Soon the meeting-place had to be removed downstairs to occupy an entire parlour floor.

He began to instruct several chosen disciples in jnāna-yoga in order to clarify their intellects regarding the subtle truths of Vedānta, and also in rāja-yoga to teach them the science of self-control, concentration, and meditation. He was immensely happy with the result of his concentrated work. He enjoined upon these students to follow strict disciplines regarding food, choosing only the simplest. The necessity of chastity was emphasized, and they were warned against psychic and occult powers. At the same time he broadened their intellectual horizon through the teachings of Vedāntic universality. Daily he meditated with the serious students. Often he would lose all bodily consciousness and, like Śri Ramakrishna, have to be brought back to the knowledge of the world through the repetition of certain holy words that he had taught his disciples.

It was sometime about June 1895 when Swami Vivekananda finished writing his famous book Rāja-Yoga, which attracted the attention of the Harvard philosopher William James and was later to rouse the enthusiasm of Tolstoy. The book is a translation of Patanjali's Yoga aphorisms, the Swami adding his own explanations; the introductory chapters written by him are especially illuminating. Patanjali expounded, through these aphorisms, the philosophy of Yoga, the main purpose of which is to show the way of the soul's attaining freedom from the bondage of matter. Various methods of concentration are discussed. The book well served two purposes. First, the Swami demonstrated that religious experiences could stand on the same footing as scientific truths, being based on experimentation, observation, and verification. Therefore genuine spiritual experiences must not be dogmatically discarded as lacking rational evidence. Secondly, the Swami explained lucidly various disciplines of concentration, with the warning, however, that they should not be pursued without the help of a qualified teacher.

Miss S. Ellen Waldo of Brooklyn, a disciple of the Swami, was his amanuensis. She thus described the manner in which he dictated the book:

"In delivering his commentaries on the aphorisms, he would leave me waiting while he entered into deep states of meditation or self-contemplation, to emerge therefrom with some luminous interpretation. I had always to keep the pen dipped in the ink. He might be absorbed for long periods of time, and then suddenly his silence would be broken by some eager expression or some long, deliberate teaching."

SWAMI VIVEKANANDA AT THOUSAND ISLAND PARK

By the middle of the year 1895 the Swami was completely exhausted. The numerous classes and lectures, the private instruction, the increasing correspondence, and the writing of Rāja-Yoga had tired him both physically and mentally. It was a herculean task to spread the message of Hinduism in an alien land

and at the same time to mould the lives of individuals according to the highest
ideal of renunciation. Besides there were annoyances from zealous but well-
meaning friends, especially women. Some suggested that he should take elocu-
tion lessons, some urged him to dress fashionably in order to influence society
people, others admonished him against mixing with all sorts of people. At times
he would be indignant and say: "Why should I be bound down with all this
nonsense? I am a monk who has realized the vanity of all earthly nonsense!
I have no time to give my manners a finish. I cannot find time enough to give my
message. I will give it after my own fashion. Shall I be dragged down into the
narrow limits of your conventional life? Never!" Again, he wrote to a devotee:
"I long, oh, I long for my rags, my shaven head, my sleep under the trees,
and my food from begging."

The Swami needed rest from his strenuous work, and accepted the invitation
of his devoted friend Francis H. Leggett to come to his summer camp at Percy,
New Hampshire, and rest in the silence of the pine woods. In the meantime
Miss Elizabeth Dutcher, one of his students in New York, cordially asked the
Swami to take a vacation in her summer cottage at Thousand Island Park
on the St. Lawrence River. The Swami gratefully accepted both invitations.

About his life at the camp, he wrote to a friend on June 7, 1895: "It gives
me a new lease of life to be here. I go into the forest alone and read my Gītā
and am quite happy." After a short visit at Percy, he arrived in June at Thousand
Island Park, where he spent seven weeks. This proved to be a momentous period
in his life in the Western world.

When the students who had been attending Swami Vivekananda's classes in
New York heard of Miss Dutcher's proposal, they were immensely pleased,
because they did not want any interruption of their lessons. The Swami, too,
after two years' extensive work in America, had become eager to mould the
spiritual life of individual students and to train a group that would carry on
his work in America in the future. He wrote to one of his friends that he
intended to manufacture "a few yogis" from the materials of the classes. He
wanted only those to follow him to Thousand Island Park who were completely earnest in their practice of spiritual disciplines, and he said that he
would gladly recognize these as his disciples.

By a singular coincidence just twelve disciples were taught by him at the
summer retreat, though all were not there the full seven weeks; ten was the
largest number present at any one time. Two, Mme. Marie Louise and Mr. Leon
Landsberg, were initiated at Thousand Island Park into the monastic life. The
former, French by birth but a naturalized American, a materialist and socialist,
a fearless, progressive woman worker known to the press and platform, was
given the name Abhayananda. The latter, a Russian Jew and member of the
staff of a prominent New York newspaper, became known as Kripananda. Both
took the vows of poverty and chastity.

In many respects the sojourn in Miss Dutcher's cottage was ideal for the
Swami's purpose. Here, to this intimate group, he revealed brilliant flashes of
illumination, lofty flights of eloquence, and outpourings of the most profound
wisdom. The whole experience was reminiscent of the Dakshineswar days

when the Swami, as the young Narendra, had been initiated into the mysteries
of the spiritual life at the feet of his Master, Ramakrishna.

Thousand Island Park, near the western tip of Wellesley Island, the second
largest of the seventeen hundred islands in the St. Lawrence River, has for its
setting one of the scenic show-places of America. A prosperous village during
the last part of the nineteenth century, it was, at the time of the Swami's visit,
a stronghold of orthodox Methodist Christianity. The local tabernacle, where
celebrated preachers were invited to conduct the divine service on Sunday
mornings, attracted people from the neighbouring islands. Since secular activities were not allowed on the Sabbath, the visitors would arrive at Thousand
Island Park the previous day and spend the night camping out. No such pro-
fanities as public drinking, gambling, or dancing were allowed in the summer
resort—a rule that is still enforced half a century later. Only people of serious
mind went there for their vacation.

Miss Dutcher's cottage[10] was ideally located on a hill, which on the north
and west sloped down towards the river. It commanded a grand view of many
distant islands, the town of Clayton on the American mainland, and the
Canadian shores to the north. At night the houses and hotels were brightly
illuminated by Chinese lanterns.

Miss Dutcher, an artist, had built her cottage literally "on a rock," with huge
boulders lying all around. It was surrounded by rock-gardens with bright-coloured
flowers. At that time the trees at the base of the hill had not grown high;
people from the village often visited the upstairs porch to survey the magnificent
sweep of the river.

After inviting the Swami, Miss Dutcher added a new wing to the cottage
for his accommodation. This wing, three storeys high, stood on a steep slope
of rock, like a great lantern-tower with windows on three sides. The room at
the top was set apart exclusively for the Swami's use; the lowest room was
occupied by a student; the room between, with large windows, and several doors
opening on the main part of the house, was used as the Swami's classroom. Miss
Dutcher thoughtfully added an outside stairway to the Swami's room so that
he might go in and out without being noticed by the others.

On the roofed-in porch upstairs, extending along the west side of the cottage,
the students met the Swami for his evening talks. There, at one end, close to
the door of his room, he would take his seat and commune with his pupils
both in silence and through the spoken word. In the evening the cottage was
bathed in perfect stillness except for the murmur of insects and the whisper
of the wind through the leaves. The house being situated, as it were, among
the tree-tops, a breeze always relieved the summer heat. The centre of the village
was only a five minutes' walk from the cottage, and yet, on account of the
woods around it, not a single house could be seen. Many of the islands that
dotted the river were visible in the distance and, especially in the evening,

[10] The cottage, which was acquired by the Ramakrishna-Vivekananda Center of New
York in December 1947 and extensively restored without interfering with the original
design, is now used as a summer retreat for Swamis of the Ramakrishna Order. It has
been dedicated as "Vivekananda Cottage" and Swami Vivekananda's room has been set
apart as a shrine for the devotions of the inmates.

appeared like a picture. The glow of the sunset on the St. Lawrence was breath-taking in its beauty, and the moon at night was mirrored in the shining waters beneath.

In this ideal retreat, "the world forgetting, by the world forgot," the devoted students spent seven weeks with their beloved teacher, listening to his words of wisdom and receiving his silent benediction. Immediately after the evening meal they would assemble on the upstairs porch. Soon the Swami would come from his room and take his seat. Two hours and often much longer would be spent together. One night, when the moon was almost full, he talked to them until it set below the western horizon, both the teacher and the students being unaware of the passage of time. During these seven weeks the Swami's whole heart was in his work and he taught like one inspired.

Miss Dutcher, his hostess, was a conscientious little woman and a staunch Methodist. When the Swami arrived at the house, he saw on the walls of his living quarters scrolls bearing the words "Welcome to Vivekananda" painted in bold letters. But as the teaching began, Miss Dutcher often felt distressed by the Swami's revolutionary ideas. All her ideals, her values of life, her concepts of religion, were, it seemed to her, being destroyed. Sometimes she did not appear for two or three days. "Don't you see?" the Swami said. "This is not an ordinary illness. It is the reaction of the body against the chaos that is going on in her mind. She cannot bear it."

The most violent attack came one day after a timid protest on her part against something he had told them in the class. "The idea of duty is the midday sun of misery, scorching the very soul," he had said. "Is it not our duty—" she had begun, but got no farther. For once the great free soul broke all bounds in his rebellion against the idea that anyone should dare bind with fetters the soul of man. Miss Dutcher was not seen for some days.

Referring to the students who had gathered around the Swami, a village shopkeeper said to a new arrival who inquired for the cottage, "Yes, there are some queer people living up on the hill; among them there is a foreign-looking gentleman." A young girl of sixteen, living with her family at the foot of the hill, one day expressed the desire to talk to the Swami. "Don't go near him," her mother said sternly. "He is a heathen." Mr. Tom Mitchell, a carpenter who helped to restore the cottage for the Ramakrishna-Vivekananda Center in 1948, and had originally built the Swami's quarters in 1895, told the present writer that he had read the Swami's lectures in Chicago from the newspapers long before his arrival at the island.

The students wanted, at first, to live as a community without servants, each doing a share of the work. Nearly all of them, however, were unaccustomed to housework and found it uncongenial. The result was amusing; as time went on it threatened to become disastrous. When the tension became too great, the Swami would say with utmost sweetness, "Today, I shall cook for you." At this Landsberg would ejaculate, in an aside, "Heaven save us!" By way of explanation he declared that in New York, whenever the Swami cooked, he, Landsberg, would tear his hair, because it meant that afterwards every dish in the house required washing. After a few days an outsider was engaged to help with the housework.

Swami Vivekananda started his class at Thousand Island Park on Wednesday, June 19. Not all the students had arrived. But his heart was set on his work; so he commenced at once with the three or four who were with him. After a short meditation, he opened with the Gospel according to Saint John, from the Bible, saying that since the students were all Christians, it was proper that he should begin with the Christian scriptures. As the classes went on, he taught from the Bhagavad Gītā, the Upanishads, the Vedānta Sutras, the Bhakti Sutras of Nārada, and other Hindu scriptures. He discussed Vedānta in its three aspects: the non-dualism of Śankara, the qualified non-dualism of Rāmānuja, and the dualism of Madhva. Since the subtleties of Śankara appeared difficult to the students, Rāmānuja remained the favourite among them. The Swami also spoke at length about Śri Ramakrishna, of his own daily life with the Master, and of his struggles with the tendency to unbelief and agnosticism. He told stories from the inexhaustible storehouse of Hindu mythology to illustrate his abstruse thoughts.

The ever recurring theme of his teaching was God-realization. He would always come back to the one, fundamental, vital point: "Find God. Nothing else matters." He emphasized morality as the basis of the spiritual life. Without truth, non-injury, continence, non-stealing, cleanliness, and austerity, he repeated, there could be no spirituality. The subject of continence always stirred him deeply. Walking up and down the room, getting more and more excited, he would stop before someone as if there were no one else present. "Don't you see," he would say eagerly, "there is a reason why chastity is insisted on in all monastic orders? Spiritual giants are produced only where the vow of chastity is observed. Don't you see there must be a reason? There is a connexion between chastity and spirituality. The explanation is that through prayer and meditation the saints have transmuted the most vital force in the body into spiritual energy. In India this is well understood and yogis do it consciously. The force so transmuted is called ojas, and it is stored up in the brain. It has been lifted from the lowest centre to the highest. 'And I, if I be lifted up, will draw all men unto me.'" He would plead with the students as if to beg them to act upon this teaching as something most precious. Further, they could not be the disciples he required if they were not established in chastity. He demanded a conscious transmutation. "The man who has no temper has nothing to control," he said. "I want a few, five or six, who are in the flower of their youth."

He would frequently exhort the students to attain freedom. As the words came in torrents from the depths of his soul, the atmosphere would be charged with the yearning to break free from the bondage of the body, a degrading humiliation. As he touched upon "this indecent clinging to life," the students would feel as if the curtain that hid the region beyond life and death were lifted for them, and they would long for that glorious freedom. "Āzād! Āzād! the Free! the Free!" he would cry, pacing back and forth like a caged lion; but for him the bars of the cage were not of iron, but of bamboo. "Let us not be caught this time," would be his refrain on other occasions.

Some of these precious talks were noted down by his disciple Miss S. Ellen Waldo and later published as Inspired Talks. Students of Swami Vivekananda will for ever remain indebted to her for faithfully preserving his immortal words, and the title of this book was well chosen, for they were indeed inspired. One day Miss Waldo was reading her notes to some tardy arrivals in the cottage while the Swami strode up and down the floor, apparently unconscious of what was going on. After the travellers had left the room, the Swami turned to Miss Waldo and said: "How could you have caught my thought and words so perfectly? It was as if I heard myself speaking."

During these seven weeks of teaching the Swami was most gentle and lovable. He taught his disciples as Śri Ramakrishna had taught him at Dakshineswar: the teaching was the outpouring of his own spirit in communion with himself. The Swami said later that he was at his best at Thousand Island Park. The ideas he cherished and expressed there grew, during the years that followed, into institutions, both in India and abroad.

The Swami's one consuming passion, during this time, was to show his students the way to freedom. "Ah," he said one day, with touching pathos, "if I could only set you free with a touch!" Two students arrived at the Park one dark and rainy night. One of them said, "We have come to you as we would go to Jesus if he were still on the earth and ask him to teach us." The Swami looked at them kindly and gently said, "If I only possessed the power of the Christ to set you free!" No wonder that Miss Waldo one day exclaimed, "What have we ever done to deserve all this?" And so felt the others also.

One cannot but be amazed at the manifestation of Swami Vivekananda's spiritual power at Thousand Island Park. Outwardly he was a young man of thirty-two. All his disciples at the cottage, except one, were older than himself. Yet everyone looked upon him as a father or mother. He had attained an unbelievable maturity. Some marvelled at his purity, some at his power, some at his intellectuality, some at his serenity, which was like the depths of the ocean, unperturbed by the waves of applause or contumely. When had he acquired all these virtues which had made him, at thirty, a teacher of men? From the foregoing pages the reader will have formed an idea of him as a stormy person, struggling, in early youth, against poverty and spiritual unbelief. Afterwards he is seen wandering from the Himalayas to Cape Comorin, raging against the grievances and sufferings of the Indian masses. During his first two years in America he had had to fight tooth and nail against malicious critics in order to establish his reputation as a religious teacher. When had he, then, tapped the secret spring of inner calmness and assurance without which a teacher cannot transmit spirituality to his disciples?

One must not forget that Vivekananda, as Ramakrishna had said, was not an ordinary man, but a nityasiddha, perfect even before birth, an Iśvarakoti, or special messenger of God born on earth to fulfil a divine mission. The silent but powerful influence of the guru always guided his feet. The outer world saw only the struggles and restlessness of his wandering days, but not the inner transformation brought about through the practice of purity, detachment, self-control, and meditation. The veil of māyā, without which no physical embodiment is possible, and which in him was very thin, was rent through the spiritual struggle of a few years. People were astonished to see his blossoming forth at Thousand Island Park.

At Dakshineswar, though Śri Ramakrishna had offered young Naren various supernatural powers of Yoga as a help for his future work, the disciple had refused to accept them, as being possible impediments to spiritual progress. But later these powers began to manifest themselves as the natural fruit of his spiritual realizations. Thus one sees him at Thousand Island Park reading the inmost soul of his followers before giving them initiation, and foretelling their future careers. He prophesied for Sister Christine extensive travels in Oriental countries and work in India. He explained that his method of foresight was simple, at least in the telling. He first thought of space—vast, blue, and extending everywhere. As he meditated on that space intently, pictures appeared, and he then gave interpretations of them which would indicate the future life of the person concerned.

Even before his arrival at Thousand Island Park the Swami had had other manifestations of such Yoga powers. For instance, while busy with his lecture tour, sometimes giving twelve or fourteen speeches a week, he would feel great physical and mental strain and often wonder what he would speak of the next day. Then he would hear, at dead of night, a voice shouting at him the very thoughts he was to present. Sometimes it would come from a long distance and then draw nearer and nearer, or again, it would be like someone delivering a lecture beside him as he lay listening in bed. At other times two voices would argue before him, discussing at great length ideas, some of which he had never before consciously heard or thought of, which he would find himself repeating the following day from the pulpit or the platform.

Sometimes people sleeping in the adjoining rooms would ask him in the morning: "Swami, with whom were you talking last night? We heard you talking loudly and enthusiastically and we were wondering." The Swami often explained these manifestations as the powers and potentialities of the soul generally called inspiration. He denied that they were miracles.

At that time he experienced the power of changing a person's life by a touch, or clearly seeing things happening at a great distance. But he seldom used these and the other powers he had acquired through Yoga. One day, much later, Swami Turiyananda entered the room while the Swami was lying on his bed, and beheld, in place of Vivekananda's physical body, a mass of radiance. It is no wonder that today in America, half a century later, one meets men and women who saw or heard Swami Vivekananda perhaps once, and still remember him vividly.

But it must not be thought that the Swami did not show his lighter mood at Thousand Island Park. He unfailingly discovered the little idiosyncrasies of the students and raised gales of laughter at the dinner-table, with some quip or jest—but never in sarcasm or malice. One of the inmates of the Dutcher Cottage was Dr. Wight, a very cultured man of well over seventy who had attended the Swami's classes and lectures in New York. He became so absorbed in the class talks that at the end of every discourse he would invariably ask the teacher: "Well, Swami, it all amounts to this in the end, doesn't it?—I *am* Brahman, I *am* the Absolute." The Swami would smile indulgently and answer gently, "Yes, Dockie, you are Brahman, you are the Absolute, in the real essence of your being." Later, when the learned doctor came to the table a trifle late, the Swami, with the utmost gravity but with a merry twinkle in his eyes, would say, "Here comes Brahman" or "Here is the Absolute."

Sometimes he would say, "Now I am going to cook for you, 'brethren.'" The food he cooked would be delicious, but too hot for Western tastes. The students, however, made up their minds to eat it even if it strangled them. After the meal was cooked, the Swami would stand in the door with a white napkin draped over his arm, in the fashion of the negro waiters in a dining-car, and intone in perfect imitation their call for dinner: "Last call fo' the dining cah. Dinner served." And the students would rock with laughter.

One day he was telling the disciples the story of Sitā and of the pure womanhood of India. The question flashed in the mind of one of the women as to how some of the beautiful society queens would appear to him, especially those versed in the art of allurement. Even before the thought was expressed, the Swami said gravely, "If the most beautiful woman in the world were to look at me in an immodest or unwomanly way, she would immediately turn into a hideous green frog, and one does not, of course, admire frogs."

At last the day of the Swami's departure from Thousand Island Park arrived. It was Wednesday, August 7, 1895. In the morning he, Mrs. Funke, and Sister Christine went for a walk. They strolled about half a mile up the hill, where all was forest and solitude, and sat under a low-branched tree. The Swami suddenly said to them: "Now we shall meditate. We shall be like Buddha under the Bo-tree." He became still as a bronze statue. A thunderstorm came up and it poured; but the Swami did not notice anything. Mrs. Funke raised her umbrella and protected him as much as possible. When it was time to return, the Swami opened his eyes and said, "I feel once more I am in Calcutta in the rains." It is reported that one day at Thousand Island Park he experienced nirvikalpa samādhi.

At nine o'clock in the evening the Swami boarded the steamer for Clayton, where he was to catch the train for New York. While taking leave of the Islands he said, "I bless these Thousand Islands." As the steamer moved away, he boyishly and joyously waved his hat to the disciples still standing at the pier.

Some of his devotees thought that the Swami had planned at Thousand Island Park to start an organization. But they were mistaken. He wrote to a disciple:

We have no organization, nor want to build any. Each one is quite independent to teach, quite free to teach, whatever he or she likes. If you have the spirit within, you will never fail to attract others. . . . Individuality is my motto. I have no ambition beyond training individuals. I know very little; that little I teach without reserve; where I am ignorant I confess it. . . . I am a sannyāsin. As such I hold myself as a servant, not as a master, in this world.

Vivekananda, the awakener of souls, was indeed too great to be crammed within the confines of a narrow organization. He had had a unique experience of inner freedom at Thousand Island Park, which he expressed eloquently in his poem "The Song of the Sannyāsin." He wrote from there to a friend: "I am free, my bonds are cut, what do I care whether this body goes or does not go?

I have a truth to teach—I, the child of God. And He that gave me the truth will send me fellow workers from earth's bravest and best."

IN THE COMPANY OF SOME NOTABLES

A month after his return from Thousand Island Park, Swami Vivekananda sailed for Europe. Before we take up that important chapter of his life, however, it will be well to describe some of his interesting experiences in America, especially his meeting with noted personalities.

Robert Ingersoll, the famous orator and agnostic, and Swami Vivekananda had several conversations on religion and philosophy. Ingersoll, with a fatherly solicitude, asked the young enthusiast not to be too bold in the expression of his views, on account of people's intolerance of all alien religious ideas. "Forty years ago," he said, "you would have been hanged if you had come to preach in this country, or you would have been burnt alive. You would have been stoned out of the villages if you had come even much later." The Swami was surprised. But Ingersoll did not realize that the Indian monk, unlike him, respected all religions and prophets, and that he wanted to broaden the views of the Christians about Christ's teachings.

One day, in the course of a discussion, Ingersoll said to the Swami, "I believe in making the most of this world, in squeezing the orange dry, because this world is all we are sure of." He would have nothing to do with God, soul, or hereafter, which he considered as meaningless jargon. "I know a better way to squeeze the orange of this world than you do," the Swami replied, "and I get more out of it. I know I cannot die, so I am not in a hurry. I know that there is no fear, so I enjoy the squeezing. I have no duty, no bondage of wife and children and property, so I can love all men and women. Everyone is God to me. Think of the joy of loving man as God! Squeeze your orange my way, and you will get every single drop!" Ingersoll, it is reported, asked the Swami not to be impatient with his views, adding that his own unrelenting fight against traditional religions had shaken men's faith in theological dogmas and creeds, and thus helped to pave the way for the Swami's success in America.

Nikola Tesla, the great scientist who specialized in the field of electricity, was much impressed to hear from the Swami his explanation of the Sāmkhya cosmogony and the theory of cycles given by the Hindus. He was particularly struck by the resemblance between the Sāmkhya theory of matter and energy and that of modern physics. The Swami also met in New York Sir William Thomson (afterwards Lord Kelvin) and Professor Helmholtz, two leading representatives of Western science. Sarah Bernhardt, the famous French actress, had an interview with the Swami and greatly admired his teachings.

Madame Emma Calvé, the well-known prima donna, described the Swami as one who "truly walked with God." She came to see him in a state of physical and mental depression. The Swami, who did not at that time know even her name, talked to her about her worries and various personal problems. It was clear that he was familiar with them, even though she had never revealed them to him or to anyone else. When Madame Calvé expressed surprise, the Swami assured her that no one had talked to him about her. "Do you think that is necessary?" he asked. "I read you as I would an open book." He gave her this parting advice: "You must forget. Be gay and happy again. Do not dwell in silence upon your sorrows. Transmute your emotions into some form of external expression. Your spiritual health requires it. Your art demands it."

Madame Calvé later said: "I left him, deeply impressed by his words and his personality. He seemed to have emptied my brain of all its feverish complexities and placed there instead his clean and calming thoughts. I became once again vivacious and cheerful, thanks to the effect of his powerful will. He used no hypnosis, no mesmerism—nothing of that sort at all. It was the strength of his character, the purity and intensity of his purpose, that carried conviction. It seemed to me, when I came to know him better, that he lulled one's chaotic thoughts into a state of peaceful acquiescence, so that one could give complete and undivided attention to his words."

Like many people, Madame Calvé could not accept the Vedāntic doctrine of the individual soul's total absorption in the Godhead at the time of final liberation. "I cannot bear the idea," she said. "I cling to my individuality—unimportant though it may be. I don't want to be absorbed into an eternal unity." To this the Swami answered: "One day a drop of water fell into the vast ocean. Finding itself there, it began to weep and complain, just as you are doing. The giant ocean laughed at the drop of water. 'Why do you weep?' it asked. 'I do not understand. When you join me, you join all your brothers and sisters, the other drops of water of which I am made. You become the ocean itself. If you wish to leave me you have only to rise up on a sunbeam into the clouds. From there you can descend again, little drop of water, a blessing and a benediction to the thirsty earth.' "

Did not the Swami thus explain his own individuality? Before his present embodiment, he had remained absorbed in communion with the Absolute. Then he accepted the form of an individual to help humanity in its spiritual struggle. A giant soul like his is not content to remain eternally absorbed in the Absolute. Such also was the thought of Buddha.

In the company of great men and women, the Swami revealed his intellectual and spiritual power. But one sees his human side especially in his contact with humble people. In America he was often taken to be a negro. One day, as he alighted from a train in a town where he was to deliver a lecture, he was given a welcome by the reception committee. The most prominent townspeople were all there. A negro porter came up to him and said that he had heard how one of his own people had become great and asked the privilege of shaking hands with him. Warmly the Swami shook his hand, saying, "Thank you! Thank you, brother!" He never resented being mistaken for a negro. It happened many times, especially in the South, that he was refused admittance to a hotel, a barber shop, or a restaurant, because of his dark skin. When the Swami related these incidents to a Western disciple, he was promptly asked why he did not tell people that he was not a negro but a Hindu. "What!" the Swami replied indignantly. "Rise at the expense of another? I did not come to earth for that."

Swami Vivekananda was proud of his race and his dark complexion. "He was scornful," wrote Sister Nivedita, "in his repudiation of the pseudo-ethnology of privileged races. 'If I am grateful to my white-skinned Āryan ancestors,' he said, 'I am far more so to my yellow-skinned Mongolian ancestors, and most of all to the black-skinned negroids.' He was immensely proud of his physiognomy, especially of what he called his 'Mongolian jaw,' regarding it as a sign of 'bulldog tenacity of purpose.' Referring to this particular racial characteristic, which is believed to be behind every Āryan people, he one day exclaimed: 'Don't you see? The Tartar is the wine of the race! He gives energy and power to every blood.' "

The Swami had a strange experience in a small American town, where he was confronted by a number of college boys who had been living there on a ranch as cowboys. They heard him describe the power of concentration, through which a man could become completely oblivious of the outside world. So they decided to put him to test and invited him to lecture to them. A wooden tub was placed, with bottom up, to serve as a platform. The Swami commenced his address and soon appeared to be lost in his subject. Suddenly shots were fired in his direction, and bullets went whizzing past his ears. But the Swami continued his lecture as though nothing was happening. When he had finished, the young men flocked about him and congratulated him as a good fellow.

In his lectures and conversations the Swami showed a wonderful sense of humour. It was a saving feature in his strenuous life, and without it he might have broken down under the pressure of his intense thinking. Once, in one of his classes in Minneapolis, the Swami was asked by a student if Hindu mothers threw their children to the crocodiles in the river. Immediately came the reply: "Yes, Madam! They threw me in, but like your fabled Jonah, I got out again!" Another time, a lady became rather romantic about the Swami and said to him, "Swami! You are my Romeo and I am your Desdemona!" The Swami said quickly, "Madam, you'd better brush up your Shakespeare."

As already stated, Swami Vivekananda was particularly friendly with Mr. and Mrs. Hale, of Chicago, and their young daughters and two nieces, named Mary, Isabel, Harriet, and Jean. He affectionately called Mr. Hale "Father Pope" and Mrs. Hale "Mother Church." The girls he addressed as "sisters" or "babies." A very sweet and warm relationship grew up between them and the Swami. His relationship with the eldest girl, Mary, was especially close. He wrote to her many light-hearted letters. In a letter to the sisters, dated July 26, 1894, the Swami said:

Now, don't let my letters stray beyond the circle, please—I had a beautiful letter from Sister Mary—See how I am getting the dash—Sister Jeany teaches me all that—She can jump and run and play and swear like a devil and talk slang at the rate of five hundred a minute—only she does not much care for religion—only a little. . . . Darn it, I forget everything—I had duckings in the sea like a fish—I am enjoying every bit of it—What nonsense was the song Harriet taught me, "Dans la Plaine"—the deuce take it!—I told it to a French scholar and he laughed and laughed till the fellow was wellnigh burst at my wonderful translation—That is the way you would have taught me French—You are a pack of fools and heathens, I tell you—How you are gasping for breath like huge fish stranded—I am glad that you are sizzling[11]—Oh! how nice and cool it is here—and it is increased a hundredfold when I think about the gasping, sizzling, boiling, frying four old maids—and how cool and nice I am here—Whoooooo! ! ! . . .

Well—dear old maids—you sometimes have a glimpse of the lake and on very hot

[11] Referring to the summer heat of Chicago.

noons think of going down to the bottom of the lake—down—down—down—until it is cool and nice, and then to lie down on the bottom, with just that coolness above and around—and lie there still—silent—and just doze—not sleep, but a dreamy, dozing, half unconscious sort of bliss—very much like that which opium brings—That is delicious—and drinking lots of iced water—Lord bless my soul!—I had such cramps several times as would have killed an elephant—So I hope to keep myself away from the cold water—

May you all be happy, dear fin de siècle young ladies, is the constant prayer of VIVEKANANDA.

One realizes how deeply Swami Vivekananda had entered into the American spirit, when one sees how facile he was in his use of American slang. Surely this letter is an example. As we have stated before, the Swami also needed diversions of this kind in order to obtain relief from his intensely serious life and thinking in America. One recalls that Śri Ramakrishna, too, would often indulge in light talk in order to keep his mind on the level of ordinary consciousness.

Shortly after his success at the Parliament of Religions, the Swami began, as we have seen, to write to his devotees in India, giving them his plans for India's regeneration. He urged them to take up work that would lead to better systems of education and hygiene throughout India. He wanted a magazine to be started for disseminating among his fellow countrymen the broad truths of Vedānta, which would create confidence in their minds regarding their power and potentialities, and give them back their lost individuality. He exhorted his devotees to work especially for the uplift of women and the masses, without whose help India would never be able to raise herself from her present state of stagnation. He sent them money, earned through his lectures, for religious, educational, and other philanthropic activities. His enthusiastic letters inspired them. But they wanted him to return and take up the leadership. They were also distressed to see the malicious propaganda against him by the Christian missionaries in India. The Swami, however, repeatedly urged them to depend upon themselves. "Stand on your own feet!" he wrote to them. "If you are really my children, you will fear nothing, stop at nothing. You will be like lions. You must rouse India and the whole world."

About the criticism from the Christian missionaries, he wrote: "The Christianity that is preached in India is quite different from what one sees here. You will be astonished to hear that I have friends in this country amongst the clergy of the Episcopal and Presbyterian Churches, who are as broad-minded, as liberal, and as sincere as you are in your own religion. The real spiritual man—everywhere—is broad-minded. His love forces him to be so. They to whom religion is a trade are forced to become narrow-minded and mischievous by their very introduction into religion of the competitive, fighting, selfish methods of the world." He requested the Indian devotees not to pay any heed to what the missionaries were saying either for or against him. "I shall work incessantly," he wrote, "until I die, and even after death I shall work for the good of the world. Truth is infinitely more weighty than untruth. . . . It is the force of character, of purity, and of truth—of personality. So long as I have these things, you can feel easy; no one will be able to injure a hair of my head. If they try, they will fail, saith the Lord."

For some time Swami Vivekananda had been planning a visit to London. He wished to sow the seed of Vedānta in the capital of the mighty British Empire. Miss Henrietta Muller had extended to him a cordial invitation to come to London, and Mr. E. T. Sturdy had requested him to stay at his home there. Mr. Leggett, too, had invited the Swami to come to Paris as his guest.

Mr. Francis H. Leggett, whose hospitality the Swami had already enjoyed at Percy, was a wealthy business man of New York. He and two ladies of his acquaintance, Mrs. William Sturges and Miss Josephine MacLeod (who were sisters), had attended the Swami's lectures in New York during the previous winter. They were all impressed by the Swami's personality and his message, and Mr. Leggett remarked, one day, that the teacher was a man of "great common sense." An intimate relationship gradually developed between the Swami, the two sisters, and Mr. Leggett. Mrs. Sturges, who was a widow, and Mr. Leggett became engaged and announced their engagement at the summer camp at Percy. They decided to be married in Paris, and Mr. Leggett invited the Swami to be a witness at the ceremony.

This invitation, coming at the same time as Miss Muller's and Mr. Sturdy's, seemed to the Swami, as he described it in a letter, a "divine call." The Swami's New York friends thought that a sea voyage would be most beneficial for his weary body and mind. At this time the Swami began to feel a premonition of his approaching end. One day he even said, "My day is done." But the awareness of his unfulfilled mission made him forget his body.

The Swami and Mr. Leggett sailed from New York about the middle of August 1895, reaching Paris by the end of the month. The French metropolis with its museums, churches, cathedrals, palaces, and art galleries impressed him as the centre of European culture, and he was introduced to a number of enlightened French people.

When Swami Vivekananda arrived in London he was enthusiastically greeted by Miss Muller, who had already met him in America, and Mr. Sturdy, who had studied Sanskrit and had to a certain degree practised asceticism in the Himālayas. The Swami's mind, one can imagine, was filled with tumultuous thoughts as he arrived in the great city. He was eager to test his ability as an interpreter of the spiritual culture of India in the very citadel of the English-speaking nations. He also knew that he belonged to a subject race, which had been under the imperialistic domination of England for the past one hundred and fifty years. He attributed India's suffering, at least in part, to this alien rule. He was not unaware of the arrogance of the British ruling class in India, to whom India was a benighted country steeped in superstition. Would the Britishers give a patient hearing to the religion and philosophy of his ancestors, of which he was so proud? Would they not rather think that nothing good could ever come "out of Nazareth"? He did not, as we learn from his own confession, set foot on English soil with the friendliest of feelings. But how he felt when he left England after his short visit will be presently described.

After a few days' rest the Swami quietly began his work. Through friends he was gradually introduced to people who were likely to be interested in his thoughts; he also devoted part of his time to visiting places of historical interest. Within three weeks of his arrival he was already engaged in strenuous activity. A class was started and soon the hall was found inadequate to accommodate the students. Newspapers interviewed him and called him the "Hindu yogi." Lady Isabel Margesson and several other members of the nobility became attracted to the Swami's teachings. His first public lecture was attended by many educated and thoughtful people; some of the leading newspapers were enthusiastic about it. The *Standard* compared his moral stature with that of Rammohan Roy and Keshab Chandra Sen. The *London Daily Chronicle* wrote that he reminded people of Buddha. Even the heads of churches showed their warm appreciation.

But the Swami's greatest acquisition in London was Miss Margaret E. Noble, who later became his disciple, consecrating her life to women's education in India. She also espoused the cause of India's political freedom and inspired many of its leaders with her written and spoken words.

Miss Noble, the fourth child of Samuel Noble, was born in Northern Ireland in 1867. Both her grandfather and her father were Protestant ministers in the Wesleyan church and took active part in the political agitation for the freedom of Ireland. Her grandmother and her father gave her instruction in the Bible.

Her father, who died at the age of thirty-four, had a premonition of his daughter's future calling. One of the last things he whispered to his wife was about Margaret. "When God calls her," he said, "let her go. She will spread her wings. She will do great things."

After finishing her college education, Margaret took the position of a teacher at Keswick, in the English Lake District, where contact with the High Church stirred her religious emotions. Next she taught in an orphanage in Rugby, where she shared the manual labour of the pupils. At twenty-one, Miss Noble was appointed as mistress at the secondary school in Wrexham, a large mining centre, and participated in the welfare activities of the town, visiting slum households and looking for waifs and strays. Next she went to Chester and taught a class of eighteen-year-old girls. Here she delved into the educational systems of Pestalozzi and Froebel. And finally she came to London, where, in the autumn of 1895, she opened her own school, the Ruskin School, in Wimbledon.

The metropolis of the British Empire offered Miss Noble unlimited opportunities for the realization of her many latent desires—political, literary, and educational. Here she joined the "Free Ireland" group, working for Ireland's home rule. She was also cordially received at Lady Ripon's exclusive salon, where art and literature were regularly discussed. This salon later developed into the Sesame Club, with rooms in Dover Street, where Bernard Shaw, T. H. Huxley, and other men of literature and science discussed highly intellectual subjects. Margaret Noble became the secretary of the club, and lectured on "The Psychology of the Child" and "The Rights of Women." Thus even before she met Swami Vivekananda she was unconsciously preparing the ground for her future activities in India.

At this time Margaret suffered a cruel blow. She was deeply in love with a man and had even set the wedding date. But another woman suddenly snatched him away. A few years before, another young man, to whom she was about to be engaged, had died of tuberculosis. These experiences shocked her profoundly, and she began to take a more serious interest in religion. She was very fond of a simple prayer by Thomas à Kempis: "Be what thou prayest to be made."

One day her art teacher, Ebenezer Cook, said to Margaret: "Lady Isabel Margesson is inviting a few friends to her house to hear a Hindu Swami speak. Will you come?" Swami Vivekananda had already been a topic of discussion among certain members of the Sesame Club. Mr. E. T. Sturdy and Miss Henrietta Muller had told of his extraordinary success in America as a preacher and orator.

Miss Noble first met Swami Vivekananda on a Sunday evening in the drawing-room of Lady Isabel Margesson, situated in the fashionable West End of London. He was to address a group of people on Hindu thought. Miss Noble was one of the last to arrive. Fifteen people sat in the room in absolute silence. She nervously felt as if all eyes were turned on her, and as she took the first vacant chair, she gathered her skirt to sit down without making any noise. The Swami sat facing her. A coal fire burnt on the hearth behind him. She noticed that he was tall and well built and possessed an air of deep serenity. The effect of his long practice of meditation was visible in the gentleness and loftiness of his look, which, as she was to write later, "Raphael has perhaps painted for us on the brow of the Sistine Child."

The Swami looked at Lady Isabel with a sweet smile, as she said: "Swamiji, all our friends are here." He chanted some Sanskrit verses. Miss Noble was impressed by his melodious voice. She heard the Swami say, among other things: "All our struggle is for freedom. We seek neither misery nor happiness, but freedom, freedom alone."

It was at first difficult for Miss Noble to accept Swami Vivekananda's views. But before he left London she had begun to address him as "Master."

Recalling those first meetings in London, and their decisive influence on her life, Nivedita wrote in 1904 to a friend: "Suppose he had not come to London that time! Life would have been like a headless dream, for I always knew that I was waiting for something. I always said that a call would come. And it did. But if I had known more of life, I doubt whether, when the time came, I should certainly have recognized it. Fortunately, I knew little and was spared that torture. . . . Always I had this burning voice within, but nothing to utter. How often and often I sat down, pen in hand, to speak, and there was no speech! And now there is no end to it! As surely I am fitted to my world, so surely is my world in need of me, waiting—ready. The arrow has found its place in the bow. But if he had not come! If he had meditated, on the Himālayan peaks! . . . I, for one, had never been here."

Swami Vivekananda and Mr. Sturdy soon began an English translation of the Bhakti aphorisms of Nārada. At this time the idea came to the Swami's mind that a religion could not have a permanent hold upon people without organization and rituals. A mere loose system of philosophy, he realized, soon lost its appeal. He saw the need, therefore, of formulating rituals, on the basis of the

Upanishadic truths, which would serve a person from birth to death—rituals that would prepare for the ultimate realization of the supra-mental Absolute.

His stay in England was very short, but his insight enabled him to appraise the English character with considerable accuracy. He wrote to a devotee on November 18, 1895: "In England my work is really splendid. I am astonished myself at it. The English do not talk much in the newspapers, but they work silently. I am sure of having done more work in England than in America." And in another letter, written on November 13, to a brother disciple in India: "Every enterprise in this country takes some time to get started. But once John Bull sets his hand to a thing, he will never let it go. The Americans are quick, but they are somewhat like straw on fire, ready to be extinguished."

The Swami had been receiving letters from American devotees asking him to come back; a rich lady from Boston promised to support his work in New York throughout the winter. Before leaving England, however, he arranged that Mr. Sturdy should conduct the classes in London till the arrival of a new Swami from India, about the need of whom he was writing constantly to his brother disciples at the Baranagore monastery.

ESTABLISHING THE WORK IN AMERICA

On December 6, 1895, Swami Vivekananda returned to New York, after his two months' stay in England, in excellent health and spirits. During his absence abroad, regular classes had been carried on by his American disciples Kripananda, Abhayananda, and Miss Waldo, who taught rāja-yoga in both its practical and its theoretical aspects.

Together with Kripananda he took up new quarters, consisting of two spacious rooms, which could accommodate one hundred and fifty persons. The Swami at once plunged into activity and gave a series of talks on work as a spiritual discipline. These talks were subsequently published as Karma-Yoga, which is considered one of his best books. In the meantime the devotees of the Swami had been feeling the need of a stenographer to take down his talks in the classes and on public platforms. Many of his precious speeches had already been lost because there had been no reporter to record them. Fortunately there appeared on the scene an Englishman, J. J. Goodwin, who was at first employed as a professional stenographer; in a few days, however, he was so impressed by the Swami's life and message that he became his disciple and offered his services free, with the remark that if the teacher could give his whole life to help mankind, he, the disciple, could at least give his services as an offering of love. Goodwin followed the Swami like a shadow in America, Europe, and India; he recorded many of the public utterances of Vivekananda, now preserved in published books, and thereby earned the everlasting gratitude of countless men and women.

The Swami spent Christmas of 1895 with Mr. and Mrs. Leggett at their country home, Ridgely Manor, which he frequently visited in order to enjoy a respite from his hard work in New York. But even there he would give exalted spiritual discourses, as will be evident from the following excerpt from a letter written by Mr. Leggett on January 10, 1896, to Miss MacLeod:

One night at Ridgely we were all spellbound by his eloquence. Such thought I have never heard expressed by mortal man—such as he uttered for two and a half hours. We were all deeply affected. And I would give a hundred dollars for a typewritten verbatim report of it. Swami was inspired to a degree that I have never seen before or since. He leaves us soon and perhaps we shall never see him again, but he will leave an ineffaceable impress on our hearts that will comfort us to the end of our earthly careers.

After a short visit to Boston as the guest of Mrs. Ole Bull, the Swami commenced a series of public lectures in New York at Hardeman Hall, the People's Church, and later at Madison Square Garden, which had a seating capacity of fifteen hundred people. In the last mentioned place he gave his famous lectures on love as a spiritual discipline, which were subsequently published as *Bhakti-Yoga*. Both the lectures of the Swami and his personality received favourable comment from the newspapers. He initiated into monastic life Dr. Street, who assumed the name of Yogananda.

Mrs. Ella Wheeler Wilcox, one of the founders of the New Thought movement in America, spoke highly of the Swami's teachings. She and her husband first went to hear him out of curiosity, and what happened afterwards may be told in her own words:

Before we had been ten minutes in the audience, we felt ourselves lifted up into an atmosphere so rarefied, so vital, so wonderful, that we sat spellbound and almost breathless to the end of the lecture. When it was over we went out with new courage, new hope, new strength, new faith, to meet life's daily vicissitudes. . . . It was that terrible winter of financial disasters, when banks failed and stocks went down like broken balloons, and business men walked through the dark valleys of despair, and the whole world seemed topsy-turvy. Sometimes after sleepless nights of worry and anxiety, my husband would go with me to hear the Swami lecture, and then he would come out into the winter gloom and walk down the street smiling and say: "It is all right. There is nothing to worry over." And I would go back to my own duties and pleasures with the same uplifted sense of soul and enlarged vision. . . . "I do not come to convert you to a new belief," he said. "I want you to keep your own belief; I want to make the Methodist a better Methodist, the Presbyterian a better Presbyterian, the Unitarian a better Unitarian. I want to teach you to live the truth, to reveal the light within your own soul." He gave the message that strengthened the man of business, that caused the frivolous society woman to pause and think; that gave the artist new aspirations; that imbued the wife and mother, the husband and father, with a larger and a holier comprehension of duty.

Having finished his work in New York, the Swami, accompanied by Goodwin, left for Detroit. The main theme of his lectures and class talks there was bhakti, or love of God. At that time he was all love. A kind of divine madness seemed to have taken possession of him, as if his heart would burst with longing for the beloved Mother. He gave his last public lecture at Temple Beth-El, of which Rabbi Louis Grossman, an ardent admirer of the Swami, was the leader. The Swami cast a spell, as it were, over the whole audience. "Never," wrote Mrs. Funke, "had I seen the Master look as he looked that night. There was something in his beauty not of earth. It was as if the spirit had almost burst the bonds of flesh, and it was then that I saw a foreshadowing of the end. He was much exhausted from the years of overwork, and it was even then to be seen that he was not long for this world. I tried to close my eyes to it, but in my heart I knew the truth. He had needed rest but felt that he must go on."

The idea that his years were numbered came to Swami Vivekananda again and again. He would often say at this time, "Oh, the body is a terrible bondage!" or "How I wish that I could hide myself for ever!" The note-book that he had carried during his wanderings in India contained these significant words: "Now to seek a corner and lay myself down to die!" In a letter to a friend, he quoted these words and said: "Yet all this karma remained. I hope I have now worked it out. It appears like a hallucination that I was in these childish dreams of doing this and doing that. I am getting out of them. . . . Perhaps these mad desires were necessary to bring me over to this country. And I thank the Lord for the experience."

On March 25, 1896, he delivered his famous lecture on "The Philosophy of Vedānta" before the graduate students of the philosophy department of Harvard University. It produced such an impression that he was offered the Chair of Eastern Philosophy in the university. Later a similar offer came from Columbia University. But he declined both on the ground that he was a sannyāsin.

In February 1896, Swami Vivekananda established the Vedānta Society of New York as a non-sectarian organization with the aim of preaching the universal principles of Vedānta. Tolerance and religious universalism formed its motto, and its members generally came to be known as "Vedāntins."

In the meantime the Swami's great works Rāja-Yoga, Bhakti-Yoga, and Karma-Yoga were receiving marked attention from many thoughtful people of the country. The Swami was serious about organizing Hinduism on a sound, universal, ethical, and rational basis so that it would appeal to earnest thinkers in all parts of the world. He wanted to reinterpret, in keeping with the methods of modern science, the Hindu view of the soul, the Godhead, the relationship between matter and energy, and cosmology. Further, he wanted to classify the apparently contradictory passages of the Upanishads bearing on the doctrines of dualism, qualified non-dualism, and absolute non-dualism, and show their ultimate reconciliation. In order to achieve this end, he asked his devotees in India to send him the Upanishads and the Vedānta Sutras with their commentaries by the leading āchāryas, and also the Brāhmana portions of the Vedas, and the Purānas. He himself wanted to write this Maximum Testamentum, this Universal Gospel, in order to translate Hindu thought into Western language. He expressed his objective in a letter written to one of his disciples on February 17, 1896:

To put the Hindu ideas into English and then make out of dry philosophy and intricate mythology and queer, startling psychology, a religion which shall be easy, simple, popular, and at the same time meet the requirements of the highest minds, is a task which only those can understand who have attempted it. The abstract Advaita must become living—poetic—in everyday life; and out of bewildering yogism must come the most scientific and practical psychology—and all this must be put into such a form that a child may grasp it. That is my life's work. The Lord only knows how far I shall succeed. To work we have the right, not to the fruits thereof.

The Swami always wanted a healthy interchange of ideas between East and West; this was one of the aims of the Vedānta Society of New York. He felt the need of centres of vital and continual communication between the two worlds to make "open doors, as it were, through which the East and the West could pass freely back and forth, without a feeling of strangeness, as from one home to another." Already he had thought of bringing to America some of his brother disciples as preachers of Vedānta. He also wanted to send some of his American and English disciples to India to teach science, industry, technology, economics, applied sociology, and other practical things which the Indians needed in order to improve their social conditions and raise their standard of living. He often told his American disciples of his vision that the time would come when the lines of demarcation between East and West would be obliterated. From England he had already written to Swami Saradananda to prepare to come to the West.

In the spring of 1896 letters began to pour in from England beseeching Swami Vivekananda to return there and continue his activities. The Swami felt the need of concentrating on the work in both London and New York, the two great metropolises of the Western world. Therefore he made arrangements with Miss Waldo and other qualified disciples to continue his program in America during his absence. Mr. Francis Leggett was made the president of the Vedānta Society.

The Swami had also been receiving letters from his friends in India begging for his return. He said he would come as soon as possible, but he encouraged them to organize the work, warning them against the formation of any new cult around the person of Śri Ramakrishna, who, to the Swami, was the demonstration of the eternal principles of Hinduism. On April 14, 1896, he wrote to India: "That Ramakrishna Paramahamsa was God—and all that sort of thing—has no go in countries like this. M——— has a tendency to put that stuff down everybody's throat; but that will make our movement a little sect. You keep separate from such attempts; at the same time, if people worship him as God, no harm. Neither encourage nor discourage. The masses will always have the person; the higher ones, the principle. We want both. But principles are universal, not persons. Therefore stick to the principles he taught, and let people think whatever they like of his person."

The Swami now made definite arrangements to leave for London on April 15, and, after carrying out his plans there, to sail for his motherland.

It should be apparent to readers of Swami Vivekananda's life that he worked under great pressure, from a fraction of which a lesser person would have collapsed in no time. Naturally he spent his few spare moments in fun and joking. He would read a copy of Punch or some other comic paper, and laugh till tears rolled down his cheeks. He loved to tell the story of a Christian missionary who was sent to preach to the cannibals. The new arrival proceeded to the chief of the tribe and asked him, "Well, how did you like my predecessor?" The cannibal replied, smacking his lips, "Simply de-li-cious!"

Another was the story of a "darky" clergyman who, while explaining the creation, shouted to his congregation: "You see, God was a-makin' Adam, and He was a-makin' him out o' mud. And when He got him made, He stuck him up agin a fence to dry. And den—" "Hold on, dar, preacher!" suddenly cried out a learned listener. "What's dat about dis 'ere fence? Who's made dis fence?" The preacher replied sharply: "Now you listen 'ere, Sam Jones. Don't you be askin' sich questions. You'll be a-smashin' up all theology!"

By way of relaxation he would often cook an Indian meal at a friend's house. On such occasions he brought out from his pockets tiny packets of finely ground spices. He would make hot dishes which his Western disciples could hardly eat without burning their tongues. They were, no doubt, soothing to his high-strung temperament.

But the Swami's brain was seething with new ideas all the time. He very much wanted to build a "Temple Universal" where people of all faiths would gather to worship the Godhead through the symbol Om, representing the un-differentiated Absolute. At another time, in the beginning of the year 1895, he wrote to Mrs. Bull about buying one hundred and eight acres of land in the Catskill Mountains where his students would build camps and practice medi-tation and other disciplines during the summer holidays.

A touching incident, which occurred in 1894, may be told here; it shows the high respect in which some of the ladies of Cambridge, Massachusetts, held the Swami and his mother. The Swami one day spoke to them about "The Ideals of Indian Women," particularly stressing the ideal of Indian motherhood. They were greatly moved. The following Christmas they sent the Swami's mother in India a letter together with a beautiful picture of the Child Jesus on the lap of the Virgin Mary. They wrote in the letter: "At this Christmastide, when the gift of Mary's son to the world is celebrated and rejoiced over with us, it would seem the time of remembrance. We, who have your son in our midst, send you greetings. His generous service to men, women, and children in our midst was laid at your feet by him, in an address he gave us the other day on the Ideals of Motherhood in India. The worship of his mother will be to all who heard him an inspiration and an uplift."

The Swami often spoke to his disciples about his mother's wonderful self-control, and how on one occasion she had gone without food for fourteen days. He acknowledged that her character was a constant inspiration to his life and work.

The love and adoration in which the Swami was held by his Western disciples can hardly be over-emphasized. Some described him as the "lordly monk," and some as a "grand seigneur." Mrs. Leggett said that in all her experience she had met only two celebrated personages who could make one feel perfectly at ease without for an instant losing their own dignity, and one of them was Swami Vivekananda. Sister Nivedita described him aptly as a Plato in thought and a modern Savonarola in his fearless outspokenness. William James of Harvard addressed him as "Master" and referred to him in *Varieties of Religious Experi-ence* as the "paragon of Vedāntists."

MEETING WITH MAX MÜLLER

A pleasant surprise awaited Swami Vivekananda on his arrival in London. Swami Saradananda had already come and was staying as the guest of Mr. Sturdy. The two Swamis had not seen each other in a very long time. Swami

Vivekananda was told all the news of his spiritual brothers at the Alambazar monastery and their activities in India. It was a most happy occasion.

Swami Vivekananda soon plunged into a whirlwind of activity. From the beginning of May he conducted five classes a week and a Friday session for open discussion. He gave a series of three Sunday lectures in one of the galleries of the Royal Institute of Painters in Water-Colours, in Piccadilly, and also lectured at Princes' Hall and the Lodge of Annie Besant, in addition to speaking at many clubs, and in educational institutions and drawing-rooms. His audiences consisted mostly of intellectual and serious-minded people. His speeches on jnāna-yoga, containing the essence of the Vedānta philosophy, were mostly given in England. Canon Wilberforce held a reception in the Swami's honour, to which he invited many distinguished people.

At one of the meetings, at the close of his address, a white-haired and well-known philosopher said to the Swami: "You have spoken splendidly, sir, but you have told us nothing new." Quick came the Swami's reply: "Sir, I have told you the Truth. That, the Truth, is as old as the immemorial hills, as old as humanity, as old as creation, as old as the Great God. If I have told you in such words as will make you think, make you live up to your thinking, do I not do well in telling it?" Loud applause greeted him at the end of these remarks.

The Swami was quick in repartee. During the question period a man, who happened to be a native of Scotland, asked, "What is the difference between a baboo and a baboon?"[12] "Oh, not much," was the instantaneous reply of the Swami. "It is like the difference between a sot and a Scot—just the difference of a letter."

In one of his public lectures in England he paid the most touching tribute to his Master, Śri Ramakrishna. He said that he had not one little word of his own to utter, not one infinitesimal thought of his own to unfold; everything, every single thing, all that he was himself, all that he could be to others, all that he might do for the world, came from that single source, from that pure soul, from that illimitable inspiration, from him who, seated "there in my beloved India, had solved the tremendous secret, and bestowed the solution on all, ungrudgingly and with divine prodigality." The Swami's own self was utterly forgotten, altogether ignored. "I am what I am, and what I am is always due to him; whatever in me or in my words is good and true and eternal came to me from his mouth, his heart, his soul. Śri Ramakrishna is the spring of this phase of the earth's religious life, of its impulses and activities. If I can show the world one glimpse of my Master, I shall not have lived in vain."

It was Ramakrishna who brought him in contact with Max Müller, the great German Sanskritist and Indologist, who had been impressed by the eloquence of Keshab Chandra Sen and his religious fervour, and had also come to know of the influence that Śri Ramakrishna had exerted in the development of Keshab's life. From the information that he had been able to gather from India, Max Müller had already published an article on Ramakrishna in the

[12] In Northern India the word baboo is used at the end of a man's first name as a sign of respect, somewhat as the English word Mr. before the name of a gentleman. The questioner was evidently making fun of the Swami.

Nineteenth Century, entitled "A Real Mahātman." Now he was eager to meet a direct disciple of the Master, and invited Swami Vivekananda to lunch with him in Oxford on May 28, 1896.

The Swami was delighted to meet the savant. When the name of Ramakrishna was mentioned, the Swami said, "He is worshipped by thousands today, Professor."

"To whom else shall worship be accorded, if not to such?" was Max Müller's reply.

Regarding Max Müller and his wife, the Swami later wrote:

The visit was really a revelation to me. That little white house, its setting in a beautiful garden, the silver-haired sage, with a face calm and benign, and forehead smooth as a child's in spite of seventy winters, and every line in that face speaking of a deep-seated mine of spirituality somewhere behind; that noble wife, the helpmate of his life through his long and arduous task of exciting interest, overriding opposition and contempt, and at last creating a respect for the thoughts of the sages of ancient India—the trees, the flowers, the calmness, and the clear sky—all these sent me back in imagination to the glorious days of ancient India, the days of our brahmarshis[13] and rājarshis,[14] the days of the great vānaprasthins,[15] the days of Arundhatis and Vasishthas.[16] It was neither the philologist nor the scholar that I saw, but a soul that is every day realizing its oneness with the universe.

The Swami was deeply affected to see Max Müller's love for India. "I wish," he wrote enthusiastically, "I had a hundredth part of that love for my motherland. Endowed with an extraordinary, and at the same time an intensely active, mind, he has lived and moved in the world of Indian thought for fifty years or more, and watched the sharp interchange of light and shade in the interminable forest of Sanskrit literature with deep interest and heartfelt love, till they have sunk into his very soul and coloured his whole being."

The Swami asked Max Müller: "When are you coming to India? All men there would welcome one who has done so much to place the thoughts of their ancestors in a true light."

The face of the aged sage brightened up; there was almost a tear in his eye, a gentle nodding of the head, and slowly the words came out: "I would not return then; you would have to cremate me there."

Further questions on the Swami's part seemed an unwarranted intrusion into realms wherein were stored the holy secrets of a man's heart.

Max Müller asked the Swami, "What are you doing to make Śri Ramakrishna known to the world?" He himself was eager to write a fuller biography of the Master if he could only procure the necessary materials. At the Swami's request, Swami Saradananda wrote down the sayings of Śri Ramakrishna and the facts of his life. Later Max Müller embodied these in his book *The Life and Sayings of Śri Ramakrishna*.

One day Saradananda asked the Swami why he himself had not written about the Master's life for Max Müller. He answered: "I have such deep feeling for

[13] Sages illumined by the Knowledge of Brahman.

[14] Kings illumined by the Knowledge of Brahman.

[15] A vānaprasthin is a man who, during the third stage of life, lives with his wife in solitude, both devoting themselves to the contemplation of the Godhead.

[16] Arundhati was the wife of the great Hindu sage Vasishtha.

the Master that it is impossible for me to write about him for the public. If I had written the article Max Müller wanted, then I would have proved, quoting from philosophies, the scriptures, and even the holy books of the Christians, that Ramakrishna was the greatest of all prophets born in this world. That would have been too much for the old man. You have not thought so deeply about the Master as I have; hence you could write in a way that would satisfy Max Müller. Therefore I asked you to write."

Max Müller showed the Swami several colleges in Oxford and the Bodleian Library, and at last accompanied him to the railroad station. To the Swami's protest that the professor should not take such trouble, the latter said, "It is not every day that one meets with a disciple of Ramakrishna Paramahamsa."

Besides doing intensive public work in England, the Swami made there some important personal contacts. The names of Goodwin, Henrietta Muller, Margaret Noble, and Sturdy have already been mentioned. These knew him intimately during his second visit and had become his disciples. Now came the turn of Captain and Mrs. Sevier. The captain was a retired officer of the English army, forty-nine years old, and had served for many years in India. Both were earnest students of religion and had sought the highest truth in various sects and creeds, but had not found it anywhere. When they heard Swami Vivekananda, they intuitively realized that his teachings were what they had so long sought. They were deeply impressed by the non-dualistic philosophy of India and the Swami's personality.

Coming out of one of the Swami's lectures, Captain Sevier asked Miss MacLeod, who had already known the Swami in America: "You know this young man? Is he what he seems?"

"Yes."

"In that case one must follow him and with him find God."

The Captain went to his wife and said, "Will you let me become the Swami's disciple?"

"Yes," she replied.

She asked him, "Will you let me become the Swami's disciple?"

He replied with affectionate humour, "I am not so sure!"

The very first time the Swami met Mrs. Sevier in private he addressed her as "Mother" and asked her if she would not like to come to India, adding, "I will give you my best realizations."

A very affectionate relationship sprang up between the Swami and the Seviers, and the latter regarded him as their son. They became his intimate companions and offered him all their savings. But the Swami, anxious about their future worldly security, persuaded them to keep the greater portion of their fortune. Captain and Mrs. Sevier, together with Miss Noble and Goodwin, were the choicest among the followers that Swami Vivekananda gathered in England, and all of them remained faithful to him and his work till the last days of their lives.

Through the generosity of the Seviers, the Swami, as will be seen, established the Advaita Āsrama at Mayavati in the Himālayas for the training of his disciples, both Eastern and Western, in the contemplation of the Impersonal Godhead. After Captain Sevier's death in the monastery, Mrs. Sevier lived there

for fifteen years—the only Western woman in that remote region of the mountains, which is inaccessible for long months of the year—busying herself with
the education of the children of the neighbouring hills. Once Miss MacLeod
asked her, "Do you not get bored?" "I think of him," she replied, referring
to Swami Vivekananda.

Though preoccupied with various activities in England, the Swami never for
one moment forgot his work in India. After all, it had been his intense desire to
find means to ameliorate the condition of his countrymen that had brought him
to the West. That hope he always cherished in a corner of his mind, both in
Europe and in America. He had to train his brother disciples as future workers
in India. And so he is seen writing to them in detail regarding the organization
of the monastery at Alambazar, where they had been living for some time.

On April 27, 1896, he sent instructions about the daily life of the monks, their
food and clothing, their intercourse with the public, and about the provision of a
spacious library at the monastery, a smaller room for interviews, a big hall for
religious discussions with the devotees, a small room for an office, another for
smoking, and so forth and so on. He advised them to furnish the rooms in the
simplest manner and to keep an eye on the water for drinking and cooking. The
monastery, he suggested, should be under the management of a President and
a Secretary to be elected by vote. Study, preaching, and religious practices
should be important items among the duties of the inmates. He also desired
to establish a math for women, directly under the control of the Holy Mother.
The monks were not to visit the women's quarters. In conclusion, he recom-
mended Swami Brahmananda as the President of the math, and said: "He who
is the servant of all is their true master. He never becomes a leader in whose
love there is a consideration of high or low. He whose love knows no end and
never stops to consider high or low has the whole world lying at his feet." For
his workers the Swami wanted men with "muscles of iron and nerves of steel,
inside which dwells a mind of the same material as that of which the thunderbolt is made."

To quote the Swami's words again: "I want strength, manhood, kshatra-
virya, or the virility of a warrior, and brahma-teja, or the radiance of a brāhmin.
. . . These men will stand aside from the world, give their lives, and be ready
to fight the battle of Truth, marching on from country to country. One blow
struck outside of India is equal to a hundred thousand struck within. Well, all
will come if the Lord wills it."

TOUR IN EUROPE

The Swami was exhausted by his strenuous work in England. Three of his
intimate disciples, the Seviers and Henrietta Muller, proposed a holiday tour on
the continent. He was "as delighted as a child" at the prospect. "Oh! I long to
see the snows and wander on the mountain paths," he said. He recalled his
travels in the Himālayas. On July 31, 1896, the Swami, in the company of his
three friends, left for Switzerland. They visited Geneva, Mer-de-Glace, Mon-
treux, Chillon, Chamounix, the St. Bernard, Lucerne, the Rigi, Zermatt, and
Schaffhausen. The Swami felt exhilarated by his walks in the Alps. He wanted
to climb Mont Blanc, but gave up the idea when told of the difficulty of the

ascent. He found that Swiss peasant life and its manners and customs resembled those of the people who dwelt in the Himālayas.

In a little village at the foot of the Alps between Mont Blanc and the Little St. Bernard, he conceived the idea of founding a monastery in the Himālayas. He said to his companions: "Oh, I long for a monastery in the Himālayas, where I can retire from the labours of my life and spend the rest of my days in meditation. It will be a centre for work and meditation, where my Indian and Western disciples can live together, and I shall train them as workers. The former will go out as preachers of Vedānta to the West, and the latter will devote their lives to the good of India."

Mr. Sevier, speaking for himself and his wife, said: "How nice it would be, Swami, if this could be done. We must have such a monastery."

The dream was fulfilled through the Advaita Āśrama at Mayavati, which commands a magnificent view of the eternal snows of the Himālayas.

In the Alps the Swami enjoyed some of the most lucid and radiant moments of his spiritual life. Sometimes he would walk alone, absorbed in thought, the disciples keeping themselves at a discreet distance. One of the disciples said: "There seemed to be a great light about him, and a great stillness and peace. Never have I seen the Swami to such advantage. He seemed to communicate spirituality by a look or with a touch. One could almost read his thoughts, which were of the highest, so transfigured had his personality become."

While still wandering in the Alps, the Swami received a letter from the famous orientalist, Paul Deussen, Professor of Philosophy at the University of Kiel. The professor urgently invited the Swami to visit him. The Swami accepted the invitation and changed his itinerary. He arrived at Kiel after visiting Heidelberg, Coblenz, Cologne, and Berlin. He was impressed by the material power and the great culture of Germany.

Professor Deussen was well versed in Sanskrit, and was perhaps the only scholar in Europe who could speak that language fluently. A disciple of Schopenhauer and follower of Kant, Deussen could easily appreciate the high flights of Śankarāchārya's philosophy. He believed that the system of Vedānta, as founded on the Upanishads and the Vedānta Sutras, is one of the "most majestic structures and valuable products of the genius of man in his search for Truth, and that the highest and purest morality is the immediate consequence of Vedānta."

The Swami and the Seviers were cordially received by the German scholar. In the course of the conversation Deussen said that a movement was being made back towards the fountainhead of spirituality, a movement that would in the future probably make India the spiritual leader of the nations, the highest and the greatest spiritual influence on earth. He also found in the Swami a vivid demonstration of concentration and control of the mind. On one occasion he saw his guest turning over the pages of a poetical work and did not receive any response to a query. Afterwards the Swami apologized, saying that he had been so absorbed in the book that he did not hear the professor. Then he repeated the verses from the book. The conversation soon turned to the power of concentration as developed in the Yoga philosophy. One of the purposes of Deussen's meeting the Swami, it is said, was his desire to learn from the latter the secrets of the Yoga powers.

Deussen showed the Swami the city of Kiel. Thereafter the Swami wished to leave immediately for England, though the professor insisted that he should stay at Kiel a few days more. As that was not possible, Deussen joined the party in Hamburg and they travelled together in Holland. After spending three days in Amsterdam all arrived in London, and for two weeks Deussen met with the Swami daily. The Swami also visited Max Müller again at Oxford.

Swami Vivekananda spent another two months in England, giving lectures and seeing important men of their day, such as Edward Carpenter, Frederick Myers, Canon Wilberforce, and Moncure D. Conway. The most notable lectures he gave at this time were those on māyā, about which he spoke on three occasions, dealing with its various aspects. It is said that some members of the British royal family attended these lectures incognito. He created such an intense atmosphere during these talks that the whole audience was transported into a realm of ecstatic consciousness, and some burst into tears. The lectures were the most learned and eloquent among his speeches on non-dualistic Vedānta.

Swami Abhedananda arrived from India, and Vivekananda was immensely pleased to have his brother disciple assist him in his foreign work. The maiden speech of Abhedananda at a club in Bloomsbury Square, on October 27, was highly appreciated by all, and the Swami said about his spiritual brother, "Even if I perish on this plane, my message will be sounded through these dear lips, and the world will hear it." The report of the continued popularity of Swami Saradananda, who had in the meantime gone to New York, likewise gratified him.

Despite the rush of his European work Swami Vivekananda maintained his contact with America. He took a personal interest in the spiritual development of his students. The affectionate relationship of the Swami with the Hale family of Chicago has been mentioned before, especially with the four unmarried girls. Hearing of the proposed marriage of Harriet, he wrote to her on September 17, 1896, "Marriage is the truest goal for ninety-nine per cent of the human race, and they will live the happiest life as soon as they have learnt and are ready to abide by the eternal lesson—that we are bound to bear and forbear and that to everyone life must be a compromise." He sent the young lady his blessings in these terms: "May you always enjoy the undivided love of your husband, helping him in attaining all that is desirable in this life, and when you have seen your children's children, and the drama of life is nearing its end, may you help each other in reaching that infinite ocean of Existence, Knowledge, and Bliss, at the touch of whose waters all distinctions melt away and we all become One."

But Mary Hale could not make a decision between marriage and lifelong celibacy. She was full of idealism and the spirit of independence; but she was warm in her affection. Swami Vivekananda was particularly fond of Mary. On the day he wrote to Harriet he also wrote to Mary, congratulating Harriet for her discrimination, and prophesying for her a life of joy and sweetness, since she was "not so imaginative and sentimental as to make a fool of herself and has enough of common sense and gentleness to soften the hard points of life which must come to everyone." But he wanted to tell Mary "the truth, and my language is plain." He wrote:

My dear Mary, I will tell you a great lesson I have learnt in this life. It is this: "The higher your ideal is, the more miserable you are," for such a thing as an ideal cannot be attained in the world—or in this life, even. He who wants perfection in the world is a madman—for it cannot be. How can you find the infinite in the finite?

You, Mary, are like a mettlesome Arab—grand, splendid. You would make a splendid queen—physically, mentally—you would shine alongside of a dashing, bold, adventurous, heroic husband. But, my dear sister, you will make one of the worst wives. You will take the life out of our easy-going, practical, plodding husbands of the everyday world. Mind, my sister, although it is true that there is much more romance in actual life than in any novel, yet it is few and far between. Therefore my advice to you is that until you bring down your ideals to a more practical level, you ought not to marry. If you do, the result will be misery for both of you. In a few months you will lose all regard for a common-place, good, nice young man, and then life will become insipid. . . .

There are two sorts of persons in the world—the one strong-nerved, quiet, yielding to nature, not given to much imagination, yet good, kind, sweet, etc. For such is this world—they alone are born to be happy. There are others, again, with high-strung nerves, tremendously imaginative, with intense feeling—always going high, and coming down the next moment. For them there is no happiness. The first class will have almost an even tenor of happiness. The second will have to run between ecstasy and misery. But of these alone what we call geniuses are made. There is some truth in a recent theory that genius is "a sort of madness."

Now persons of this class, if they want to be great, must fight to be so—clear the deck for battle. No encumbrance—no marriage—no children, no undue attachment to anything except the one idea, and live and die for that. I am a person of this sort. I have taken up the one idea of "Vedānta," and I have "cleared the deck for action." You and Isabel are made of this metal—but let me tell you, though it is hard, you are spoiling your lives in vain. Either take up one idea, clear the deck, and to it dedicate the life, or be contented and practical, lower the ideal, marry, and have a happy life. Either "bhoga" or "yoga"—either enjoy this life or give up and be a yogi. None can have both in one. Now or never—select quick. "He who is very particular gets nothing," says the proverb. Now sincerely and really and for ever determine to "clear the deck for the fight," take up anything—philosophy or science or religion or literature—and let that be your God for the rest of your life. Achieve happiness or achieve greatness. I have no sympathy with you and Isabel—you are neither for this nor for that. I wish to see you happy, as Harriet is, or great. Eating, drinking, dressing, and society nonsense are not things to throw away a life upon—especially for you, Mary. You are rusting away a splendid brain and abilities, for which there is not the least excuse. You must have ambition to be great. I know you will take these rather harsh remarks from me in the right spirit, knowing I like you really as much as or more than what I call you, my sister. I had long had a mind to tell you this and as experience is gathering I feel like telling you. The joyful news from Harriet urged me to tell you this. I will be over-joyed to hear that you are married also, and happy so far as happiness can be had here, or would like to hear of your doing great deeds.

Mary Hale later married a gentleman from Florence, and became known as Mme. Matteini.

For some time the Swami had been feeling an inner urge to return to India. From Switzerland he wrote to friends in India: "Do not be afraid. Great things are going to be done, my children. Take heart. . . . In the winter I am going back to India and will try to set things on their feet there. Work on, brave hearts, fail not—no saying nay; work on—the Lord is behind the work. Mahāśakti, the Great Power, is with you."

On November 29, 1896, he wrote to a disciple in India about his proposed Himālayan monastery. He further said that his present plan was to start two centres, one in Madras and the other in Calcutta, and later others in Bombay and Allahabad. He was pleased to see that the magazine *Brahmavādin*, published in English in Madras, was disseminating his ideas; he was planning to start similar magazines in the vernaculars also. He also intended to start a paper, under the management of writers from all nations, in order to spread his ideas to every corner of the globe. "You must not forget," he wrote, "that my interests are international and not Indian alone."

Swami Vivekananda could no longer resist the voice of India calling him back. Sometime during the middle of November, after a class lecture, he called Mrs. Sevier aside and quietly asked her to purchase four tickets for India. He planned to take with him the Seviers and Mr. Goodwin. Reservations were accordingly made on the "Prinz Regent Luitpold," of the North German Lloyd Steamship Line, sailing from Naples for Ceylon on December 20, 1896. The Seviers wanted to lead a retired life in India, practising spiritual disciplines and helping the Swami in carrying out the idea of building a monastery in the Himālayas. Faithful Goodwin, who had already taken the vows of a brahma-chārin, would work as the Swami's stenographer. It was also planned that Miss Muller and Miss Noble would follow the party some time after, the latter to devote her life to the cause of women's education in India.

The Swami was given a magnificent farewell by his English friends, devotees, and admirers on December 13 at the Royal Society of Painters in Water-Colours, in Piccadilly. There were about five hundred people present. Many were silent, tongue-tied and sad at heart. Tears were very near in some eyes. But the Swami, after his farewell address, walked among the assembled friends and repeated over and over again, "Yes, yes, we shall meet again, we shall." It was decided that Swami Abhedananda would continue the work after the Swami's departure.

Of the impressions left by the Swami's teachings in England, Margaret Noble writes:

To not a few of us the words of Swami Vivekananda came as living water to men perishing of thirst. Many of us have been conscious for years past of that growing uncertainty and despair, with regard to religion, which has beset the intellectual life of Europe for half a century. Belief in the dogmas of Christianity has become impossible for us, and we had no tool, such as now we hold, by which to cut away the doctrinal shell from the kernel of Reality, in our faith. To these, the Vedānta has given intellectual confirmation and philosophical expression of their own mistrusted intuitions. "The people that walked in darkness have seen a great light." . . .

It was the Swami's *I am God* that came as something always known, only never said before. . . . Yet again, it was the Unity of Man that was the touch needed to rationalize all previous experiences and give logical sanction to the thirst for absolute service, never boldly avowed in the past. Some by one gate, and some by another, we have all entered into a great heritage, and we know it.

The practical Englishman saw in the Swami's life the demonstration of fearlessness which was the necessary corollary of his teaching regarding the divinity of the soul. It was revealed in many incidents.

One in particular illustrates this. He was one day walking with Miss Muller and an English friend across some fields when a mad bull came tearing towards them. The Englishman frankly ran, and reached the other side of the hill in safety. Miss Muller ran as far as she could, and then sank to the ground, incapable of further effort. Seeing this, and unable to aid her, the Swami— thinking, "So this is the end, after all"—took up his stand in front of her, with folded arms.

He told afterwards how his mind was occupied with a mathematical calculation as to how far the bull would be able to throw him. But the animal suddenly stopped a few paces off, and then, raising its head, retreated sullenly. The Englishman felt ashamed of his cowardly retreat and of having left the Swami alone to face the bull. Miss Muller asked the Swami how he could muster courage in such a dangerous situation. He said that in the face of danger and death he felt—and he took two pebbles in his hands and struck the one against the other—as strong as flint, for "I have touched the feet of God." He had shown a like courage in his early youth, when he quickly stepped up to a runaway horse and caught it, in a street of Calcutta, thus saving the life of a woman who occupied the carriage behind.

Regarding his experience and work in England, he told the Hale sisters, in a letter, that it was a roaring success. To another American friend he wrote that he believed in the power of the English to assimilate great ideas, and that though the process of assimilation might be slow, it would be all the more sure and abiding. He believed that the time would come when distinguished ecclesiastics of the Church of England, imbued with the idealism of Vedānta, would form a liberal community within the Anglican Church itself, supporting the universality of religion both in vision and in practice.

But what he admired most in England was the character of the English people—their steadiness, thoroughness, loyalty, devotion to the ideal, and perseverance to finish any work that they undertook. His preconceived idea about the English was thoroughly changed when he came to know them intimately. "No one," he said later, addressing the Hindus of Calcutta, "ever landed on English soil feeling more hatred in his heart for a race than I did for the English. [The iniquities of the colonial rule in India were deeply impressed in his mind.] . . . There is none among you who loves the English people more than I do."

He wrote to the Hale sisters on November 28, 1896: "The English are not so bright as the Americans, but once you touch their heart it is yours for ever. . . . I now understand why the Lord has blessed them above all other races— steady, sincere to the backbone, with great depths of feeling, only with a crust of stoicism on the surface. If that is broken you have your man." In another letter: "You know, of course, the steadiness of the English; they are, of all nations, least jealous of each other and that is why they dominate the world. They have solved the secret of obedience without slavish cringing—great freedom with law-abidingness." On still another occasion he called the English "a nation of heroes, the true kshattriyas. . . . Their education is to hide their feelings and never to show them. If you know how to reach the English heart, he is your friend for ever. If he has once an idea put into his brain, it never comes out; and the immense practicality and energy of the race makes it sprout up and immediately bear fruit."

The Swami felt that the finger of God had brought about the contact between India and England. The impact created by the aggressive British rule, on the one hand, awakened the Hindu race from its slumber of ages, and on the other hand, offered India opportunities to spread her spiritual message throughout the Western world.

He wrote to Mr. Leggett on July 6, 1896:

The British Empire with all its evils is the greatest machine that ever existed for the dissemination of ideas. I mean to put my ideas in the centre of this machine, and it will spread them all over the world. Of course, all great work is slow and the difficulties are too many, especially as we Hindus are a conquered race. Yet that is the very reason why it is bound to work, for spiritual ideals have always come from the downtrodden. The downtrodden Jews overwhelmed the Roman Empire with their spiritual ideals. You will be pleased to learn that I am also learning my lesson every day in patience and above all in sympathy. I think I am beginning to see the Divine even inside the bullying Anglo-Indians. I think I am slowly approaching to that state when I would be able to love the very "Devil" himself, if there were any.

Though Swami Vivekananda himself spoke highly of the effect of his teachings in England, he did not start any organized work there as he did in the United States of America. From his letters and conversations one learns that he was growing weary of the world. Though he was at the peak of his success, as far as public activity was concerned, he began to feel a longing for the peace that comes from total absorption in the Supreme Spirit. He sensed that his earthly mission was over. On August 23, 1896, he wrote to a friend, from Lucerne:

"I have begun the work, let others work it out. So you see, to set the work going I had to defile myself by touching money and property for a time.[17] Now I am sure my part of the work has been done, and I have no more interest in Vedānta or any philosophy in the world, or in the work itself. I am getting ready to depart, to return no more to this hell, this world. . . . Even its religious utility is beginning to pall on me. . . . These works and doing good, and so forth, are just a little exercise to cleanse the mind. I have had enough of it."[18] He was losing interest even in the American programme, which he himself had organized.

In the letter quoted above, the Swami wrote: "If New York or Boston or any other place in the U. S. needs Vedānta teachers, they must receive them, keep them, and provide for them. As for me, I am as good as retired. I have played my part in the world." To Swami Abhedananda he confided one day, about this time, that he was going to live for five or six years at the most. The brother disciple said in protest that he was a young man and that he should not think of death. "But," Vivekananda said, "you are a fool; you do not understand.

[17] Where money was concerned, he shared the physical repulsion towards it of Śri Ramakrishna.

[18] That work serves as a discipline for the realization of freedom, and is not freedom itself, has been fully discussed by Swami Vivekananda in his Karma-Yoga.

My soul is getting bigger and bigger every day; the body can hardly contain
it. Any day it may burst this cage of flesh and bone!"

The world was leaving him. The string of the kite by which it was fastened
to earth was breaking.

The reader may recall that Śri Ramakrishna spoke of Vivekananda as a free
soul whom he had dragged down from the realm of the Absolute to help him
in his mission on earth. A temporary veil, necessary for physical embodiment
and work, was put on this soul so that it might dwell in the world to help men
in their search for spiritual freedom. But now, as the veil was becoming thinner,
the Swami began to get a glimpse of the real freedom. He realized that the
world was the lilā, the play, of the Divine Mother, and it would continue as
long as She wanted it. On August 8, 1896, he wrote from Switzerland to
Goodwin:

> I am much refreshed now. I look out of the window and see the huge glaciers just
> before me—and feel that I am in the Himālayas. I am quite calm. My nerves have
> regained their accustomed strength, and little vexations like those you write of do not
> touch me at all. How shall I be disturbed by this child's play? The whole world is mere
> child's play—preaching, teaching, and all included. "Know him to be a sannyāsin who
> neither hates nor desires." What is to be desired in this little mud-puddle of a world,
> with its ever recurring misery, disease, and death? "He who has given up all desires, he
> alone is happy." This rest—eternal, peaceful rest—I am catching a glimpse of it now
> in this beautiful spot. "If a man knows the Ātman as 'I am this,' then desiring what
> and for whose sake will he suffer in the wake of the body?"
>
> I feel as if I have had my share of experience in what they call "work." I am finished.
> I am longing to get out now.

With this growing detachment from the world, the idea of good and evil,
without the consciousness of which no work is possible, began to drop away.
The Swami was realizing an intense love for God. In that mood a great exaltation would come over him, and the whole universe would seem to him
an Eternal Garden where an Eternal Child plays an Eternal Game. In that
mood of delirious joy he had written on July 6, 1896, to Francis Leggett, his
friend and disciple:

> At twenty I was a most unsympathetic, uncompromising fanatic. I would not walk on
> the foot-path on the theatre side of the street in Calcutta. At thirty-three I can live in the
> same house with prostitutes and never would think of saying a word of reproach to them.
> Is it degeneration? Or is it that I am broadening out into that universal love which is
> the Lord Himself? . . . Some days I get into a sort of ecstasy. I feel that I must bless
> everyone, every being, love and embrace every being, and I literally see that evil is a
> delusion. . . . I bless the day I was born. I have had so much of kindness and love here,
> and that Love Infinite who brought me into being has guided every one of my actions,
> good or bad (don't be frightened); for what am I, what was I ever, but a tool in His
> hands—for whose service I have given up everything—my Beloved, my Joy, my Life,
> my Soul? He is my playful darling, I am His playfellow. There is neither rhyme nor
> reason in the universe. What reason binds Him? He, the Playful One, is playing—these
> tears and laughter are all parts of the play. Great fun, great fun! as Joe[19] says.
>
> It is a funny world, and the funniest chap you ever saw is He, the Beloved. Infinite

[19] Referring to Miss MacLeod.

fun, is it not? Brotherhood or playmatehood? A shoal of romping children let out to play in this playground of the world, isn't it? Whom to praise, whom to blame? It is all His play. They want an explanation, but how can you explain Him? He is brain-less, nor has He any reason. He is fooling us with little brains and reasons, but this time He won't find me napping—"you bet." I have learnt a thing or two. Beyond, beyond reason and learning and talking is the feeling, the "Love," the "Beloved." Ay, "Sake,"[20] fill the cup and we will be mad.—Yours ever in madness, VIVEKANANDA.

In a philosophical mood he spoke about the illusion of progress. He did not believe in the possibility of transforming this earth into a heaven where misery would be totally eliminated and happiness alone would reign in its place. True freedom and bliss could be attained only by the individual and not by the masses as a whole. He wrote to Goodwin on August 8, 1896: " 'A good world,' 'a happy world,' 'social progress' are equally intelligible as 'hot ice,' 'dark light,' etc. If it were good it would not be the world. The soul foolishly thinks of manifesting the Infinite in finite matter—the intelligence through gross particles—and at last finds out its error and tries to escape. This going back is the beginning of religion, and its method, destruction of self, that is, love. Not love for wife or child or anybody else, but love for everything else except this little self. Never be deluded by the tall talk, of which you will hear a lot in America, about 'human progress' and such stuff. There is no progress without regression."

On November 1, 1896, in the course of a letter to Mary Hale, Swami Vivekananda wrote from London:

"An objective heaven or millennium therefore has existence only in the fancy, but a subjective one is already in existence. The musk-deer, after vain search for the cause of the scent of the musk, at last will have to find it in himself."

But Swami Vivekananda's mission to the world was not yet finished. An arduous task was awaiting him in his beloved motherland. The Indian work had to be organized before he could bid farewell to this earth. He left England on December 16, 1896, and travelled overland for the port of departure at Naples.

The party headed directly for Milan, passing through Dover, Calais, and Mont Cenis. The Swami enjoyed the railroad journey and entertained his companions, the Seviers, with his stimulating conversation. But a part of his mind was drawn to India. He said to the Seviers: "Now I have but one thought, and that is India. I am looking forward to India." On the eve of his departure from London, an English friend had asked him, "Swami, how will you like your motherland after three years' experience in the luxurious and powerful West?" His significant reply was: "India I loved before I came away. Now the very dust of India has become holy to me, the very air is now holy to me; it is the holy land, the place of pilgrimage." Often the Swami said that the West was the karma-bhumi, the land of action, where through selfless work a man purified his heart; and India was the punya-bhumi, the land of holiness, where the pure in heart communed with God.

In Milan the Swami was much impressed by the great cathedral and by

[20] Friend.

Leonardo's "Last Supper." Pisa, with the leaning tower, and Florence, with its magnificent achievements in art, immensely delighted him. But the peak of his happiness was reserved for Rome, where he spent Christmas week. Many things there reminded him of India: the tonsure of the priests, the incense, the music, the various ceremonies of the Catholic Church, and the Holy Sacrament—the last of these recalling to his mind the prasādam of the Hindu temples, the food partaken of by devotees after it has been offered to God.

When asked by a lady companion about the church ritual, the Swami said, "If you love the Personal God, then give Him your best—incense, flowers, fruit, and silk." But he was a little bewildered by the imposing High Mass at St. Peter's on Christmas Day, and whispered to the Seviers: "Why all this pageantry and ostentatious show? Can it be possible that the Church which loves such a display of pomp and ceremonies is the true follower of the humble Jesus, who had nowhere to lay his head?" He could never forget that Christ was a sannyāsin, a world-renouncing monk, and that the essence of his teachings was renunciation and detachment.

He enjoyed his visit to the catacombs, associated with the memories of early Christian martyrs and saints. The Christmas festival at Santa-Maria d'Ara Coeli, with the stalls where sweets, toys, and cheap pictures of the Bambino were sold, reminded him of similar religious fairs in India. Christmas in Rome filled his heart with a warm devotion for Jesus Christ, who was an Asiatic and whom Asia had offered to the West as a gift to awaken its spiritual consciousness.

The Swami spent a few days in Naples, visiting Vesuvius, Pompeii, and other places of interest. Then the ship at last arrived from Southampton with Mr. Goodwin as one of her passengers. The Swami and his friends sailed from Naples on December 30, 1896, expecting to arrive in Colombo on January 15, 1897.

On board the ship the Swami had a significant vision. One night, somewhere between Naples and Port Said, he saw in a vivid dream a venerable, bearded old man, like a rishi of India, who said: "Observe carefully this place. You are now in the Island of Crete. This is the land where Christianity began. I am one of the Therapeutae who used to live here." The apparition uttered another word, which the Swami could not remember. It might have been "Essene," a sect to which John the Baptist belonged.

Both the Therapeutae and the Essenes had practised renunciation and cherished a liberal religious outlook. According to some scholars, the word Therapeutae may be derived from the Buddhist word sthaviraputta, meaning the sons or disciples of the Theras, or Elders, the superiors among the Buddhist monks. The word Essene may have some relation with Iśiyāna, meaning the Path of the Lord, a well-known sect of Buddhist monks. It is now admitted that the Buddhists at an early time had monasteries in Asia Minor, Egypt, and generally along the eastern part of the Mediterranean.

The old man in the dream concluded his statement by saying: "The truths and ideas preached by us were presented as the teachings of Jesus. But Jesus the person was never born. Various proofs attesting this fact will be brought to light when this place is dug up." At that moment—it was midnight—the

Swami awoke and asked a sailor where the ship was; he was told that it was fifty miles off Crete.

The Swami was startled at this singular coincidence. The idea flashed in his mind that the Acts of the Apostles might have been an older record than the Gospels, and that Buddhist thought, coming through the Therapeutae and the Essenes, might have helped in the formulation of Christianity. The person of Christ might be a later addition. He knew that Alexandria had been a meeting-place of Indian and Egyptian thought. Later, when the old sites in Crete were excavated, evidence was found connecting early Christianity with foreign sources.

But Swami Vivekananda never refused to accept the historical Christ. Like Krishna, Christ, too, has been revealed in the spiritual experiences of many saints. That, for Vivekananda, conferred upon him a reality which was more real than historical realities. While travelling in Switzerland, the Swami one day plucked some wild flowers and asked Mrs. Sevier to offer them at the feet of the Virgin in a little chapel in the mountains, with the remark, "She too is the Mother." One of his disciples, another day, gave him a picture of the Sistine Madonna to bless. But he refused in all humility, and piously touching the feet of the child said, "I would have washed his feet, not with my tears, but with my heart's blood." It may be remembered that the monastic Order of Ramakrishna was started on Christmas Eve.

During the two weeks' voyage, Swami Vivekananda had ample time to reflect on the experiences of his three years in the Western world. His mind was filled with memories of sweet friendship, unflinching devotion, and warm appreciation from both sides of the Atlantic. Three years before, he had come to America, unknown and penniless, and was regarded somewhat as a curiosity from the glamorous and inscrutable East. Now he was returning to his native land, a hero and prophet worshipped by hundreds and admired by thousands. Guided by the finger of God he had gone to Chicago. In the New World he had seen life at its best and its worst. He found there a society based on the ideals of equality, justice, and freedom, where a man—in sad contrast with India— was given every opportunity to develop his potentialities. There the common people had reached a high standard of living and enjoyed their well-earned prosperity in a way unimaginable in any other part of the world. The American mind was alert, inquisitive, daring, receptive, and endowed with a rare ethical sensitivity. He saw in America, in her men and women of letters, wealth, and position, sparks of spirituality which kindled at the touch of his magic words. He was impressed to see the generous confidence and richness of heart manifested through the pure and candid souls who gave themselves to him once they had recognized him as a trustworthy spiritual guide. They became his noble friends and slaves of love, and did not shrink from the highest sacrifice to help in the fulfilment of his mission.

But withal, the Swami saw the vulgarity, garishness, greed, lust for power, and sensuality among this vast country's heterogeneous elements. People had been swept off their feet by the newly acquired prosperity created with the aid of science, technology, and human ingenuity. They often appeared to him naïve and noisy, and he may have wondered if this new nation, l'enfant terrible, the last hope of Western culture and also the source of potential fear for the rest of the world, would measure up to the expectations of its Founding Fathers and act as the big brother of the world, sharing with all the material amenities of life.

America had given him the first recognition and he was aware of it. In America he had started the work of Vedānta in an organized form, and he hoped America would be the spiritual bridge between the East and the West. Though his scholarly and conservative mind often felt at home among the intellectuals of England and Germany, yet to America his heart was devoted. The monuments of Western culture no doubt fascinated him, but, as he wrote to Mary Hale from London, in May 1896: "I love the Yankee land—I like to see new things. I do not care a fig to loaf about old ruins and mope a life out about old histories and keep sighing about the ancients. I have too much vigour in my blood for that. In America is the place, the people, the opportunity for everything new. I have become horribly radical."

In that same letter he wrote, too, that he wished he could infuse some of the American spirit into India, into "that awful mass of conservative jelly-fish, and then throw overboard all old associations and start a new thing, entirely new—simple, strong, new and fresh as the first-born baby—throw all of the past overboard and begin anew."

Swami Vivekananda bestowed equally high praise upon the Englishman. He felt that in a sense his work in England was more satisfactory than his work in America. There he transformed the life of individuals. Goodwin and Margaret Noble embraced his cause as their own, and the Seviers accompanied him to India, deserting Europe and all their past to follow him.

But what of Swami Vivekananda's early dream of gathering from America the material treasures to remedy the sufferings of the Indian masses and raise their standard of living? He had come to America to obtain, in exchange for India's spiritual wealth, the needed monetary help and scientific and technological knowledge to rebuild the physical health of his own people. Though on his return he did not take with him American scientists and technologists, or carry in his pocket gold and silver from the New World, yet he had left behind a vast storehouse of goodwill and respect for India. He had been India's first spiritual ambassador to America, India's herald, who, remembering the dignity of the royal land whence he had come, had spoken in her name and delivered her message with appropriate dignity.

The full effect of this contact will be known only in years to come; but a beginning can be seen even now. Half a century after Swami Vivekananda's visit to America, India gained her freedom from British rule. When she thus obtained facilities to arrange her national affairs in her own way, India sent thousands of students to the New World to acquire advanced knowledge in the physical sciences and technology. Further, American money is now being spent to improve the material condition of the Indian masses. Thus it appears that, after all, Swami Vivekananda was not a mere visionary, but had insight into the shape of things to come.

The immediate task before him, the Swami felt, was to work for India's regeneration from within the country itself. India could be liberated by her own efforts alone. But he was carrying from the West a priceless asset to help him in his herculean task: The West had given him an authority which, it appears, he did not have before in the land of his birth. He had been successful in planting the seeds of India's spiritual ideas in the very heart of the English-speaking world—in New York and London. Did he know then that within a half century these ideas would be broadcast over the Western world, and earn its respect for his motherland? Though he had come to America as a giver, he was now, in a sense, going back to India as a gift from the New World.

THE RETURN TO INDIA

Swami Vivekananda enjoyed the sea voyage back to India, relaxing from his strenuous activities in the West. But his mind was full of ideas regarding his future plan of work in his motherland.

There were on the boat, among other passengers, two Christian missionaries who, in the course of a heated discussion with the Swami, lost their tempers and savagely criticized the Hindu religion. The Swami walked to one of them, seized him by the collar, and said menacingly, "If you abuse my religion again, I will throw you overboard."

"Let me go, sir," the frightened missionary apologized; "I'll never do it again."

Later, in the course of a conversation with a disciple in Calcutta, he asked, "What would you do if someone insulted your mother?" The disciple answered, "I would fall upon him, sir, and teach him a good lesson."

"Bravo!" said the Swami. "Now, if you had the same positive feeling for your religion, your true mother, you could never see any Hindu brother converted to Christianity. Yet you see this occurring every day, and you are quite indifferent. Where is your faith? Where is your patriotism? Every day Christian missionaries abuse Hinduism to your face, and yet how many are there amongst you whose blood boils with righteous indignation and who will stand up in its defense?"

When the boat stopped at Aden, the party went ashore and visited the places of interest. The Swami saw from a distance a Hindusthāni betel-leaf seller smoking his hookah, or hubble-bubble. He had not enjoyed this Indian way of smoking for the past three years. Going up to him, the Swami said, "Brother, do give me your pipe." Soon he was puffing at it with great joy and talking to him as to an intimate friend.

Mr. Sevier later on said to Swamiji teasingly: "Now we see! It was this pipe that made you run away from us so abruptly!" Speaking of this incident, the Swami's companions said later: "The shopkeeper could not have resisted him; for he had such an endearing way about him, when asking for anything, that he was simply irresistible. We shall never forget that ingenuous look on his face when he said to the shopkeeper, with childlike sweetness, 'Brother, do give me your pipe.'"

In the early morning of January 15, 1897, the coast of Ceylon with its majestic coco palms and gold-coloured beach was seen at a distance. The Swami's heart leapt with joy; and his disciples caught his excitement as the boat approached the beautiful harbour of Colombo. But no one in the party had the slightest idea of what they were to witness while disembarking.

Since the day of his success at the Parliament of Religions in Chicago, which had filled with joy and pride the hearts of his countrymen, especially of his disciples and brother monks at the Baranagore Math, Swami Vivekananda had been inspiring his faithful followers to lay down their lives for the uplift of the masses of India, and in particular to help the hungry and illiterate. In his heart of hearts he felt that India would not be able to resist his appeal. Many months before, while discussing with some of his disciples in Detroit the great difficulties that he had encountered in presenting Hinduism to bigoted Christians in America, he had said: "But India shall listen to me. I will shake India to her foundations. I will send an electric thrill through her veins. Wait! You will see how India receives me. It is India, my own India, that knows truly how to appreciate what I have given so freely here, and with my life's blood. India will receive me in triumph."

When the news of Swami Vivekananda's departure from Europe reached India, the hearts of the people were stirred. The spiritual ambassador of their ancient land was coming back after fulfilling his mission. They must give a regal welcome to this great crusader. In big towns committees were formed for his reception. His brother disciples and friends were impatient. Swami Shivananda came ahead of time to Madras and Swami Niranjanananda to Colombo; so also many of his disciples from Bengal and the Northern Provinces came to Madras to await his arrival. The newspapers published articles eulogizing his personality and work.

A gaily decorated steam launch carried the Swami and his party from the ship to the harbour. When the monk with his yellow robe and luminous eyes touched the dust of his motherland, a mighty shout arose from the human throng crowding the quays. Thousands flung themselves on the ground to touch his feet. A deputation of the notables of Ceylon welcomed him, and he was taken in a huge procession through many triumphal arches. Flags were unfurled, religious hymns chanted; an Indian band played. Rose-water and the sacred water of the Ganges were sprinkled before him, and flowers were strewn in his path. Incense was burnt before the houses as he passed. Fruit and other offerings were brought by hundreds of visitors.

Swami Vivekananda accepted all these honours without losing his poise. He was not the man to flee from triumph any more than from battle. He regarded the tributes paid to him, a penniless beggar, as tributes paid to the spiritual ideal of India. In the course of his reply to the address of welcome given in Colombo, he said: "The spirituality of the Hindus is revealed by the princely reception which they have given to a beggar sannyāsin." He pointed out that though he was not a military general, not a prince nor a wealthy man, yet men great in the transitory possessions of the world and much respected by society had nevertheless come to honour him, a homeless monk. "This," he exclaimed, "is one of the highest expressions of spirituality." He disclaimed any personal glory in the welcome he received, insisting that it was but the recognition of a principle.

Swami Vivekananda's progress from Colombo to Madras and the welcomes he received at Kandy, Anuruddhapura, Jaffna, Pamban, Rameswaram, Ramnad, Paramakudi, Madura, Trichinopoly, and Kumbhakonum demonstrated how deeply he had endeared himself to the men and women of India. At Anuruddhapura a band of fanatical Buddhists tried to break up the meeting, but did not succeed. At Rameswaram the Swami exhorted the people to "worship Śiva in the poor, the diseased, and the weak."

He received a touching welcome there from the Rājā of Ramnad, his disciple, who had encouraged him to go to America and had helped him materially for that purpose. At Ramnad the horses were unhitched from the carriage bearing the Swami, and the people themselves, the Rājā among them, drew it. At Rameswaram the Rājā erected, in the Swami's honour, a victory column forty feet high with a suitable inscription. He also gave a liberal donation to the Madras famine-relief fund to commemorate the home-coming of the Swami.

At a small railroad station near Madras, hundreds of people gathered for a glimpse of Vivekananda. The stationmaster did not want to delay the train since no stop was scheduled. But the crowd of admirers flung themselves on the track, and the train had to be halted. The Swami was visibly moved and blessed the multitude.

The enthusiasm of the people reached its peak in Madras, where extensive preparations had been made for the Swami's reception. It was Madras that had first recognized the greatness of Vivekananda and equipped him for the journey to Chicago. At that time, when he had first come there, he had been, in effect, only an obscure individual. He had spent some two months in an unknown bungalow at St. Thome, holding conversations on Hinduism. Yet even then a few educated young men of keen foresight had predicted that there was something in the man, a "power" that would lift him above all others and enable him to be a leader of men. These youths, who had been ridiculed as "misguided enthusiasts" and "dreamy revivalists," now, four years later, had the supreme satisfaction of seeing "our Swami," as they loved to call him, return to them a famous personage in both Europe and America.

The streets and thoroughfares of Madras were profusely decorated; seventeen triumphal arches were erected. The Swami's name was on everybody's lips. Thousands jammed the railway station, and as the train steamed in he was received with thundering shouts of applause. An elaborate procession was formed, and he was taken to "Castle Kernan," the palatial home of Billigiri Iyengar, where arrangements had been made for his stay in the city.

On the third day after his arrival Swami Vivekananda was honoured in a public meeting on behalf of the people of Madras. As Victoria Hall, chosen for the purpose, was too small to hold the large crowd, the people cried for an open-air gathering. The Swami came out and addressed them from the top of a coach; it was, as it were, Śri Krishna, standing in the chariot, exhorting Arjuna to give up his unmanliness and measure up to his Āryan heritage. In a brief speech he told the people how India, through her love of God, had expanded the limited love of the family into love of country and of humanity. He urged them to maintain their enthusiasm and to give him all the help he required to do great things for India.

During his short stay in Madras, Swami Vivekananda gave four public lectures, his subjects being, "My Plan of Campaign," "The Sages of India," "Vedānta in its Relation to Practical Life," and "The Future of India." In these lectures he reminded the Indians of both their greatness and their weakness, and urged them to be proud of their past and hopeful for their future.

While speaking on "My Plan of Campaign," the Swami exposed the meanness of some of the Theosophists, who had tried their utmost to injure his work in America but later claimed that they had paved the way for his success in the New World. He told the audience that when, in desperation, he had cabled to India for money, the Theosophists had come to know about it and one of them had written to a member of the Society in India: "Now the devil is going to die. God bless us all!" But it must be said that there were many among the Theosophists, especially in India, who were his genuine well-wishers.

Swami Vivekananda had hardly a moment's respite during his nine days in Madras. When asked by a disciple how he found the strength for such incessant activity, he answered, "Spiritual work never tires one in India." But he would lose patience if asked about matters that had no bearing on practical life. One day a pandit asked him to state clearly whether he was a dualist or a non-dualist. The Swami said: "As long as I have this body I am a dualist, but not otherwise. This incarnation of mine is to help put an end to useless and mischievous quarrels, which only distract the mind and make men weary of life, and even turn them into sceptics and atheists."

Meanwhile heart-warming letters had been arriving from America informing the Swami of the progress of the Vedānta work in the New World under the leadership of Swami Saradananda, and also in appreciation of his own achievements. One letter was signed by Lewis G. Janes, President of the Brooklyn Ethical Association; C. C. Everett, Dean of the Harvard Divinity School; William James and Josiah Royce, both professors of philosophy at Harvard University; Mrs. Sara C. Bull of Boston, and others. It said: "We believe that such expositions as have been given by yourself and your co-labourer, the Swami Saradananda, have more than mere speculative interest and utility—that they are of great ethical value in cementing the ties of friendship and brotherhood between distant peoples, and in helping us to realize that solidarity of human relationship and interests which has been affirmed by all the great religions of the world. We earnestly hope that your work in India may be blessed in further promoting this noble end, and that you may return to us again with assurances of fraternal regard from our distant brothers of the great Āryan family, and the ripe wisdom that comes from reflection and added experience and further contact with the life and thought of your people."

Another letter from Detroit, signed by forty-two of his friends, said in part: "We Western Āryans have been so long separated from our Eastern brothers that we had almost forgotten our identity of origin, until you came and with your beautiful presence and matchless eloquence rekindled within our hearts the knowledge that we of America and you of India are one."

Swami Vivekananda, after his strenuous work in South India, needed rest. On the advice of friends, he decided to travel to Calcutta by steamer. Monday, February 15, was the date of his sailing. Several devotees boarded the steamer to see him off, and one of them, Professor Sundarama Iyer, asked the Swami if his mission had achieved lasting good in America and Europe. The Swami said: "Not much. I hope that here and there I have sown a seed which in time may grow and benefit some at least."

Swami Vivekananda's lectures delivered during his progress from Colombo to Madras were inspiring and enthusiastic. He yearned to awaken the masses of India from the slumber of ages. He had seen the dynamic life of the West; he now felt more deeply the personality of India, which only needed his fiery exhortation to assert itself once more among the nations of the world. Again one is reminded of Krishna's admonition to Arjuna on the battlefield of Kurukshetra: "In this crisis, O Arjuna, whence comes such lowness of spirit, unbecoming to an Āryan, dishonourable, and an obstacle to the attaining of heaven? Do not yield to unmanliness, O Arjuna. It does not become you. Shake off this base faint-heartedness and arise, O scorcher of enemies!"

In his famous lecture "My Plan of Campaign," delivered in Madras, he called upon the people to assert their soul-force:

My India, arise! Where is your vital force? In your Immortal Soul. Each nation, like each individual, has one theme in this life, which is its centre, the principal note round which every other note comes to form the harmony. If any one nation attempts to throw off its national vitality, the direction which has become its own through the transmission of centuries, that nation dies. . . . In one nation political power is its vitality, as in England. Artistic life, in another, and so on. In India religious life forms the centre, the keynote of the whole music of the national life. And therefore, if you succeed in the attempt to throw off your religion and take up either politics or society, the result will be that you will become extinct. Social reform and politics have to be preached through the vitality of your religion. . . . Every man has to make his own choice; so has every nation. We made our choice ages ago. And it is the faith in an Immortal Soul. I challenge anyone to give it up. How can you change your nature?

He asked the Indians to stop complaining. Let them make use of the power that lay in their hands. That power was so great that if they only realized it and were worthy of it, they could revolutionize the world. India was the Ganges of spirituality. The material conquests of the Anglo-Saxon races, far from being able to dam its current, had helped it. England's power had united the nations of the world; she had opened paths across the seas so that the waves of the spirit of India might spread until they had bathed the ends of the earth.

What was this new faith, this word that the world was awaiting?

The other great idea that the world wants from us today—more perhaps the lower classes than the higher, more the uneducated than the educated, more the weak than the strong—is that eternal, grand idea of the spiritual oneness of the whole universe, the only Infinite Reality, that exists in you and in me and in all, in the self, in the soul. The infinite oneness of the soul—that you and I are not only brothers, but are really one—is the eternal sanction of all morality. Europe wants it today just as much as our down-trodden races do, and this great principle is even now unconsciously forming the basis of all the latest social and political aspirations that are coming up in England, in Germany, in France, and in America.[21]

[21] Extracts from the lecture "The Mission of the Vedānta."

What Swami Vivekananda preached was the essence of the non-dualistic Vedānta, the deepest and the unique expression of India's spirit.

I heard once the complaint made that I was preaching too much of Advaita, absolute non-dualism, and too little of dualism. Ay, I know what grandeur, what oceans of love, what infinite, ecstatic blessings and joy there are in dualistic religion. I know it all. But this is not the time for us to weep, even in joy; we have had weeping enough; no more is this the time for us to become soft. This softness has been with us till we have become like masses of cotton. What our country now wants is muscles of iron and nerves of steel, gigantic will, which nothing can resist, which will accomplish their purpose in any fashion, even if it means going down to the bottom of the ocean and meeting death face to face. That is what we want, and that can only be created, established, and strengthened by understanding and realizing the ideal of Advaita, that ideal of the oneness of all. Faith, faith, faith in ourselves! . . . If you have faith in the three hundred and thirty millions of your mythological gods, and in all the gods which foreigners have introduced into your midst, and still have no faith in yourselves, there is no salvation for you. Have faith in yourselves and stand upon that faith. Why is it that we three hundred and thirty millions of people have been ruled for the last thousand years by any and every handful of foreigners? Because they had faith in themselves and we had not. I read in the newspapers how, when one of our poor fellows is murdered or ill-treated by an Englishman, howls go up all over the country; I read and I weep, and the next moment comes to my mind the question of who is responsible for it all. Not the English; it is we who are responsible for all our degradation. Our aristocratic ancestors went on treading the common masses of our country underfoot till they became helpless, till under this torment the poor, poor people nearly forgot that they were human beings. They have been compelled to be merely hewers of wood and drawers of water for centuries, so that they are made to believe that they are born as slaves, born as hewers of wood and drawers of water.[22]

He exhorted the leaders to cultivate the indispensable virtue of feeling for the people: "Feel, therefore, my would-be reformers, my would-be patriots! Do you feel? Do you feel that millions and millions of the descendants of gods and of sages have become next-door neighbours to brutes? Do you feel that millions are starving today and millions have been starving for ages? Do you feel that ignorance has come over the land as a dark cloud? Does it make you restless? Does it make you sleepless? Has it made you almost mad? Are you seized with that one idea of the misery of ruin, and have you forgotten all about your name, your fame, your wives, your children, your property, even your own bodies? If so, that is the first step to becoming a patriot. For centuries people have been taught theories of degradation. They have been told that they are nothing. The masses have been told all over the world that they are not human beings. They have been so frightened for centuries that they have nearly become animals. Never were they allowed to hear of the Ātman. Let them hear of the Ātman—that even the lowest of the low have the Ātman within, who never dies and never is born—Him whom the sword cannot pierce, nor the fire burn, nor the air dry, immortal, without beginning or end, the all-pure, omnipotent, and omnipresent Ātman."[23]

[22] Extracts from "The Mission of the Vedānta."
[23] Extracts from "My Plan of Campaign."

"Ay, let every man and woman and child, without respect of caste or birth, weakness or strength, hear and learn that behind the strong and the weak, behind the high and the low, behind everyone, there is that Infinite Soul, assuring all the infinite possibility and the infinite capacity to become great and good. Let us proclaim to every soul: Arise, arise, awake! Awake from this hypnotism of weakness. None is really weak; the soul is infinite, omnipotent, and omniscient. Stand up, assert yourself, proclaim the God within you, do not deny Him!"[24]

"It is a man-making religion that we want. It is a man-making education all round that we want. It is man-making theories that we want. And here is the test of truth: Anything that makes you weak physically, intellectually, and spiritually, reject as poison; there is no life in it, it cannot be true. Truth is strengthening. Truth is purity, truth is all knowledge. Truth must be strengthening, must be enlightening, must be invigorating. Give up these weakening mysticisms and be strong. The greatest truths are the simplest things in the world, simple as your own existence.

"Therefore my plan is to start institutions in India to train our young men as preachers of the truths of our scriptures in India and outside India. Men, men—these are wanted: everything else will be ready; but strong, vigorous, believing young men, sincere to the backbone, are wanted. A hundred such and the world becomes revolutionized. The will is stronger than anything else. Everything must go down before the will, for that comes from God: a pure and strong will is omnipotent."[25]

"If the brāhmin has more aptitude for learning on the grounds of heredity than the pariah, spend no more money on the brāhmin's education, but spend all on the pariah. Give to the weak, for there all the gift is needed. If the brāhmin is born clever, he can educate himself without help. This is justice and reason as I understand it."[26]

"For the next fifty years let all other vain Gods disappear from our minds. This is the only God that is awake: our own race—everywhere His hands, everywhere His feet, everywhere His ears, He covers everything. All other Gods are sleeping. Why should we vainly go after them, when we can worship the God that we see all around us, the Virāt? The first of all worships is the worship of the Virāt, of those all around us. These are all our Gods—men and animals; and the first Gods we have to worship are our own countrymen."[27]

These stirring words did not fall on deaf ears. The spirit of India vibrated to the Swami's call. India became aware of the power of the soul—of God sleeping in man and of His illimitable possibilities. Ramakrishna and Vivekananda were the first awakeners of India's national consciousness; they were India's first nationalist leaders in the true sense of the term. Ramakrishna was the power and Vivekananda the voice. The movement for India's liberation started from Dakshineswar. The subsequent political leaders of the country, consciously or unconsciously, received their inspiration from Vivekananda's

[24] Extracts from "The Mission of the Vedānta."
[25] Extracts from "My Plan of Campaign."
[26] From "The Mission of the Vedānta."
[27] From "The Future of India."

message, and some of them openly acknowledged it. The Bengal revolutionaries were ardent readers of Vivekananda's books, some of which were frowned upon by the British Government. The uplift of the masses, the chief plank in Gandhi's platform, was Vivekananda's legacy.

Yet the militant Vivekananda was not a politician. "Let no political significance ever be attached falsely to my writings or sayings. What nonsense!"— he had said as early as September 1894. A year later he wrote: "I will have nothing to do with political nonsense. I do not believe in politics. God and Truth are the only policy in the world. Everything else is trash."

Swami Vivekananda longed for India's political freedom; but he thought of a free India in relation to her service to humanity. A free India would take her rightful place in the assembly of nations and make a vital contribution towards bringing peace and goodwill to mankind. His message was both national and international.

BACK TO BENGAL

While Swami Vivekananda was enjoying the restful boat trip from Madras to Calcutta, a reception committee was busy preparing for him a fitting welcome in the metropolis of India, the city of his birth. The steamer docked at Kidderpore, and the Swami and his party arrived by train in Calcutta. The reception was magnificent, with an enthusiastic crowd at the railroad station, triumphal arches, the unharnessed carriage drawn by students, and a huge procession with music and religious songs. A princely residence on the bank of the Ganges was placed at the Swami's disposal.

On February 28, 1897, he was given a public reception. Rājā Benoy Krishna Deb presided, and five thousand people jammed the meeting. As usual, the Swami asked the people to go back to the perennial philosophy of the Upanishads. He also paid a touching tribute to Ramakrishna, "my teacher, my master, my hero, my ideal, my God in life." "If there has been anything achieved by me," he said with deep feeling, "by thoughts or words or deeds, if from my lips has ever fallen one word that has ever helped anyone in the world, I lay no claim to it; it was his. But if there have been curses falling from my lips, if there has been hatred coming out of me, it is all mine, and not his. All that has been weak has been mine; all that has been life-giving, strengthening, pure, and holy has been his inspiration, his words, and he himself. Yes, my friends, the world has yet to know that man." A few days after, he gave another public lecture, on "Vedānta in All its Phases."

Shortly after the Swami's arrival in Calcutta the anniversary of Śri Ramakrishna's birth was celebrated at Dakshineswar. Accompanied by his brother disciples, the Swami joined the festival. He walked barefoot in the holy grounds. Deep emotions were stirred up as he visited the temples, the Master's room, the Panchavati, and other spots associated with the memory of Śri Ramakrishna. The place was a sea of human heads.

The Swami said to Girish, a beloved disciple of the Master, "Well, what a difference between those days and these!"

"I know," replied Girish, "but I have the desire to see more."

For a little while the Swami spent his days at the palatial house on the river;

nights, however, he spent with his spiritual brothers at the Alambazar monastery. He had hardly any rest. People streamed in at all times to pay him their respects or to hear his exposition of Vedānta, or just to see him. There were also people who came to argue with him on scriptural matters and to test his knowledge.

But the Swami's heart was with the educated, unmarried youths whom he could train for his future work. He longed to infuse into their hearts some of his own burning enthusiasm. He wanted them to become the preachers of his "man-making religion." The Swami deplored the physical weakness of Indian youths, denounced their early marriage, and reproached them for their lack of faith in themselves and in their national ideals.

One day a young man complained to the Swami that he could not make progress in spiritual life. He had worshipped images, following the advice of one teacher, and had tried to make his mind void according to the instruction of another, but all had been fruitless.

"Sir," the young man said, "I sit still in meditation, shutting the door of my room, and keep my eyes closed as long as I can, but I do not find peace of mind. Can you show me the way?"

"My boy," replied the Swami in a voice full of loving sympathy, "if you take my word, you will have first of all to open the door of your room and look around, instead of closing your eyes. There are hundreds of poor and helpless people in your neighbourhood; you have to serve them to the best of your ability. You will have to nurse and procure food and medicine for the sick. You will have to feed those who have nothing to eat. You will have to teach the ignorant. My advice to you is that if you want peace of mind, you shall have to serve others to the best of your ability."

Another day a well-known college professor, who was a disciple of Śri Ramakrishna, said to the Swami: "You are talking of service, charity, and doing good to the world; these, after all, belong to the domain of māyā. Vedānta says that the goal of man is the attainment of mukti, liberation, through breaking the chain of māyā. What is the use of preaching about things which keep one's mind on mundane matters?"

The Swami replied: "Is not the idea of mukti in the domain of māyā? Does not Vedānta teach that the Ātman is ever free? Why should It, then, strive for mukti?"

He said on another occasion: "When I used to roam about all over India, practising spiritual disciplines, I passed day after day in caves absorbed in meditation. Many a time I decided to starve myself to death because I could not attain mukti. Now I have no desire for mukti. I do not care for it as long as a single individual in the universe remains in bondage."

Swami Vivekananda often used to say that different forms of spiritual discipline were especially efficacious for different ages. At one period it was the practice of austerities; at another period, the cultivation of divine love; and at a third period, it was philosophical discrimination accompanied by renunciation. But in modern times, he emphasized, unselfish service of others, karma-yoga, would quickly bring spiritual results. Therefore he advocated the discipline of selfless action. He particularly advocated this discipline for the

Indians because they were under the spell of tamas, inertia. The Swami realized that only after cultivating rajas would they be able to acquire sattva and attain liberation. As regards himself, the Swami had already known mukti through the realization of oneness with Brahman in nirvikalpa samādhi. But by the will of God he had brought himself down to consciousness of the phenomenal world, and lived like a bodhisattva, devoting himself to the welfare of humanity.

Swami Vivekananda found it most difficult to convert some of his own brother disciples to his new conception of religion and its discipline and method. These brother disciples were individualists, eager for their personal salvation. They wanted to practise austerities and penances, enjoy peaceful meditation, and lead a quiet life of detachment from the world. To them God was first, and next the world. At least that was the way they understood Sri Ramakrishna's teachings. These young monks thought that for one who had taken the monastic vows the world was māyā; therefore all activities, including the charitable and philanthropic, ultimately entangled one in worldly life.

But Vivekananda's thought flowed through a different channel. Sri Ramakrishna had once admonished him to commune with God with eyes open, that is to say, through the service of the poor, the sick, the hungry, and the ignorant. During his days of wandering the Swami had seen with his own eyes the suffering of the people and had felt the voiceless appeal of India for his help. In America and Europe he had witnessed the material prosperity of the people, the dynamic social life, and the general progress made through science, technology, and organized action. Time and again he remembered the words of Ramakrishna: "Religion is not for empty stomachs."

To his brother disciples, therefore, he pointed out that the idea of personal liberation was unworthy of those who called themselves disciples of Ramakrishna, an Incarnation of God. The very fact that they had received the grace of a Saviour should have convinced them of their sure salvation. Their duty, he emphasized, was to serve others as the visible manifestations of God. He said that he wanted to create a new band of monks, who would take not only the traditional vow of personal salvation, but also a new vow of service to humanity.

The brother disciples, who respected the superior spirituality of Vivekananda and bore him great love as the one especially chosen by the Master to carry on his work, obeyed him without always agreeing with him wholeheartedly. Thus at his behest Swami Ramakrishnananda—who had been the keeper of Sri Ramakrishna's shrine for twelve long years after the passing away of the Master, regarding his worship as the supreme spiritual discipline, and had not been absent even for a single day from the monasteries at Baranagore and Alambazar—left for Madras to found a centre for the propagation of Vedānta in South India. Swami Akhandananda went to Murshidabad to carry on relief work among the famine-stricken people there. Swamis Abhedananda and Saradananda had already gone to America.

As for himself, Swami Vivekananda was constantly talking to people, instructing them in the Upanishads, and enjoining them to cultivate the inner strength that comes from the knowledge of God residing in all human hearts. The strain of work and the heat of the plains soon told upon his health. At the advice

of physicians he went for a short change to Darjeeling, in the Himālayas, and
felt somewhat refreshed. Returning to Calcutta he again devoted himself to the
work of teaching.

Several young men, inspired by the Swami's fiery words, joined the Order.
Four others, who had been practising disciplines in the monastery under the
guidance of the older Swamis while Vivekananda was abroad, were now eager
to receive the monastic initiation formally from their great leader. His brother
disciples expressed hesitation about one of them, because of some incidents
of his past life.

This aroused Swami Vivekananda's emotion. "What is this?" he said. "If
we shrink from sinners, who else will save them? Besides, the very fact that
someone has taken refuge at the monastery, in his desire to lead a better life,
shows that his intentions are good, and we must help him. Suppose a man
is bad and perverted; if you cannot change his character, why then have
you put on the ochre robe of a monk? Why have you assumed the rôle of
teachers?" All four received their monastic initiation.

On the day previous to this sacred ceremony the Swami spoke to them only
about the glories of renunciation and service. He said: "Remember, for the
salvation of his soul and for the good and happiness of many, a sannyāsin is
born in the world. To sacrifice his own life for others, to alleviate the misery
of millions rending the air with their cries, to wipe away tears from the eyes
of widows, to console the hearts of bereaved mothers, to provide the ignorant
and depressed masses with ways and means for the struggle for existence and
make them stand on their own feet, to broadcast the teachings of the scriptures
to one and all, without distinction, for their spiritual and material welfare, to
rouse the sleeping lion of Brahman in the hearts of all beings by the knowledge
of Vedānta—a sannyāsin is born in the world." Turning to his brother disciples
the Swami said: "Remember, it is for the consummation of this purpose in life
that we have taken birth, and we shall lay down our lives for it. Arise and awake,
arouse and awaken others, fulfil your mission in life, and you will reach the
highest goal." Then addressing the aspirants for the monastic life he said: "You
must renounce everything. You must not seek comfort or pleasure for yourself.
You must look upon gold and objects of lust as poison, name and fame as the
vilest filth, worldly glory as a terrible hell, pride of birth or of social position
as 'sinful as drinking spirituous liquor.' In order to be teachers of your fellow
men, and for the good of the world, you will have to attain freedom through
the knowledge of the Self."

From the following incident one can learn the depths of the Swami's compassion. Many inmates of the math thought that he was not very discriminating
in the choice of his disciples. Almost anyone could obtain spiritual initiation
from him after a little supplication, and some of them were found later to
indulge in wicked actions. One of his own monastic disciples, Swami Nirmal-
ananda, spoke to him about his lack of proper judgement and his inability to
understand human nature. The Swami's face became red with emotion. He
exclaimed: "What did you say? You think that I do not understand human
nature? About these unfortunate people I know not only all they have done
in their present lives, but also what they did in their previous ones. I am fully

aware of what they will do in the future. Then why do I show kindness to them? These hapless people have knocked at many doors for peace of mind and a word of encouragement, but everywhere have been repulsed. If I turn them down they will have no place to go."

Another incident indicating the tender and compassionate heart of Swami Vivekananda may be mentioned here. One day he was engaged in teaching a disciple the Vedas, with the abstruse commentary of Sāyanāchārya, when Girish Chandra Ghosh, the great playwright of Bengal and an intimate disciple of Śri Ramakrishna, arrived. By way of teasing him, the Swami said, addressing him by his familiar name: "Well, G. C., you have spent your whole life with Krishna and Vishnu.[28] You are quite innocent of the Vedas and other scriptures."

Girish Chandra admitted his ignorance of the scriptures and said, "Hail Śri Ramakrishna, the very embodiment of the Vedas!"

An adept in the knowledge of human nature, Girish was well aware that Swami Vivekananda, in spite of his preaching the austere philosophy of Vedānta, had a heart that was tender in the extreme. He wanted to reveal that side of the Swami's nature before the disciple, and began to paint, in his usual poetic language, a heart-rending picture of the afflictions of the Indian people—the starvation of the masses, the humiliation of Hindu women, the ill health and general suffering of the people everywhere. Suddenly, addressing the Swami, he said, "Now please tell me, do your Vedas teach us how to remedy this state of affairs?"

As the Swami listened to his friend's words, he could hardly suppress his emotion. At last it broke all bounds and he burst into tears.

Drawing the attention of the Swami's disciple to the great leader, Girish Chandra said: "Perhaps you have always admired your teacher's intellect. Now you see his great heart."

On May 1, 1897, Swami Vivekananda called a meeting of the monastic and lay devotees of Śri Ramakrishna at the house of the Master's intimate disciple Balaram Bose, for the purpose of establishing his work on an organized basis. He told them that by contrasting Hindu society with American society, he was convinced that lack of an organizing spirit was one of the great shortcomings of the Hindu character. Much of the intelligence and energy of the Hindus was being expended without producing any fruitful result. He also recalled how Buddhism had spread both in India and abroad through Buddhist organizations. Therefore he asked the co-operation of the monastic and householder disciples of Śri Ramakrishna in order to organize the educational, philanthropic, and religious activities which he had already inaugurated, but which had hitherto been carried out in an unsystematic way. Further, the Swami declared that in a country like India, in its then current state of development, it would not be wise to form an organization on a democratic basis, where each member had an equal voice and decisions were made according to the vote of the majority. Democratic principles could be followed later, when, with the spread of education, people would learn to sacrifice individual interests and

[28] An allusion to the dramas written by Girish Chandra Ghosh, in which Krishna, Vishnu, and other characters of Hindu mythology play prominent parts.

personal prejudices for the public weal. Therefore, said the Swami, the organization for the time being should be under the leadership of a "dictator," whose authority everybody must obey. In the fullness of time, it would come to be guided by the opinion and consent of others. Moreover, he himself was only acting in the capacity of a servant of the common Master, as were they all.[29]

Swami Vivekananda proposed to the members present that the Association should "bear the name of him in whose name we have become sannyāsins, taking whom as your ideal you are leading the life of householders, and whose holy name, influence, and teachings have, within twelve years of his passing away, spread in such an unthought-of way both in the East and in the West." All the members enthusiastically approved of the Swami's proposal, and the Ramakrishna Mission Association came into existence.

The aim of the Association was to spread the truths that Ramakrishna, for the good of humanity, had preached and taught through the example of his own life, and to help others to put them into practice for their physical, mental, and spiritual advancement.

The duty of the Association was to direct, in the right spirit, the activities of the movement inaugurated by Śri Ramakrishna for the establishment of fellowship among the followers of different religions, knowing them all to be so many forms of one undying Eternal Religion.

Its methods of action were to be: (a) to train men so as to make them competent to teach such knowledge and sciences as are conducive to the material and spiritual welfare of the masses; (b) to promote and encourage arts and industries; (c) to introduce and spread among the people in general Vedāntic and other ideas as elucidated in the life of Śri Ramakrishna.

The Ramakrishna Mission Association was to have two departments of action: Indian and foreign. The former, through retreats and monasteries established in different parts of India, would train such monks and householders as might be willing to devote their lives to the teaching of others. The latter would send trained members of the Order to countries outside India to start centres there for the preaching of Vedānta in order to bring about a closer relationship and better understanding between India and foreign countries.

The aims and ideals of the Ramakrishna Mission Association, being purely spiritual and humanitarian, were to have no connexion with politics.

Swami Vivekananda must have felt a great inner satisfaction after the estab-

[29] A touching incident that happened shortly afterwards and expresses the complete self-effacement of the Swami, may be narrated here. He handed over to Swami Brahmananda, the newly appointed President of the Ramakrishna Mission Association, all the money he had brought from America for the purpose of carrying on his Indian activities, with the request that "only the kids should be eaten and the mother goat be spared," meaning that the Association should spend only the interest and not touch the capital. Thus he himself was left without any personal income. A few minutes later he said that he would like to go to Calcutta and requested one of his disciples to ask Swami Brahmananda for a few pennies for the ferry-boat across the Ganges. Swami Brahmananda felt embarrassed and told him that the whole money belonged to him and that he must not ask for it in that way. But Swami Vivekananda insisted on being counted as any other member of the monastery.

lishment of the Association. His vision of employing religion, through head, heart, and hands, for the welfare of man was realized. He found no essential conflict among science, religion, art, and industry. All could be used for the worship of God. God could be served as well through His diverse manifestations as through the contemplation of His non-dual aspect. Further, as the great heart of Ramakrishna had embraced all of mankind with its love, so also the Ramakrishna Mission was pledged to promote brotherhood among different faiths, since their harmony constituted the Eternal Religion.

Swami Vivekananda, the General President, made Brahmananda and Yogananda the President and the Vice-president of the Calcutta centre. Weekly meetings were organized at Balaram's house to discuss the Upanishads, the Bhagavad Gita, the Vedanta scriptures, and religious subjects in general.[30]

Even now Swami Vivekananda could not completely convince some of his brother disciples about his new conception of religion, namely, the worship of God through the service of man. They had heard Śri Ramakrishna speak time and again against preaching, excessive study of the scriptures, and charitable activities, and exhort aspirants to intensify their love of God through prayer and meditation in solitude. Therefore they regarded Vivekananda's activities in the West as out of harmony with the Master's teachings. One of them said bluntly to the Swami, "You did not preach our Master in America; you only preached yourself." The Swami retorted with equal bluntness, "Let people understand me first; then they will understand Śri Ramakrishna."

On one occasion Swami Vivekananda felt that some of these brother disciples wanted to create a narrow sect in the name of Ramakrishna and turn the Ramakrishna Math into a cult of the Temple, where the religious activities would centre around devotional music, worship, and prayer alone. His words burst upon them like a bomb-shell. He asked them how they knew that his ideas were not in keeping with those of Śri Ramakrishna. "Do you want," he said, "to shut Śri Ramakrishna, the embodiment of infinite ideas, within your own limits? I shall break these limits and scatter his ideas broadcast all over the world. He never enjoined me to introduce his worship and the like."

[30] In 1899 Swami Vivekananda established the Belur Math, the present Headquarters of the Ramakrishna Order, and turned it over to a Board of Trustees drawn from the monastic members of the Ramakrishna Order; the main purpose of the Math was to train monks in spiritual practice and to serve humanity in all possible ways. It was, however, restricted in its public activities. With the establishment of the Belur Math, the Ramakrishna Mission Association ceased to function as an independent organization. Soon the need was felt to conduct extensive philanthropic, charitable, educational, and missionary work. Therefore a separate organization, called the Ramakrishna Mission, was set up to carry on these activities, and a legal status was given to it in 1909. Its membership was open to monks and laymen. But the management of the Ramakrishna Mission was vested in a Governing Body, which, for the time being, consisted of the Trustees of the Belur Math. Both the Ramakrishna Math at Belur, also called the Belur Math, and the Ramakrishna Mission now have branches all over India. The members of the Math devote themselves mainly to the spiritual practices of study, prayer, worship, and meditation, whereas the members of the Mission carry on public activities in various fields.

Had it not been demonstrated to Vivekananda time and again that Śri Ramakrishna was behind him in all his actions? He knew that through the Master's grace alone he had come out triumphant from all ordeals, whether in the wilderness of India or in the busy streets of Chicago.

"Śri Ramakrishna," the Swami continued, "is far greater than the disciples understand him to be. He is the embodiment of infinite spiritual ideas capable of development in infinite ways. . . . One glance of his gracious eyes can create a hundred thousand Vivekanandas at this instant. If he chooses now, instead, to work through me, making me his instrument, I can only bow to his will."

Vivekananda took great care lest sentimentalism and narrowness in one form or another should creep in, for he detested these from the bottom of his heart.

But things came to a climax one day at Balaram's house in Calcutta, when Swami Jogananda, a brother disciple whom Śri Ramakrishna had pointed out as belonging to his "inner circle" of devotees, said that the Master had emphasized bhakti alone for spiritual seekers and that philanthropic activities, organizations, homes of service for the public good, and patriotic work were the Swami's own peculiar ideas, the result of his Western education and travel in Europe and America.

The Swami at first retorted to his brother with a sort of rough humour. He said: "What do you know? You are an ignorant man. . . . What do you understand of religion? You are only good at praying with folded hands: 'O Lord! how beautiful is Your nose! How sweet are Your eyes!' and all such nonsense. . . . And you think your salvation is secured and Śri Ramakrishna will come at the final hour and take you by the hand to the highest heaven! Study, public preaching, and doing humanitarian works are, according to you, māyā, because he said to someone, 'Seek and find God first; doing good to the world is a presumption!' As if God is such an easy thing to be achieved! As if He is such a fool as to make Himself a plaything in the hands of an imbecile!

"You think you have understood Śri Ramakrishna better than myself! You think jnāna is dry knowledge to be attained by a desert path, killing out the tenderest faculties of the heart! Your bhakti is sentimental nonsense which makes one impotent. You want to preach Śri Ramakrishna as you have understood him, which is mighty little! Hands off! Who cares for your Ramakrishna? Who cares for your bhakti and mukti? Who cares what your scriptures say? I will go into a thousand hells cheerfully if I can rouse my countrymen, immersed in tamas, to stand on their own feet and be men inspired with the spirit of karma-yoga. I am not a follower of Ramakrishna or anyone, but of him only who serves and helps others without caring for his own bhakti and mukti!"

The Swami's voice was choked with emotion, his body shook, and his eyes flashed fire. Quickly he went to the next room. A few moments later some of his brother disciples entered the room and found him absorbed in meditation, tears flowing from his half-closed eyes. After nearly an hour the Swami got up, washed his face, and joined his spiritual brothers in the drawing-room. His features still showed traces of the violent storm through which he had just passed; but he had recovered his calmness. He said to them softly:

"When a man attains bhakti, his heart and nerves become so soft and delicate

Vivekananda as Hindu Teacher

BRAHMANANDA

PREMANANDA

SARADANANDA

JOGANANDA

NIRANJANANANDA

ADVAITANANDA

ADBHUTANANDA

SHIVANANDA

RAMAKRISHNANANDA

TURIYANANDA

TRIGUNATITANANDA

Akhandananda

Subodhananda

Vijnanananda

Abhedananda

Sᴿɪ Rᴀᴍᴀᴋʀɪꜱʜɴᴀ Mᴏɴᴀꜱᴛᴇʀʏ ᴀᴛ Bᴇʟᴜʀ

(Vivekananda's room is at left front of second storey.)

that he cannot bear even the touch of a flower! . . . I cannot think or talk of Śri Ramakrishna long without being overwhelmed. So I am always trying to bind myself with the iron chains of jnāna, for still my work for my mother-land is unfinished and my message to the world not fully delivered. So as soon as I find that those feelings of bhakti are trying to come up and sweep me off my feet, I give a hard knock to them and make myself firm and adamant by bringing up austere jnāna. Oh, I have work to do! I am a slave of Ramakrishna, who left his work to be done by me and will not give me rest till I have finished it. And oh, how shall I speak of him? Oh, his love for me!"

He was again about to enter into an ecstatic mood, when Swami Jogananda and the others changed the conversation, took him on the roof for a stroll, and tried to divert his mind by small talk. They felt that Vivekananda's inmost soul had been aroused, and they remembered the Master's saying that the day Naren knew who he was, he would not live in this body. So from that day the brother disciples did not again criticize the Swami's method, knowing fully well that the Master alone was working through him.

From this incident one sees how Vivekananda, in his inmost heart, relished bhakti, the love of God. But in his public utterances he urged the Indians to keep their emotionalism under control; he emphasized the study of Vedānta, because he saw in it a sovereign tonic to revivify them. He further prescribed for his countrymen both manual and spiritual work, scientific research, and service to men. Vivekananda's mission was to infuse energy and faith into a nation of "dyspeptics" held under the spell of their own sentimentality. He wished in all fields of activity to awaken that austere elevation of spirit which arouses heroism.

As with his Master, the natural tendency of Vivekananda's mind was to be absorbed in contemplation of the Absolute. Again, like Śri Ramakrishna, he had to bring down his mind forcibly to the consciousness of the world in order to render service to men. Thus he kept a balance between the burning love of the Absolute and the irresistible appeal of suffering humanity. And what makes Swami Vivekananda the patriot saint of modern India and at the same time endears him so much to the West is that at the times when he had to make a choice between the two, it was always the appeal of suffering humanity that won the day. He cheerfully sacrificed the bliss of samādhi to the amelioration of the suffering of men. The Swami's spirit acted like a contagion upon his brother disciples. One of them, Akhandananda, as stated before, fed and nursed the sufferers from famine at Murshidabad, in Bengal; another, Trigunatita, in 1897 opened a famine-relief centre at Dinajpur. Other centres were established at Deoghar, Dakshineswar, and Calcutta.

Swami Vivekananda was overjoyed to see the happy beginning of his work in India. To Mary Hale he wrote on July 9, 1897:

Only one idea was burning in my brain—to start the machine for elevating the Indian masses, and that I have succeeded in doing to a certain extent.

It would have made your heart glad to see how my boys are working in the midst of famine and disease and misery—nursing by the mat-bed of the cholera-stricken pariah and feeding the starving chandāla, and the Lord sends help to me, to them, to all. . . .
He is with me, the Beloved, and He was when I was in America, in England, when I

was roaming about unknown from place to place in India. What do I care about what they say?[31] The babies—they do not know any better. What? I, who have realized the Spirit, and the vanity of all earthly nonsense, to be swerved from my path by babies' prattle? Do I look like that? . . . I feel my task is done—at most three or four years more of life are left. I have lost all wish for my salvation. I never wanted earthly enjoyments. I must see my machine in strong working order, and then, knowing for sure that I have put in a lever for the good of humanity, in India at least, which no power can drive back, I will sleep without caring what will be next.

And may I be born again and again, and suffer thousands of miseries, so that I may worship the only God that exists, the only God I believe in, the sum total of all souls. And above all, my God the wicked, my God the miserable, my God the poor of all races, of all species, is the especial object of my worship.

IN NORTHERN INDIA

From May 1897 to the end of that year, the Swami travelled and lectured extensively in Northern India. The physicians had advised him to go as soon as possible to Almora, where the air was dry and cool, and he had been invited by prominent people in Northern India to give discourses on Hinduism. Accompanied by some of his brother disciples and his own disciples, he left Calcutta, and he was joined later by the Seviers, Miss Muller, and Goodwin.

In Lucknow he was given a cordial welcome. The sight of the Himālayas in Almora brought him inner peace and filled his mind with the spirit of detachment and exaltation of which these great mountains are the symbol. But his peace was disturbed for a moment when he received letters from American disciples about the malicious reports against his character spread by Christian missionaries, including Dr. Barrows, who had been the President of the Parliament of Religions in Chicago. Evidently they had become jealous of the Swami's popularity in India. Dr. Barrows told the Americans that the report of the Swami's reception in India was greatly exaggerated. He accused the Swami of being a liar and remarked: "I could never tell whether to take him seriously or not. He struck me as being a Hindu Mark Twain. He is a man of genius and has some following, though only temporary."

The Swami was grieved. At his request the people of Madras had given Dr. Barrows a big reception, but the missionary, lacking religious universalism, had not made much of an impression.

In a mood of weariness the Swami wrote to a friend on June 3, 1897:

As for myself, I am quite content. I have roused a good many of our people, and that was all I wanted. Let things have their course and karma its sway. I have no bonds here below. I have seen life, and it is all self—life is for self, love is for self, honour for self, everything for self. I look back and scarcely find any action I have done for self—even my wicked deeds were not for self. So I am content—not that I feel I have done anything especially good or great, but the world is so little, life so mean a thing, existence so, so servile, that I wonder and smile that human beings, rational souls, should be running after this self—so mean and detestable a prize.

This is the truth. We are caught in a trap, and the sooner one gets out the better for one. I have seen the truth—let the body float up or down, who cares? . . .

[31] Referring to some scurrilous remarks about Swami Vivekananda by certain American missionaries.

I was born for the life of a scholar—retired, quiet, poring over my books. But the Mother dispensed otherwise. Yet the tendency is there.

In Almora the Swami's health improved greatly. On May 29 he wrote to a friend: "I began to take a lot of exercise on horseback, both morning and evening. Since then I have been very much better indeed. . . . I really began to feel that it was a pleasure to have a body. Every movement made me conscious of strength—every movement of the muscles was pleasurable. . . . You ought to see me, Doctor, when I sit meditating in front of the beautiful snow-peaks and repeat from the Upanishads: 'He has neither disease, nor decay, nor death; for verily, he has obtained a body full of the fire of yoga.' "

He was delighted to get the report that his disciples and spiritual brothers were plunging heart and soul into various philanthropic and missionary activities.

From Almora he went on a whirlwind tour of the Punjab and Kashmir, sowing everywhere the seeds of rejuvenated Hinduism. In Bareilly he encouraged the students to organize themselves to carry on the work of practical Vedānta. In Ambala he was happy to see his beloved disciples Mr. and Mrs. Sevier. After spending a few days in Amritsar, Dharamsala, and Murree, he went to Kashmir.

In Jammu the Swami had a long interview with the Mahārājā and discussed with him the possibility of founding in Kashmir a monastery for giving young people training in non-dualism. In the course of the conversation he sadly remarked how the present-day Hindus had deviated from the ideals of their forefathers, and how people were clinging to various superstitions in the name of religion. He said that in olden days people were not outcasted even when they committed such real sins as adultery, and the like; whereas nowadays one became untouchable simply by violating the rules about food.

On the same topic he said a few months later, at Khetri: "The people are neither Hindus nor Vedāntins—they are merely 'don't touchists'; the kitchen is their temple and cooking-pots are their objects of worship. This state of things must go. The sooner it is given up, the better for our religion. Let the Upanishads shine in their glory, and at the same time let not quarrels exist among different sects."

In Lahore the Swami gave a number of lectures, among which was his famous speech on the Vedānta philosophy, lasting over two hours. He urged the students of Lahore to cultivate faith in man as a preparation for faith in God. He asked them to form an organization, purely non-sectarian in character, to teach hygiene to the poor, spread education among them, and nurse the sick. One of his missions in the Punjab was to establish harmony among people belonging to different sects, such as the Ārya Samājists and the orthodox Hindus. It was in Lahore that the Swami met Mr. Tirtha Ram Goswami, then a professor of mathematics, who eventually gained wide recognition as Swami Ram Tirtha. The professor became an ardent admirer of Swami Vivekananda.

Next the Swami travelled to Dehra-Dun, where, for the first ten days, he lived a rather quiet life. But soon he organized a daily class on the Hindu scriptures for his disciples and companions, which he continued to conduct during the whole trip. At the earnest invitation of his beloved disciple the Rājā of Khetri, he visited his capital, stopping on the way at Delhi and Alwar, which were familiar to him from his days of wandering prior to his going to America. Everywhere he met old friends and disciples and treated them with marked affection. The Rājā of Khetri lavished great honours upon him and also gave him a handsome donation for the Belur Math, which was being built at that time.

Before returning to Calcutta, he visited Kishengarh, Ajmere, Jodhpur, Indore, and Khandwa and thus finished his lecture tour in North India. During this tour he explained to his fellow countrymen the salient features of Hinduism and told them that they would have a glorious future if they followed the heritage of their past. He emphasized that the resurgent nationalism of India must be based on her spiritual ideals, but that healthy scientific and techno-logical knowledge from the West, also, had to be assimilated in the process of growth. The fundamental problem of India, he pointed out, was to organize the whole country around religious ideals. By religion the Swami meant not local customs which served only a contemporary purpose, but the eternal prin-ciples taught in the Vedas.

Wherever the Swami went he never wearied of trying to rebuild individual character in India, pointing out that the strength of the whole nation depended upon the strength of the individual. Therefore each individual, he urged, what-ever might be his occupation, should try, if he desired the good of the nation as a whole, to build up his character and acquire such virtues as courage, strength, self-respect, love, and service of others. To the young men, especially, he held out renunciation and service as the highest ideal. He preached the necessity of spreading a real knowledge of Sanskrit, without which a Hindu would remain an alien to his own rich culture. To promote unity among the Hindus, he encouraged intermarriage between castes and sub-castes, and wanted to revive the Indian universities so that they might produce real patriots, rather than clerks, lawyers, diplomats, and Government officials.

Swami Vivekananda's keen intellect saw the need of uniting the Hindus and Moslems on the basis of the Advaita philosophy, which teaches the oneness of all. On June 10, 1898, he wrote to a Moslem gentleman at Nainital:

The Hindus may get the credit for arriving at Advaitism earlier than other races, they being an older race than either the Hebrew or the Arab; yet practical Advaitism, which looks upon and behaves towards all mankind as one's own soul, is yet to be developed among the Hindus universally. On the other hand, our experience is that if ever the followers of any religion approach to this equality in an appreciable degree on the plane of practical work-a-day life—it may be quite unconscious generally of the deeper mean-ing and the underlying principle of such conduct, which the Hindus as a rule so clearly perceive—it is those of Islām and Islām alone.

Therefore we are firmly persuaded that without the help of practical Islām, the theories of Vedāntism, however fine and wonderful they may be, are entirely valueless to the vast mass of mankind. We want to lead mankind to the place where there is neither the Vedas nor the Bible nor the Koran; yet this has to be done by harmonizing the Vedas, the Bible, and the Koran. Mankind ought to be taught that religions are but the varied expressions of the Religion which is Oneness, so that each may choose the path that suits him best.

For our own motherland a junction of the two great systems, Hinduism and Islām— Vedāntic brain and Islāmic body—is the only hope.

I see in my mind's eye the future perfect India rising out of this chaos and strife, glorious and invincible, with Vedāntic brain and Islāmic body.

For the regeneration of India, in the Swami's view, the help of the West was indispensable. The thought of India had been uppermost in his mind when he had journeyed to America. On April 6, 1897, the Swami, in the course of a letter to the lady editor of an Indian magazine, had written: "It has been for the good of India that religious preaching in the West has been done and will be done. It has ever been my conviction that we shall not be able to rise unless the Western countries come to our help. In India no appreciation of merit can be found, no financial support, and what is most lamentable of all, there is not a bit of practicality."

TRAINING OF THE DISCIPLES

The year 1898 was chiefly devoted to the training of Vivekananda's disciples, both Indian and Western, and to the consolidation of the work already started. During this period he also made trips to Darjeeling, Almora, and Kashmir.

In February 1898, the monastery was removed from Alambazar to Nilambar Mukherjee's garden house in the village of Belur, on the west bank of the Ganges. The Swami, while in Calcutta, lived at Balaram Bose's house, which had been a favourite haunt of Śri Ramakrishna's during his lifetime. But he had no rest either in the monastery or in Calcutta, where streams of visitors came to him daily. Moreover, conducting a heavy correspondence consumed much of his time and energy; one cannot but be amazed at the hundreds of letters the Swami wrote with his own hand to friends and disciples. Most of these reveal his intense thinking, and some his superb wit.

While at the monastery, he paid especial attention to the training of the sannyāsins and the brahmachārins, who, inspired by his message, had renounced home and dedicated themselves to the realization of God and the service of humanity. Besides conducting regular classes on the Upanishads, the Bhagavad Gitā, the physical sciences, and the history of the nations, he would spend hours with the students in meditation and devotional singing. Spiritual practices were intensified on holy days.

In the early part of 1898, the site of the Belur Math, the present Head-quarters of the Ramakrishna Math and Mission, was purchased with the help of a generous donation from Miss Muller, the devoted admirer of the Swami. Mrs. Ole Bull gave another handsome gift to complete the construction, and the shrine at the Belur Math was consecrated, as we shall see, on December 9, 1898. Sometime during this period the Swami initiated into the monastic life Swami Swarupananda, whom he considered to be a real "acquisition." This qualified aspirant was given initiation after only a few days' stay at the monastery, contrary to the general rule of the Ramakrishna Order. Later he became editor of the monthly magazine *Prabuddha Bhārata*, and president of the Advaita Āśrama at Mayavati, in the Himālayas.

Among the Western devotees who lived with Swami Vivekananda at this time were Mr. and Mrs. Sevier, Mrs. Ole Bull, Miss Henrietta F. Muller, Miss Josephine MacLeod, and Miss Margaret E. Noble, all of whom travelled with him at various times in Northern India. The Seviers identified themselves completely with the work at the Mayavati Advaita Āśrama. Mrs. Ole Bull, the wife of the famous Norwegian violinist, and a lady of social position, great culture, and large heart, had been an ardent admirer of the Swami during his American trip. Miss Muller, who knew the Swami in both England and America and had helped defray, together with the Seviers and Mr. Sturdy, the expenses of his work in England, had come to India to organize an educational institution for Indian women.

Miss MacLeod had attended Swami Vivekananda's classes in New York, and for months at a time he had been the guest of her relatives at their country home, Ridgely Manor. She became his life-long friend and admirer and cherished his memory till the last day of her life, but though she was devoted to him, she never renounced her independence, nor did he demand that she should. By way of spiritual instruction, the Swami had once asked Miss MacLeod to meditate on Om for a week and report to him afterwards. When the teacher inquired how she felt, she said that "it was like a glow in the heart." He encouraged her and said: "Good, keep on." Many years later she told her friends that the Swami made her realize that she was in eternity. "Always remember," the Swami had admonished her, "you are incidentally an American and a woman, but always a child of God. Tell yourself day and night who you are. Never forget it." To her brother-in-law, Francis H. Leggett, the Swami had written, on July 6, 1896, in appreciation of Miss MacLeod: "I simply admire Joe Joe for her tact and quiet ways. She is a feminine statesman. She could wield a kingdom. I have seldom seen such strong yet good common sense in a human being."

When Miss MacLeod asked the Swami's permission to come to India, he wrote on a postcard: "Do come by all means, only you must remember this: The Europeans and Indians live as oil and water. Even to speak of living with the natives is damning, even at the capitals. You will have to bear with people who wear only a loin-cloth; you will see me with only a loin-cloth about me. Dirt and filth everywhere, and brown people. But you will have plenty of men to talk philosophy to you." He also wrote to her that she must not come to India if she expected anything else, for the Indians could not "bear one more word of criticism."

On one occasion, while travelling in Kashmir with the Swami and his party, she happened to make a laughing remark about one of his South Indian disciples with the caste-mark of the brāhmins of his sect on his forehead. This appeared grotesque to her. The Swami turned upon her "like a lion, withered her with a glance, and cried: 'Hands off! Who are you? What have you ever done?'"

Miss MacLeod was crestfallen. But later she learnt that the same poor brāhmin had been one of those who, by begging, had collected the money that had made it possible for the Swami to undertake his trip to America.

"How can I best help you," she asked the Swami when she arrived in India. "Love India," was his reply.

One day Swami Vivekananda told Miss MacLeod that since his return to India he had had no personal money. She at once promised to pay him fifty dollars a month as long as he lived and immediately gave him three hundred dollars for six months in advance. The Swami asked jokingly if it would be enough for him.

"Not if you take heavy cream every day!" she said.

The Swami gave the money to Swami Trigunatita to defray the initial expenses of the newly started Bengali magazine, the *Udbodhan*.

But of all Swami Vivekananda's Western disciples, the most remarkable was Margaret E. Noble, who was truly his spiritual daughter. She had attended the Swami's classes and lectures in London and resolved to dedicate her life to his work in India. When she expressed to him her desire to come to India, the Swami wrote to her, on July 29, 1897: "Let me tell you frankly that I am now convinced that you have a great future in the work for India. What was wanted was not a man but a woman, a real lioness, to work for the Indians—women especially. India cannot yet produce great women; she must borrow them from other nations. Your education, sincerity, purity, immense love, determination, and above all, your Celtic blood, make you just the woman wanted.

"Yet the difficulties are many. You cannot form any idea of the misery, the superstition, and the slavery that are here. You will be in the midst of a mass of half-naked men and women with quaint ideas of caste and isolation, shunning the white-skins through fear or hatred, and hated by them intensely. On the other hand, you will be looked upon by the white as a crank, and every one of your movements will be watched with suspicion.

"Then the climate is fearfully hot, our winter in most places being like your summer, and in the south it is always blazing. Not one European comfort is to be had in places out of the cities. If in spite of all this you dare venture into the work, you are welcome, a hundred times welcome. As for me, I am nobody here as elsewhere, but what little influence I have shall be devoted to your service.

"You must think well before you plunge in, and afterwards if you fail in this or get disgusted, on my part I promise you *I will stand by you unto death*, whether you work for India or not, whether you give up Vedānta or remain in it. 'The tusks of the elephant come out but never go back'—so are the words of a man never retracted. I promise you that." He further asked her to stand on her own feet and never seek help from his other Western women devotees.

Miss Noble came to India on January 28, 1898, to work with Miss Muller for the education of Indian women. The Swami warmly introduced her to the public of Calcutta as a "gift of England to India," and in March made her take the vow of brahmacharya, that is to say, the life of a religious celibate devoted to the realization of God. He also gave her the name of Nivedita, the "Dedicated," by which she has ever since been cherished by the Indians with deep respect and affection. The ceremony was performed in the chapel of the monastery. He first taught her how to worship Śiva and then made the whole ceremony culminate in an offering at the feet of Buddha.

"Go thou," he said, "and follow him who was born and gave his life for others five hundred times before he attained the vision of the Buddha."

The Swami now engaged himself in the training of Sister Nivedita along with the other Western disciples. And certainly it was a most arduous task. They were asked to associate intimately with the Holy Mother, the widow of Śri

Ramakrishna, who at once adopted them as her "children." Then the Swami
would visit them almost daily to reveal to them the deep secrets of the Indian
world—its history, folklore, customs, and traditions. Mercilessly he tried to
uproot from their minds all preconceived notions and wrong ideas about India.
He wanted them to love India as she was at the present time, with her poverty,
ignorance, and backwardness, and not the India of yore, when she had produced
great philosophies, epics, dramas, and religious systems.

It was not always easy for the Western disciples to understand the religious
ideals and forms of worship of the Hindus. For instance, one day in the great
Kāli temple of Calcutta, one Western lady shuddered at the sight of the blood
of the goats sacrificed before the Deity, and exclaimed, "Why is there blood
before the Goddess?" Quickly the Swami retorted, "Why not a little blood to
complete the picture?"

The disciples had been brought up in the tradition of Protestant Christianity,
in which the Godhead was associated only with what was benign and beautiful,
and Satan with the opposite.

With a view to Hinduizing their minds, the Swami asked his Western disciples to visit Hindu ladies at their homes and to observe their dress, food, and
customs, which were radically different from their own. Thus he put to a severe
test their love for Vedānta and India. In the West they had regarded the Swami
as a prophet showing them the path of liberation, and as a teacher of the
universal religion. But in India he appeared before them, in addition, in the
rôle of a patriot, an indefatigable worker for the regeneration of his motherland.

The Swami began to teach Nivedita to lose herself completely in the Indian
consciousness. She gradually adopted the food, clothes, language, and general
habits of the Hindus.

"You have to set yourself," he said to her, "to Hinduize your thoughts, your
needs, your conceptions, your habits. Your life, internal and external, has to
become all that an orthodox brāhmin brahmachārini's ought to be. The method
will come to you if you only desire it sufficiently. But you have to forget your
past and cause it to be forgotten." He wanted her to address the Hindus "in
terms of their own orthodoxy."

Swami Vivekananda would not tolerate in his Western disciples any trace of
chauvinism, any patronizing attitude or stupid criticism of the Indian way of
life. They could serve India only if they loved India, and they could love India
only if they knew India, her past glories and her present problems. Thus later he
took them on his trip to Northern India, including Almora and Kashmir, and
told them of the sanctity of Benares and the magnificence of Agra and Delhi;
he related to them the history of the Moghul Emperors and the Rajput heroes,
and also described the peasant's life, the duties of a farm housewife, and the
hospitality of poor villagers to wandering monks. The teacher and his disciples
saw together the sacred rivers, the dense forests, the lofty mountains, the sun-
baked plains, the hot sands of the desert, and the gravel beds of the rivers, all
of which had played their parts in the creation of Indian culture. And the
Swami told them that in India custom and culture were one. The visible manifestations of the culture were the system of caste, the duties determined by the
different stages of life, the respect of parents as incarnate gods, the appointed

hours of religious service, the shrine used for daily worship, the chanting of the Vedas by the brāhmin children, the eating of food with the right hand and its use in worship and japa, the austerities of Hindu widows, the kneeling in prayer of the Moslems wherever the time of prayer might find them, and the ideal of equality practised by the followers of Mohammed.

Nivedita possessed an aggressively Occidental and intensely English outlook. It was not easy for her to eradicate instinctive national loyalties and strong personal likes and dislikes. A clash between the teacher and the disciple was inevitable. Ruthlessly the Swami crushed her pride in her English upbringing. Perhaps, at the same time, he wanted to protect her against the passionate adoration she had for him. Nivedita suffered bitter anguish.

The whole thing reached its climax while they were travelling together, some time after, in the Himālayas. One day Miss MacLeod thought that Nivedita could no longer bear the strain, and interceded kindly and gravely with the Swami. "He listened," Sister Nivedita wrote later, "and went away. At evening, however, he returned, and finding us together on the veranda, he turned to her (Miss MacLeod) and said with the simplicity of a child: 'You were right. There must be a change. I am going away to the forests to be alone, and when I come back I shall bring peace.' Then he turned away and saw that above us the moon was new, and a sudden exaltation came into his voice as he said: 'See, the Mohammedans think much of the new moon. Let us also, with the new moon, begin a new life.' " As he said these words, he lifted his hand and blessed his rebellious disciple, who by this time was kneeling before him. It was assuredly a moment of wonderful sweetness of reconciliation.

That evening in meditation Nivedita found herself gazing deep into an Infinite Good, to the recognition of which no egotistic reasoning had led her. "And," she wrote, "I understood for the first time that the greatest teachers may destroy in us a personal relation only in order to bestow the Impersonal Vision in its place."

To resume our story, on March 30, 1898, the Swami left for Darjeeling, for he badly needed a change to the cool air of the Himālayas. Hardly had he begun to feel the improvement in his health, when he had to come down to Calcutta, where an outbreak of plague was striking terror.

Immediately he made plans for relief work with the help of the members of the monastery and volunteers from Calcutta.

When a brother disciple asked him where he would get funds, the Swami replied: "Why, we shall sell if necessary the land which has just been purchased for the monastery. We are sannyāsins; we must be ready to sleep under the trees and live on alms as we did before. Must we care for the monastery and possessions when by disposing of them we could relieve thousands of helpless people suffering before our own eyes?" Fortunately this extreme step was not necessary; the public gave him money for the relief work.

The Swami worked hard to assuage the suffering of the afflicted people. Their love and admiration for him knew no bounds as they saw this practical application of Vedānta at a time of human need.

The plague having been brought under control, the Swami left Calcutta for

Nainital on May 11, accompanied by, among others, his Western disciples. From there the party went to Almora where they met the Seviers. During this tour the Swami never ceased instructing his disciples. For his Western companions it was a rare opportunity to learn Indian history, religion, and philosophy direct from one who was an incarnation of the spirit of India. Some of the talks the Swami gave were recorded by Sister Nivedita in her charming book *Notes of Some Wanderings with the Swami Vivekananda.*

In Almora the Swami received news of the deaths of Pavhari Baba and Mr. Goodwin. He had been closely drawn to the former during his days of wandering. Goodwin died on June 2. Hearing of this irreparable loss, the Swami exclaimed in bitter grief, "My right hand is gone!" To Goodwin's mother he wrote a letter of condolence in which he said: "The debt of gratitude I owe him can never be repaid, and those who think they have been helped by any thought of mine ought to know that almost every word of it was published through the untiring and most unselfish exertions of Mr. Goodwin. In him I have lost a friend true as steel, a disciple of never-failing devotion, a worker who knew not what tiring was, and the world is less rich by the passing away of one of those few who are born, as it were, to live only for others."

The Swami also sent her the following poem, which he had written in memory of Goodwin, bearing witness to the affection of the teacher for the disciple:

REQUIESCAT IN PACE

Speed forth, O soul! upon thy star-strewn path;
Speed, blissful one! where thought is ever free,
Where time and space no longer mist the view;
Eternal peace and blessings be with thee!

Thy service true, complete thy sacrifice;
Thy home the heart of love transcendent find!
Remembrance sweet, that kills all space and time,
Like altar roses, fill thy place behind!

Thy bonds are broke, thy quest in bliss is found,
And one with That which comes as death and life,
Thou helpful one! unselfish e'er on earth,
Ahead, still help with love this world of strife!

Before the Swami left Almora, he arranged to start again the monthly magazine *Prabuddha Bhārata,* which had ceased publication with the death of its gifted editor, B. R. Rajam Iyer. Swami Swarupananda became its new editor, and Captain Sevier, the manager. The magazine began its new career at Almora. Then, on June 11, the Swami, in the company of his Western disciples, left for Kashmir as the guest of Mrs. Ole Bull.

The trip to Kashmir was an unforgettable experience for the Westerners. The natural beauty of the country, with its snow-capped mountains reflected in the water of the lakes, its verdant forests, multi-coloured flowers, and stately poplar and chennar trees, make the valley of Kashmir a paradise on earth. Throughout the journey the Swami poured out his heart and soul to his disciples. At first he was almost obsessed with the ideal of Śiva, whom he had worshipped since boyhood, and for days he told the disciples legends relating to the great God of renunciation. The party spent a few days in house-boats, and in the afternoons the Swami would take his companions for long walks across the fields. The conversations were always stimulating. One day he spoke of Genghis Khan and declared that he was not a vulgar aggressor; he compared the Mongol Emperor to Napoleon and Alexander, saying that they all wanted to unify the world and that it was perhaps the same soul that had incarnated itself three times in the hope of bringing about human unity through political conquest. In the same way, he said, one Soul might have come again and again as Krishna, Buddha, and Christ, to bring about the unity of mankind through religion.

In Kashmir the Swami pined for solitude. The desire for the solitary life of a monk became irresistible; and he would often break away from the little party to roam alone. After his return he would make some such remark as: "It is a sin to think of the body," "It is wrong to manifest power," or "Things do not grow better; they remain as they are. It is we who grow better, by the changes we make in ourselves." Often he seemed to be drifting without any plan, and the disciples noticed his strange detachment. "At no time," Sister Nivedita wrote, "would it have surprised us had someone told us that today or tomorrow he would be gone for ever, that we were listening to his voice for the last time."

This planlessness was observed in him more and more as his earthly existence drew towards its end. Two years later, when Sister Nivedita gave him a bit of worldly advice, the Swami exclaimed in indignation: "Plans! Plans! That is why you Western people can never create a religion! If any of you ever did, it was only a few Catholic saints who had no plans. Religion was never, never preached by planners!"

About solitude as a spiritual discipline, the Swami said one day that an Indian could not expect to know himself till he had been alone for twenty years, whereas from the Western standpoint a man could not live alone for twenty years and remain quite sane. On the Fourth of July the Swami gave a surprise to his American disciples by arranging for its celebration in an appropriate manner. An American flag was made with the help of a brāhmin tailor, and the Swami composed the following poem:

TO THE FOURTH OF JULY

Behold, the dark clouds melt away
That gathered thick at night and hung
So like a gloomy pall above the earth!
Before thy magic touch the world
Awakes. The birds in chorus sing.
The flowers raise their star-like crowns,
Dew-set, and wave thee welcome fair.
The lakes are opening wide, in love,
Their hundred thousand lotus-eyes
To welcome thee with all their depth.
All hail to thee, thou lord of light!
A welcome new to thee today,
O sun! Today thou sheddest liberty!

Bethink thee how the world did wait
And search for thee, through time and clime!
Some gave up home and love of friends
And went in quest of thee, self-banishèd,
Through dreary oceans, through primeval forests,
Each step a struggle for their life or death;
Then came the day when work bore fruit,
And worship, love, and sacrifice,
Fulfilled, accepted, and complete.
Then thou, propitious, rose to shed
The light of freedom on mankind.

Move on, O lord, in thy resistless path,
Till thy high noon o'erspreads the world,
Till every land reflects thy light,
Till men and women, with uplifted head,
Behold their shackles broken and know
In springing joy their life renewed!

As the Swami's mood changed he spoke of renunciation. He showed scorn for the worldly life and said: "As is the difference between a fire-fly and the blazing sun, between a little pond and the infinite ocean, a mustard seed and the mountain of Meru, such is the difference between the householder and the sannyāsin." Had it not been for the ochre robe, the emblem of monasticism, he pointed out, luxury and worldliness would have robbed man of his manliness.

Thus the party spent their time on the river, the teacher providing a veritable university for the education of his disciples. The conversation touched upon all subjects—Vedic rituals, Roman Catholic doctrine, Christ, St. Paul, the growth of Christianity, Buddha.

Of Buddha, the Swami said that he was the greatest man that ever lived. "Above all, he never claimed worship. Buddha said: 'Buddha is not a man, but a state. I have found the way. Enter all of you!' "

Then the talk would drift to the conception of sin among the Egyptian, Semitic, and Āryan races. According to the Vedic conception, the Swami said, the Devil is the Lord of Anger, and with Buddhists he is Māra, the Lord of Lust. Whereas in the Bible the creation was under the dual control of God and Satan, in Hinduism Satan represented defilement, never duality.

Next the Swami would speak about the chief characteristics of the different nations. "You are so morbid, you Westerners," he said one day. "You worship sorrow! All through your country I found that. Social life in the West is like a peal of laughter, but underneath it is a wail. The whole things ends in a sob. The fun and frivolity are all on the surface; really, it is full of tragic intensity. Here it is sad and gloomy on the outside, but underneath are detachment and merriment."

Once, at Islamabad, as the group sat round him on the grass in an apple orchard, the Swami repeated what he had said in England after facing a mad bull. Picking up two pebbles in his hand, he said: "Whenever death approaches me all weakness vanishes. I have neither fear nor doubt nor thought of the external. I simply busy myself making ready to die. I am as hard as that"

—and the stones struck each other in his hand—"for I have touched the feet of God!"

At Islamabad the Swami announced his desire to make a pilgrimage to the great image of Śiva in the cave of Amarnāth in the glacial valley of the Western Himālayas. He asked Nivedita to accompany him so that she, a future worker, might have direct knowledge of the Hindu pilgrim's life. They became a part of a crowd of thousands of pilgrims, who formed at each halting-place a whole town of tents.

A sudden change came over the Swami. He became one of the pilgrims, scrupulously observing the most humble practices demanded by custom. He ate one meal a day, cooked in the orthodox fashion, and sought solitude as far as possible to tell his beads and practise meditation. In order to reach the destination, he had to climb up rocky slopes along dangerous paths, cross several miles of glacier, and bathe in the icy water of sacred streams.

On August 2 the party arrived at the enormous cavern, large enough to contain a vast cathedral. At the back of the cave, in a niche of deepest shadow, stood the image of Śiva, all ice. The Swami, who had fallen behind, entered the cave, his whole frame shaking with emotion. His naked body was smeared with ashes, and his face radiant with devotion. Then he prostrated himself in the darkness of the cave before that glittering whiteness.

A song of praise from hundreds of throats echoed in the cavern. The Swami almost fainted. He had a vision of Śiva Himself. The details of the experience he never told anyone, except that he had been granted the grace of Amarnāth, the Lord of Immortality, not to die until he himself willed it.

The effect of the experience shattered his nerves. When he emerged from the grotto, there was a clot of blood in his left eye; his heart was dilated and never regained its normal condition. For days he spoke of nothing but Śiva. He said: "The image was the Lord Himself. It was all worship there. I have never seen anything so beautiful, so inspiring."

On August 8 the party arrived at Srinagar, where they remained until September 30. During this period the Swami felt an intense desire for meditation and solitude. The Mahārājā of Kashmir treated him with the utmost respect and wanted him to choose a tract of land for the establishment of a monastery and a Sanskrit college. The land was selected and the proposal sent to the British Resident for approval. But the British Agent refused to grant the land. The Swami accepted the whole thing philosophically.

A month later his devotion was directed to Kāli, the Divine Mother, whom Ramakrishna had called affectionately "my Mother."

A unique symbol of the Godhead, Kāli represents the totality of the universe: creation and destruction, life and death, good and evil, pain and pleasure, and all the pairs of opposites. She seems to be black when viewed from a distance, like the water of the ocean; but to the intimate observer She is without colour, being one with Brahman, whose creative energy She represents.

In one aspect She appears terrible, with a garland of human skulls, a girdle of human fingers, her tongue dripping blood, a decapitated human head in one hand and a shining sword in the other, surrounded by jackals that haunt the cremation ground—a veritable picture of terror. The other side is benign and gracious, ready to confer upon Her devotees the boon of immortality. She reels as if drunk: who could have created this mad world except in a fit of drunkenness? Kāli stands on the bosom of Her Divine Consort, Śiva, the symbol of Brahman; for Kāli, or Nature, cannot work unless energized by the touch of the Absolute. And in reality Brahman and Kāli, the Absolute and Its Creative Energy, are identical, like fire and its power to burn.

The Hindu mind does not make a sweepingly moralistic distinction between good and evil. Both are facts of the phenomenal world and are perceived to exist when māyā hides the Absolute, which is beyond good and evil. Ramakrishna emphasized the benign aspect of the Divine Mother Kāli and propitiated Her to obtain the vision of the Absolute. Swami Vivekananda suddenly felt the appeal of Her destructive side. But is there really any difference between the process of creation and destruction? Is not the one without the other an illusion of the mind?

Vivekananda realized that the Divine Mother is omnipresent. Wherever he turned, he was conscious of the presence of the Mother, "as if She were a person in the room." He felt that it was She "whose hands are clasped with my own and who leads me as though I were a child." It was touching to see him worship the four-year-old daughter of his Mohammedan boatman as the symbol of the Divine Mother.

His meditation on Kāli became intense, and one day he had a most vivid experience. He centred "his whole attention on the dark, the painful, and the inscrutable" aspect of Reality, with a determination to reach by this particular path the Non-duality behind phenomena. His whole frame trembled, as if from an electric shock. He had a vision of Kāli, the mighty Destructress lurking behind the veil of life, the Terrible One, hidden by the dust of the living who pass by, and all the appearances raised by their feet. In a fever, he groped in the dark for pencil and paper and wrote his famous poem "Kāli the Mother"; then he fell exhausted:

> The stars are blotted out,
> The clouds are covering clouds,
> It is darkness, vibrant, sonant;
> In the roaring, whirling wind
> Are the souls of a million lunatics,
> Loosed from the prison-house,
> Wrenching trees by the roots,
> Sweeping all from the path.
> The sea has joined the fray
> And swirls up mountain-waves
> To reach the pitchy sky.
> The flash of lurid light
> Reveals on every side
> A thousand thousand shades
> Of death, begrimed and black.
>
> Scattering plagues and sorrows,
> Dancing mad with joy,
> Come, Mother, come!

For terror is Thy name,
Death is in Thy breath,
And every shaking step
Destroys a world for e'er.
Thou Time, the All-destroyer,
Come, O Mother, come!

Who dares misery love,
And hug the form of death.
Enjoy destruction's dance—
To him the Mother comes.

The Swami now talked to his disciples only about Kāli, the Mother, describing Her as "time, change, and ceaseless energy." He would say with the great Psalmist: "Though Thou slay me, yet I will trust in Thee."

"It is a mistake," the Swami said, "to hold that with all men pleasure is the motive. Quite as many are born to seek pain. There can be bliss in torture, too. Let us worship terror for its own sake.

"Learn to recognize the Mother as instinctively in evil, terror, sorrow, and annihilation as in that which makes for sweetness and joy!

"Only by the worship of the Terrible can the Terrible itself be overcome, and immortality gained. Meditate on death! Meditate on death! Worship the Terrible, the Terrible, the Terrible! And the Mother Herself is Brahman! Even Her curse is a blessing. The heart must become a cremation ground—pride, selfishness, and desire all burnt to ashes. Then, and then alone, will the Mother come."

The Western disciples, brought up in a Western faith which taught them to see good, order, comfort, and beauty alone in the creation of a wise Providence, were shaken by the typhoon of a Cosmic Reality invoked by the Hindu visionary. Sister Nivedita writes:

And as he spoke, the underlying egoism of worship that is devoted to the kind God, to Providence, the consoling Deity, without a heart for God in the earthquake or God in the volcano, overwhelmed the listener. One saw that such worship was at bottom, as the Hindu calls it, merely "shopkeeping," and one realized the infinitely greater boldness and truth of teaching that God manifests through evil as well as through good. One saw that the true attitude for the mind and will that are not to be baffled by the personal self, was in fact that determination, in the stern words of Swami Vivekananda, "to seek death, not life, to hurl oneself upon the sword's point, to become one with the Terrible for evermore."

Heroism, to Vivekananda, was the soul of action. He wanted to see Ultimate Truth in all its terrible nakedness, and refused to soften it in any shape or manner. His love of Truth expected nothing in return; he scorned the bargain of "giving to get in return" and all its promise of paradise.

But the gentle Ramakrishna, though aware of the Godhead in all its aspects, had emphasized Its benign side. One day several men had been arguing before him about the attributes of God, attempting to find out, by reason, their meaning. Śri Ramakrishna stopped them, saying: "Enough, enough! What is the use of disputing whether the divine attributes are reasonable or not? . . . You say that God is good: can you convince me of His goodness by this reasoning? Look at the flood that has just caused the death of thousands. How can you prove that a benevolent God ordered it? You will perhaps reply that the same flood swept away uncleanliness and watered the earth, and so on. But could not a good God do that without drowning thousands of innocent men, women, and children?"

Thereupon one of the disputants said, "Then ought we to believe that God is cruel?"

"O idiot," cried Ramakrishna, "who said that? Fold your hands and say humbly, 'O God, we are too feeble and too weak to understand Thy nature and Thy deeds. Deign to enlighten us!' Do not argue. Love!"

God is no doubt Good, True, and Beautiful; but these attributes are utterly different from their counterparts in the relative world.

The Swami, during these days, taught his disciples to worship God like heroes. He would say: "There must be no fear, no begging, but demanding —demanding the Highest. The true devotees of the Mother are as hard as adamant and as fearless as lions. They are not in the least upset if the whole universe suddenly crumbles into dust at their feet. Make Her listen to you. None of that cringing to Mother! Remember, She is all-powerful; She can make heroes out of stones."

On September 30 Swami Vivekananda retired to a temple of the Divine Mother, where he stayed alone for a week. There he worshipped the Deity, known as Kshirbhavāni, following the time-honoured ritual, praying and meditating like a humble pilgrim. Every morning he also worshipped a brāhmin's little daughter as the symbol of the Divine Virgin. And he was blessed with deep experiences, some of which were most remarkable and indicated to him that his mission on earth was finished.

He had a vision of the Goddess and found Her a living Deity. But the temple had been destroyed by the Moslem invaders, and the image placed in a niche surrounded by ruins. Surveying this desecration, the Swami felt distressed at heart and said to himself: "How could the people have permitted such sacrilege without offering strenuous resistance? If I had been here then, I would never have allowed such a thing. I would have laid down my life to protect the Mother." Thereupon he heard the voice of the Goddess saying: "What if unbelievers should enter My temple and defile My image? What is that to you? Do you protect Me, or do I protect you?" Referring to this experience after his return, he said to his disciples: "All my patriotism is gone. Everything is gone. Now it is only 'Mother! Mother!' I have been very wrong. . . . I am only a little child." He wanted to say more, but could not; he declared that it was not fitting that he should go on. Significantly, he added that spiritually he was no longer bound to the world.

Another day, in the course of his worship, the thought flashed through the Swami's mind that he should try to build a new temple in the place of the present dilapidated one, just as he had built a monastery and temple at Belur to Śri Ramakrishna. He even thought of trying to raise funds from his wealthy American disciples and friends. At once the Mother said to him: "My child!

If I so wish I can have innumerable temples and monastic centres. I can even this moment raise a seven-storied golden temple on this very spot."

"Since I heard that divine voice," the Swami said to a disciple in Calcutta much later, "I have ceased making any more plans. Let these things be as Mother wills."

Śri Ramakrishna had said long ago that Narendranath would live in the physical body to do the Mother's work and that as soon as this work was finished, he would cast off his body by his own will. Were the visions at the temple of Kshirbhavāni a premonition of the approaching dissolution?

When the Swami rejoined his disciples at Srinagar, he was an altogether different person. He raised his hand in benediction and then placed some marigolds, which he had offered to the Deity, on the head of every one of his disciples. "No more 'Hari Om!' " he said. "It is all 'Mother' now!" Though he lived with them, the disciples saw very little of him. For hours he would stroll in the woods beside the river, absorbed within himself. One day he appeared before them with shaven head, dressed as the simplest sannyāsin and with a look of unapproachable austerity on his face. He repeated his own poem "Kāli the Mother" and said, "It all came true, every word of it; and I have proved it, for I have hugged the form of death."

Sister Nivedita writes: "The physical ebb of the great experience through which he had just passed—for even suffering becomes impossible when a given point of weariness is reached; and similarly, the body refuses to harbour a certain intensity of the spiritual life for an indefinite period—was leaving him, doubtless, more exhausted than he himself suspected. All this contributed, one imagines, to a feeling that none of us knew for how long a time we might now be parting."

The party left Kashmir on October 11 and came down to Lahore. The Western disciples went to Agra, Delhi, and the other principal cities of Northern India for sight-seeing, and the Swami, accompanied by his disciple Sadananda, arrived at Belur on October 18. His brother disciples saw that he was very pallid and ill. He suffered from suffocating attacks of asthma; when he emerged from its painful fits, his face looked blue, like that of a drowning man. But in spite of all, he plunged headlong into numerous activities.

On November 12, 1898, the day of the worship of Kāli, the Nivedita Girls' School was opened in Calcutta. At the end of the inaugural ceremony the Holy Mother, Śri Ramakrishna's consort, "prayed that the blessing of the Great Mother of the universe might be upon the school and that the girls it should train might be ideal girls." Nivedita, who witnessed the ceremony with the Swamis of the Order, said: "I cannot imagine a grander omen than her blessing spoken over the educated Hindu womanhood of the future."

The dedication of the school was the beginning of Nivedita's work in India. The Swami gave her complete freedom about the way to run it. He told her that she was free from her collaborators if she so chose; and that she might, if she wished, give the work a "definite religious colour" or even make it sectarian. Then he added, "You may wish through a sect to rise beyond all sects."

On December 9, 1898, the Ramakrishna Monastery at Belur was formally consecrated by the Swami with the installation of the Master's image in the chapel. The plot of land, as already stated, had been purchased the previous year and had been consecrated with proper religious ceremony in March that year. The Swami himself had performed the worship on that occasion and afterwards had carried on his shoulder the copper vessel containing the Master's sacred relics. While bearing it he said to a disciple: "The Master once told me, 'I will go and live wherever you take me, carrying me on your shoulder, be it under a tree or in the humblest cottage.' With faith in that gracious promise I myself am now carrying him to the site of our future Math. Know for certain, my boy, that so long as his name inspires his followers with the ideal of purity, holiness, and charity for all men, even so long shall he, the Master, sanctify this place with his presence."

Of the glorious future he saw for the monastery the Swami said: "It will be a centre in which will be recognized and practised a grand harmony of all creeds and faiths as exemplified in the life of Śri Ramakrishna, and religion in its universal aspect, alone, will be preached. And from this centre of universal toleration will go forth the shining message of goodwill, peace, and harmony to deluge the whole world." He warned all of the danger of sectarianism's creeping in if they became careless.

After the ceremony, he addressed the assembled monks, brahmachārins, and lay devotees as follows: "Do you all, my brothers, pray to the Lord with all your heart and soul that He, the Divine Incarnation of the age, may bless this place with his hallowed presence for ever and ever, and make it a unique centre, a holy land, of harmony of different religions and sects, for the good of the many, for the happiness of the many."

Swami Vivekananda was in an ecstatic mood. He had accomplished the great task of finding a permanent place on which to build a temple for the Master, with a monastery for his brother disciples and the monks of the future that should serve as the headquarters of the Ramakrishna Order for the propagation of Śri Ramakrishna's teachings. He felt as if the heavy responsibility that he had carried on his shoulders for the past twelve years had been lifted. He wanted the monastery at Belur to be a finished university where Indian mystical wisdom and Western practical science would be taught side by side. And he spoke of the threefold activities of the monastery: annadāna, the gift of food; vidyādāna, the gift of intellectual knowledge; and jnānadāna, the gift of spiritual wisdom. These three, properly balanced, would, in the Swami's opinion, make a complete man. The brahmachārins of the monastery, through unselfish service of men, would purify their minds and thus qualify themselves for the supreme knowledge of Brahman.

Swami Vivekananda in his vivid imagination saw the different sections of the monastery allotted to different functions—the free kitchen for the distribution of food to the hungry, the university for the imparting of knowledge, the quarters for devotees from Europe and America, and so forth and so on. The spiritual ideals emanating from the Belur Math, he said, would influence the thought-currents of the world for eleven hundred years.

"All these visions are rising before me"—these were his very words.

It was a few months before the buildings of the new monastery were com-

Miss J. MacLeod   Mrs. Ole Bull   Vivekananda   Sister Nivedita
(Photograph taken in India, 1898)

TRIGUNATITANANDA   SHIVANANDA   TURIYANANDA

SADANANDA   VIVEKANANDA   BRAHMANANDA

pleted and the monastery was finally removed to its present site. The date of the momentous occasion was January 2, 1899. The Bengali monthly magazine, the *Udbodhan*, was first published on January 4 of the same year, and regarding its policy, the Swami declared that nothing but positive ideas for the physical, mental, and spiritual improvement of the race should find a place in it; that instead of criticizing the thoughts and aspirations of ancient and modern man, as embodied in literature, philosophy, poetry, and the arts, the magazine should indicate the way in which those thoughts and aspirations might be made conducive to progress; and finally that the magazine should stand for universal harmony as preached by Śri Ramakrishna, and disseminate his ideals of love, purity, and renunciation.

The Swami was happy to watch the steady expansion of the varied activities of the Order. At his request Swami Saradananda had returned from America to assist in the organization of the Belur Math. Together with Swami Turiyananda, he conducted regular classes at the Math for the study of Sanskrit and of Eastern and Western philosophy. Somewhat later the two Swamis were sent on a preaching mission to Gujrat, in Western India, and for the same purpose two of the Swami's own disciples were sent to East Bengal. Swami Shivananda was deputed to Ceylon to preach Vedānta. Reports of the excellent work done by Swamis Ramakrishnananda and Abhedananda in Madras and America were received at the Math. Swami Akhandananda's work for the educational uplift of the villages and also in establishing homes for the orphans elicited praise from the Government.

One of the most remarkable institutions founded by Swami Vivekananda was the Advaita Āśrama at Mayavati in the Himālayas. Ever since his visit to the Alps in Switzerland, the Swami had been cherishing the desire to establish a monastery in the solitude of the Himālayas where non-dualism would be taught and practised in its purest form. Captain and Mrs. Sevier took up the idea, and the Āśrama was established at Mayavati, at an altitude of 6800 feet. Before it there shone, day and night, the eternal snow-range of the Himālayas for an extent of over six hundred miles, with Nandā Devi rising to a height of 25,500 feet.

Spiritual seekers, irrespective of creed and race, were welcome at the monastery at Mayavati. No external worship of any kind was permitted within its boundaries. Even the formal worship of Śri Ramakrishna was excluded. It was required of the inmates and guests always to keep before their minds the vision of the nameless and formless Spirit.

Swami Vivekananda in the following lines laid down the ideals and principles of this Himālayan āśrama:

"In Whom is the Universe, Who is in the Universe, Who is the Universe; in Whom is the Soul, Who is in the Soul, Who is the Soul of man; to know Him, and therefore the Universe, as our Self, alone extinguishes all fear, brings an end to misery, and leads to infinite freedom. Wherever there has been expansion in love or progress in well-being of individuals or numbers, it has been through the perception, realization, and the practicalization of the Eternal Truth—*the Oneness of All Beings.* 'Dependence is misery. Independence is happiness.' The Advaita is the only system which gives unto man complete possession of himself and takes off all dependence and its associated superstitions, thus making us brave to suffer, brave to do, and in the long run to attain to Absolute Freedom.

"Hitherto it has not been possible to preach this Noble Truth entirely free from the settings of dualistic weakness; this alone, we are convinced, explains why it has not been more operative and useful to mankind at large.

"To give this ONE TRUTH a freer and fuller scope in elevating the lives of individuals and leavening the mass of mankind, we start this Advaita Āśrama on the Himālayan heights, the land of its first formulation.

"Here it is hoped to keep Advaita free from all superstitions and weakening contaminations. Here will be taught and practised nothing but the Doctrine of Unity, pure and simple; and though in entire sympathy with all other systems, this Āśrama is dedicated to Advaita and Advaita alone."

After the Swami's return from Kashmir his health had begun to deteriorate visibly. His asthma caused him great suffering. But his zeal for work increased many times.

"Ever since I went to Amarnāth," he said one day, "Śiva Himself has entered into my brain. He will not go."

At the earnest request of the brother monks, he visited Calcutta frequently for treatment; yet even there he had no respite from work. Visitors thronged about him for religious instruction from morning till night, and his large heart could not say no to them. When the brother monks pressed him to receive people only at appointed hours, he replied: "They take so much trouble to come, walking all the way from their homes, and can I, sitting here, not speak a few words to them, merely because I risk my health a little?"

His words sounded so much like those of Śri Ramakrishna during the latter's critical illness, no wonder that Swami Premananda said to him one day, "We do not see any difference between Śri Ramakrishna and you."

But the Swami's greatest concern was the training of the sannyāsins and brahmachārins—the future bearers of his message—and to this task he addressed himself with all his soul. He encouraged them in their meditation and manual work, himself setting the example. Sometimes he would cook for them, sometimes knead bread, till the garden, or dig a well. Again, he would train them to be preachers by asking them to speak before a gathering without preparation. Constantly he reminded the monks of their monastic vows, especially chastity and renunciation, without which deep spiritual perception was impossible. He attached great importance to physical exercise and said: "I want sappers and miners in the army of religion! So, boys, set yourselves to the task of training your muscles! For ascetics, mortification is all right. For workers, well developed bodies, muscles of iron and nerves of steel!" He urged them to practise austerities and meditation in solitude. For the beginners he laid down strict rules about food. They were to rise early, meditate, and perform their religious duties scrupulously. Health must not be neglected and the company of worldly people should be avoided. But above all, he constantly admonished them to give up idleness in any shape or form.

Of himself he said: "No rest for me! I shall die in harness! I love action! Life is a battle, and one must always be in action, to use a military phrase. Let me live and die in action!" He was a living hymn of work.

To a disciple who wanted to remain absorbed in the Brahman of Vedānta, the Swami thundered: "Why? What is the use of remaining always stupefied in samādhi? Under the inspiration of non-dualism why not sometimes dance like Śiva, and sometimes remain immersed in superconsciousness? Who enjoys a delicacy more—he who eats it all by himself, or he who shares it with others? Granted, by realizing Ātman in meditation you attain mukti; but of what use is that to the world? We have to take the whole world with us to mukti. We shall set a conflagration in the domain of great Māyā. Then only will you be established in the Eternal Truth. Oh, what can compare with that Bliss immeasurable, 'infinite as the skies'! In that state you will be speechless, carried beyond yourself, by seeing your own Self in every being that breathes, and in every atom of the universe. When you realize this, you cannot live in this world without treating everyone with exceeding love and compassion. This is indeed practical Vedānta."

He wanted his disciples to perform with accuracy and diligence the everyday tasks of life. "He who knows even how to prepare a smoke properly, knows also how to meditate. And he who cannot cook well cannot be a perfect sannyāsin. Unless cooking is performed with a pure mind and concentration, the food is not palatable."

Work cannot produce real fruit without detachment on the part of the worker. "Only a great monk," the Swami said one day, "can be a great worker; for he is without attachment. . . . There are no greater workers than Buddha and Christ. No work is secular. All work is adoration and worship."

The first duty of the inmates of the monastery was renunciation. How the Swami idolized the monastic life! "Never forget, service to the world and the realization of God are the ideals of the monk! Stick to them! The monastic is the most immediate of the paths. Between the monk and his God there are no idols! 'The sannyāsin stands on the head of the Vedas!' declare the Vedas, for he is free from churches and sects and religions and prophets and scriptures. He is the visible God on earth. Remember this, and go thou thy way, sannyāsin bold, carrying the banner of renunciation—the banner of peace, of freedom, of blessedness!"

To a disciple who wanted to practise spiritual discipline to attain his own salvation, the Swami said: "You will go to hell if you seek your own salvation! Seek the salvation of others if you want to reach the Highest. Kill out the desire for personal mukti. This is the greatest spiritual discipline. Work, my children, work with your whole heart and soul! That is the thing. Mind not the fruit of work. What if you go to hell working for others? That is worth more than to gain heaven by seeking your own salvation. . . . Śri Ramakrishna came and gave his life for the world. I will also sacrifice my life. You also, every one of you, should do the same. All these works and so forth are only a beginning. Believe me, from the shedding of our lifeblood will arise gigantic, heroic workers and warriors of God who will revolutionize the whole world."

He wanted his disciples to be all-round men. "You must try to combine in your life immense idealism with immense practicality. You must be prepared to go into deep meditation now, and the next moment you must be ready to go and cultivate the fields. You must be prepared to explain the intricacies of the scriptures now, and the next moment to go and sell the produce of the fields in the market. . . . The true man is he who is strong as strength itself and yet possesses a woman's heart."

He spoke of the power of faith: "The history of the world is the history of a few men who had faith in themselves. That faith calls out the inner divinity. You can do anything. You fail only when you do not strive sufficiently to manifest infinite power. As soon as a man loses faith in himself, death comes. Believe first in yourself and then in God. A handful of strong men will move the world. We need a heart to feel, a brain to conceive, and a strong arm to do the work. . . . One man contains within him the whole universe. One particle of matter has all the energy of the universe at its back. In a conflict between the heart and the brain, follow your heart."

"His words," writes Romain Rolland, "are great music, phrases in the style of Beethoven, stirring rhythms like the march of Handel choruses. I cannot touch these sayings of his, scattered as they are through the pages of books at thirty years' distance, without receiving a thrill through my body like an electric shock. And what shocks, what transports must have been produced when in burning words they issued from the lips of the hero!"

The Swami felt he was dying. But he said: "Let me die fighting. Two years of physical suffering have taken from me twenty years of life. But the soul changes not, does it? It is there, the same madcap—Ātman—mad upon one idea, intent and intense."

SECOND VISIT TO AMERICA

On December 16, 1898, Swami Vivekananda announced his plan to go to the West to inspect the work he had founded and to fan the flame. The devotees and friends welcomed the idea since they thought the sea voyage would restore his failing health. He planned to take with him Sister Nivedita and Swami Turiyananda.

Versed in the scriptures, Turiyananda had spent most of his life in meditation and was averse to public work. Failing to persuade him by words to accompany him to America, Vivekananda put his arms round his brother disciple's neck and wept like a child, saying: "Dear brother, don't you see how I am laying down my life inch by inch in fulfilling the mission of my Master? Now I have come to the verge of death! Can you look on without trying to relieve part of my great burden?"

Swami Turiyananda was deeply moved and offered to follow the Swami wherever he wanted to go. When he asked if he should take with him some Vedānta scriptures, Vivekananda said: "Oh, they have had enough of learning and books! The last time they saw a warrior;[32] now I want to show them a brāhmin."

June 20, 1899, was fixed as their date of sailing from Calcutta. On the night of the 19th a meeting was held at the Belur Math at which the junior members

---

[32] Referring to himself, who had delivered his message in a combative spirit.

of the monastery presented addresses to the two Swamis. The next day the Holy Mother entertained them and other monks with a sumptuous feast.

The steamship "Golconda," carrying the Swami and his two companions, touched Madras, but the passengers were not allowed to land on account of the plague in Calcutta. This was a great disappointment to Swami Vivekananda's South Indian friends. The ship continued to Colombo, Aden, Naples, and Marseilles, finally arriving in London on July 31.

The voyage in the company of the Swami was an education for Turiyananda and Nivedita. From beginning to end a vivid flow of thought and stories went on. One never knew what moment would bring the flash of intuition and the ringing utterance of some fresh truth. That encyclopaedic mind touched all subjects: Christ, Buddha, Krishna, Ramakrishna, folklore, the history of India and Europe, the degradation of Hindu society and the assurance of its coming greatness, different philosophical and religious systems, and many themes more. All was later admirably recorded by Sister Nivedita in *The Master as I Saw Him*, from which the following fragments may be cited.

"Yes," the Swami said one day, "the older I grow, the more everything seems to me to lie in manliness. This is my new gospel. Do even evil like a man! Be wicked, if you must, on a grand scale!" Some time before, Nivedita had complimented India on the infrequency of crime; on that occasion the Swami said in sorrowful protest: "Would to God it were otherwise in my land! For this is verily the virtuousness of death." Evidently, according to him, the vilest crime was not to act, to do nothing at all.

Regarding conservative and liberal ideas he said: "The conservative's whole ideal is submission. Your ideal is struggle. Consequently it is we who enjoy life, and never you! You are always striving to change yours to something better, and before a millionth part of the change is carried out, you die. The Western ideal is to be doing; the Eastern, to be suffering. The perfect life would be a wonderful harmony between doing and suffering. But that can never be."

To him selfishness was the greatest barrier to spiritual progress:

"It is selfishness that we must seek to eliminate. I find that whenever I have made a mistake in my life, it has always been because *self* entered into the calculation. Where self has not been involved, my judgement has gone straight to the mark."

"You are quite wrong," he said again, "when you think that fighting is the sign of growth. It is not so at all. Absorption is the sign. Hinduism is the very genius of absorption. We have never cared for fighting. Of course, we struck a blow now and then in defense of our homes. That was right. But we never cared for fighting for its own sake. Everyone had to learn that. So let these races of new-comers whirl on! They all will be taken into Hinduism in the end."

In another mood, the theme of his conversation would be Kāli, and the worship of the Terrible. Then he would say: "I love terror for its own sake, despair for its own sake, misery for its own sake. Fight always. Fight and fight on, though always in defeat. That's the ideal! That's the ideal!" Again: "Worship the Terrible! Worship Death! All else is vain. All struggle is vain. This is the last lesson. Yet this is not the coward's love of death, not the love of the weak or the suicide. It is the welcome of the strong man, who has sounded everything to the depths and knows that there is no alternative." And who is Kāli, whose will is irresistible? "The totality of all souls, not the human alone, is the Personal God. The will of the totality nothing can resist. It is what we know as Law. And this is what we mean by Śiva and Kāli and so on."

Concerning true greatness: "As I grow older I find that I look more and more for greatness in little things. I want to know what a great man eats and wears, and how he speaks to his servants. I want to find a Sir Philip Sidney greatness. Few men would remember to think of others in the moment of death.

"But anyone will be great in a great position! Even the coward will grow brave in the glow of the footlights. The world looks on. Whose heart will not throb? Whose pulse will not quicken, till he can do his best? More and more the true greatness seems to me that of the worm, doing its duty silently, steadily, from moment to moment and hour to hour."

Regarding the points of difference between his own schemes for the regeneration of India and those preached by others: "I disagree with those who are for giving *their* superstitions back to my people. Like the Egyptologist's interest in Egypt, it is easy to feel an interest in India that is purely selfish. One may desire to see again the India of one's books, one's studies, one's dreams. My hope is to see the strong points of that India, reinforced by the strong points of this age, only in a natural way. The new state of things must be a *growth* from within. So I preach only the Upanishads. If you look you will find that I have never quoted anything but the Upanishads. And of the Upanishads, it is only that one idea—strength. The quintessence of the Vedas and Vedānta and all, lies in that one word. Buddha's teaching was of non-resistance or non-injury. But I think ours is a better way of teaching the same thing. For behind that non-injury lay a dreadful weakness—the weakness that conceives the idea of resistance. But I do not think of punishing or escaping from a drop of sea-spray. It is nothing to me. Yet to the mosquito it would be serious. Now, I will make all injury like that. Strength and fearlessness. My own ideal is that giant of a saint whom they killed in the Sepoy Mutiny, and who broke his silence, when stabbed to the heart, to say—'And thou also art He.'"

About India and Europe the Swami said: "I see that India is a young and living organism. Europe is also young and living. Neither has arrived at such a stage of development that we can safely criticize its institutions. They are two great experiments, neither of which is yet complete." They ought to be mutually helpful, he went on, but at the same time each should respect the free development of the other. They ought to grow hand in hand.

Thus time passed till the boat arrived at Tilbury Dock, where the party was met by the Swami's disciples and friends, among whom were two American ladies who had come all the way to London to meet their teacher. It was the off-season for London, and so the two Swamis sailed for New York on August 16.

The trip was beneficial to the Swami's health; the sea was smooth and at night the moonlight was enchanting. One evening as the Swami paced up and down the deck enjoying the beauty of nature, he suddenly exclaimed, "And if all this māyā is so beautiful, think of the wondrous beauty of the Reality behind it!" Another evening, when the moon was full, he pointed to the sea and sky, and said, "Why recite poetry when there is the very essence of poetry?"

The afternoon that Swami Vivekananda arrived in New York, he and his brother disciple went with Mr. and Mrs. Leggett to the latter's country home, Ridgely Manor, at Stone Ridge in the Catskill Mountains, Swami Abhedananda being at that time absent from New York on a lecture tour. A month later Nivedita came to Ridgely, and on September 21, when she decided to assume the nun's garb, the Swami wrote for her his beautiful poem "Peace." The rest and good climate were improving his health, and he was entertaining all with his usual fun and merriment.

One day Miss MacLeod asked him how he liked their home-grown strawberries, and he answered that he had not tasted any. Miss MacLeod was surprised and said, "Why Swami, we have been serving you strawberries with cream and sugar every day for the past week." "Ah," the Swami replied, with a mischievous twinkle in his eyes, "I am tasting only cream and sugar. Even tacks taste sweet that way."

In November the Swami returned to New York and was greeted by his old friends and disciples. He was pleased to see how the work had expanded under the able guidance of Swami Abhedananda. Swami Vivekananda gave some talks and conducted classes.

At one of the public meetings in New York, after addressing a tense audience for about fifteen minutes, the Swami suddenly made a formal bow and retired. The meeting broke up and the people went away greatly disappointed. A friend asked him, when he was returning home, why he had cut short the lecture in that manner, just when both he and the audience were warming up. Had he forgotten his points? Had he become nervous? The Swami answered that at the meeting he had felt that he had too much power. He had noticed that the members of the audience were becoming so absorbed in his ideas that they were losing their own individualities. He had felt that they had become like soft clay and that he could give them any shape he wanted. That, however, was contrary to his philosophy. He wished every man and woman to grow according to his or her own inner law. He did not wish to change or destroy anyone's individuality. That was why he had had to stop.

Swami Turiyananda took up his work at Montclair, New Jersey, a short distance from New York, and began to teach children the stories and folklore of India. He also lectured regularly at the Vedanta Society of New York. His paper on Sankarāchārya, read before the Cambridge Conference, was highly praised by the Harvard professors.

One day, while the Swami was staying at Ridgely Manor, Miss MacLeod had received a telegram informing her that her only brother was dangerously ill in Los Angeles. As she was leaving for the West coast, the Swami uttered a Sanskrit benediction and told her that he would soon meet her there. She proceeded straight to the home of Mrs. S. K. Blodgett, where her brother was staying, and after spending a few minutes with the patient, asked Mrs. Blodgett whether her brother might be permitted to die in the room in which he was then lying; for she had found a large picture of Vivekananda, hanging on the wall at the foot of the patient's bed. Miss MacLeod told her hostess of her surprise on seeing the picture, and Mrs. Blodgett replied that she had heard Vivekananda at the Parliament of Religions in Chicago and thought that if ever there was a

God on earth, it was that man.[33] Miss MacLeod told her that she had just left the Swami at Ridgely Manor, and further, that he had expressed the desire to come to Los Angeles. The brother died within a few days, and the Swami started for the West Coast on November 22. He broke his trip in Chicago to visit his old friends, and upon his arrival in Los Angeles became the guest of Mrs. Blodgett, whom he described in a letter to Mary Hale as "fat, old, extremely witty, and very motherly."

The impression the Swami left in the mind of this good woman can be gathered from the following lines of a letter written by her to Miss MacLeod after Swamiji's passing away:

I am ever recalling those swift, bright days in that never-to-be-forgotten winter, lived in simple freedom and kindliness. We could not choose but to be happy and good. . . . I knew him personally but a short time, yet in that time I could see in a hundred ways the child side of Swamiji's character, which was a constant appeal to the mother quality in all good women. . . . He would come home from a lecture, where he had been compelled to break away from his audience—so eagerly would they gather around him—and rush into the kitchen like a boy released from school, with "Now we will cook!" Presently Joe would appear and discover the culprit among the pots and pans, and in his fine dress, who was by thrifty, watchful Joe admonished to change to his home garments. . . . In the homely, old-fashioned kitchen, you and I have seen Swamiji at his best.

Swami Vivekananda gave many lectures before large audiences in Los Angeles and Pasadena; but alas! there was no Goodwin to record them, and most of what he said was consequently lost. Only a little has been preserved in the fragmentary notes of his disciples.

At the Universalist Church of Pasadena he gave his famous lecture "Christ, the Messenger"; and this was the only time, Miss MacLeod said later, that she saw him enveloped in a halo. The Swami, after the lecture, was returning home wrapped in thought, and Miss MacLeod was following at a little distance, when suddenly she heard him say, "I know it, I know it!"

"What do you know?" asked Miss MacLeod.

"How they make it."

"How they make what?"

"Mulligatawny soup. They put in a dash of bay leaf for flavour." And then he burst into a laugh.

The Swami spent about a month at the headquarters of the "Home of Truth" in Los Angeles, conducted regular classes, and gave several public lectures, each of which was attended by over a thousand people. He spoke many times on the different aspects of rāja-yoga, a subject in which Californians seemed to be especially interested.

The Swami endeared himself to the members of the Home of Truth by his simple manner, his great intellect, and his spiritual wisdom. *Unity*, the magazine of the organization, said of him: "There is a combination in the Swami Vivekananda of the learning of a university president, the dignity of an archbishop, with the grace and winsomeness of a free and natural child. Getting

---

[33] See p. 62.

upon the platform, without a moment's preparation, he would soon be in the midst of his subject, sometimes becoming almost tragic as his mind would wander from deep metaphysics to the prevailing conditions in Christian countries of today, whose people go and seek to reform the Filipinos with the sword in one hand and the Bible in the other, or in South Africa allow children of the same Father to cut each other to pieces. In contrast to this condition of things, he described what took place during the last great famine in India, where men would die of starvation beside their cows rather than stretch forth a hand to kill."

The members of the Home of Truth were not permitted to smoke. One evening the Swami was invited for dinner by a member of the organization along with several other friends who were all opposed to the use of tobacco. After dinner the hostess was absent from the room for a few minutes, when the Swami, perhaps due to his ignorance of the rule about tobacco, took out his pipe, filled it up, and began to puff. The guests were aghast, but kept quiet. When the hostess returned, she flew into a rage and asked the Swami if God intended men to smoke, adding that in that case He would have furnished the human head with a chimney for the smoke to go out.

"But He has given us the brain to invent a pipe," the Swami said with a smile.

Everybody laughed, and the Swami was given freedom to smoke while living as a guest in the Home of Truth.

Swami Vivekananda journeyed to Oakland as the guest of Dr. Benjamin Fay Mills, the minister of the First Unitarian Church, and there gave eight lectures to crowded audiences which often numbered as high as two thousand. He also gave many public lectures in San Francisco and Alameda. People had already read his Rāja-Yoga. Impressed by his lectures, they wanted a centre in San Francisco. The Swami was offered a gift of land, measuring a hundred and sixty acres, in the southern part of the San Antone valley; surrounded by forest and hills, and situated at an altitude of 2500 feet, the property was only twelve miles from the Lick Observatory on Mt. Hamilton. He at once thought of Swami Turiyananda, who could be given charge of the place to train earnest students in meditation.

During his trip back to New York, across the American continent, the Swami was very much fatigued. He stopped in Chicago and Detroit on the way. In Chicago he was the guest of the Hale family, and many old reminiscences were exchanged. On the morning of his departure, Mary came to the Swami's room and found him sad. His bed appeared to have been untouched, and on being asked the reason, he confessed that he had spent the whole night without sleep. "Oh," he said, almost in a whisper, "it is so difficult to break human bonds!" He knew that this was the last time he was to visit these devoted friends.

In New York the Swami gave a few lectures at the Vedānta Society, which by this time had enlisted the active co-operation of several professors of Harvard and Columbia University. At the earliest opportunity he spoke to Turiyananda about the proposed gift of land in northern California, but the latter hesitated to accept any responsibility. The Swami said, "It is the will of the Mother that you should take charge of the work there."

Swami Turiyananda was amused and said with good humour: "Rather say it is your will. Certainly you have not heard the Mother communicate Her will to you in that way. How can you hear the words of the Mother?"

"Yes, brother," the Swami said with great emotion. "Yes, the words of the Mother can be heard as clearly as we hear one another. But one requires a fine nerve to hear Mother's words."

Swami Vivekananda made this statement with such fervour that his brother disciple felt convinced that the Divine Mother was speaking through him. He cheerfully agreed, therefore, to take charge of Śanti Āśrama, the Peace Retreat, as the new place was called.

In parting, the Swami said to Turiyananda: "Go and establish the Āśrama in California. Hoist the flag of Vedānta there; from this moment destroy even the memory of India! Above all, lead the life and Mother will see to the rest."

The Swami visited Detroit again for a week and on July 20 sailed for Paris.

GLIMPSES OF THE SWAMI'S MIND

Before continuing the thread of Swami Vivekananda's life, it will be interesting for the reader to get a glimpse of his state of mind. During the past two years, the Swami wrote to his friends, he had gone through great mental anguish. His message, to be sure, had begun to reach an ever increasing number of people both in India and in America, and naturally he had been made happy by this fact; yet he had suffered intensely on account of "poverty, treachery, and my own foolishness," as he wrote to Mary Hale on February 20, 1900. Though his outward appearance was that of a stern non-dualist, he possessed a tender heart that was often bruised by the blows of the world. To Margaret Noble he wrote on December 6, 1899: "Some people are made that way—to love being miserable. If I did not break my heart over the people I was born amongst, I would do it for somebody else. I am sure of that. This is the way of some—I am coming to see it. We are all after happiness, true, but some are only happy in being unhappy—queer, is it not?"

How sensitive he was to the sufferings of men! "I went years ago to the Himālayas," he wrote to an American friend on December 12, 1899, "never to come back—and my sister committed suicide, the news reached me there, and that weak heart flung me off from the prospect of peace! It is the weak heart that has driven me out of India to seek some help for those I love, and here I am! Peace have I sought, but the heart, that seat of bhakti, would not allow me to find it. Struggle and torture, torture and struggle! Well, so be it then, since it is my fate; and the quicker it is over, the better."

His health had been indifferent even before he had left for the West. "This sort of nervous body," he wrote on November 15, 1899, "is just an instrument to play great music at times, and at times to moan in darkness." While in America, he was under the treatment of an osteopath and a "magnetic healer," but received no lasting benefit. At Los Angeles he got the news of the serious illness of his brother disciple Niranjan. Mr. Sturdy, his beloved English disciple, had given up the Swami because he felt that the teacher was not living in the West the life of an ascetic. Miss Henrietta Muller, who had helped him financially to buy the Belur Math, left him on account of his illness; she could not associate sickness with holiness. One of the objects of the Swami's visit to California was to raise money to promote his various activities in India: people came to his meetings in large numbers, but of money he received very little. He suffered a bereavement in the passing away of his devoted friend Mr. George Hale of Chicago. Reports about the work in New York caused him much anxiety. Swami Abhedananda was not getting on well with some of Vivekananda's disciples, and Mr. Leggett severed his relationship with the Society. All these things, like so many claws, pierced Vivekananda's heart. Further, perhaps he now felt that his mission on earth was over. He began to lose interest in work. The arrow, however, was still flying, carried by its original impetus; but it was approaching the end, when it would fall to the ground.

The Swami longed to return to India. On January 17, 1900, he wrote to Mrs. Ole Bull that he wanted to build a hut on the bank of the Ganges and spend the rest of his life there with his mother: "She has suffered much through me. I must try to smooth her last days. Do you know, this was just exactly what the great Śankarāchārya himself had to do. He had to go back to his mother in the last few days of her life. I accept it. I am resigned."

In the same letter to Mrs. Ole Bull he wrote: "I am but a child; what work have I to do? My powers I passed over to you. I see it. I cannot any more *tell* from the platform. Don't tell it to anyone—not even to Joe. I am glad. I want rest; not that I am tired, but the next phase will be the *miraculous touch and not the tongue*—like Ramakrishna's. The word has gone to you, the boys, and to Margot."[34]

He was fast losing interest in active work. On April 7, 1900, he wrote to a friend:

"My boat is nearing the calm harbour from which it is never more to be driven out. Glory, glory unto Mother![35] I have no wish, no ambition now. Blessed be Mother! I am the servant of Ramakrishna. I am merely a machine. I know nothing else. Nor do I want to know."

To another friend he wrote, on April 12, in similar vein:

Work always brings dirt with it. I paid for the accumulated dirt with bad health. I am glad my mind is all the better for it. There is a mellowness and a calmness in life now, which never was before. I am learning now how to be attached as well as detached —and mentally becoming my own master. . . . Mother is doing Her own work. I do not worry much now. Moths like me die by the thousands every minute. Her work goes on all the same. Glory unto Mother! . . . For me—alone and drifting about in the will-current of the Mother has been my life. The moment I have tried to break it, that moment I was hurt. Her will be done. . . . I am happy, at peace with myself, and more of the sannyāsin than I ever was. The love for my own kith and kin is growing less every day—for Mother, increasing. Memories of long nights of vigil with Śri Rama-krishna, under the Dakshineswar banyan tree, are waking up once more. And work? What is work? Whose work? Whom to work for? I am free. I am Mother's child. She works, She plays. Why should I plan? What shall I plan? Things came and went, just

---

[34] Referring to Sister Nivedita.
[35] Referring to the Divine Mother of the Universe.

as She liked, without my planning, in spite of my planning. We are Her automata. She is the wire-puller.

With the approaching end of his mission and earthly life, he realized ever more clearly how like a stage this world is. In August 1899 he wrote to Miss Marie Halboister: "This toy world would not be here, this play could not go on, if we were knowing players. We must play blindfolded. Some of us have taken the part of the rogue of the play; some, of the hero—never mind, it is all play. This is the only consolation. There are demons and lions and tigers and what not on the stage, but they are all muzzled. They snap but cannot bite. The world cannot touch our souls. If you want, even if the body be torn and bleeding, you may enjoy the greatest peace in your mind. And the way to that is to attain hopelessness. Do you know that? Not the imbecile attitude of despair, but the contempt of the conqueror for the things he has attained, for the things he has struggled for and then thrown aside as beneath his worth."

To Mary Hale, who "has been always the sweetest note in my jarring and clashing life," he wrote on March 26, 1900:

This is to let you know "I am very happy." Not that I am getting into a shadowy optimism, but my power of suffering is increasing. I am being lifted up above the pestilential miasma of this world's joys and sorrows. They are losing their meaning. It is a land of dreams. It does not matter whether one enjoys or weeps—they are but dreams, and as such must break sooner or later. . . . I am attaining peace that passeth understanding—which is neither joy nor sorrow, but something above them both. Tell Mother[36] that. My passing through the valley of death—physical, mental—these last two years, has helped me in this. Now I am nearing that *Peace*, the eternal *Silence*. Now I mean to see things as they are—everything in that Peace—perfect in its way. "He whose joy is only in himself, whose desires are only in himself," he has *learnt* his lessons. This is the great lesson that we are here to learn through myriads of births and heavens and hells: There is nothing to be sought for, asked for, desired, beyond one's self. The greatest thing I can obtain is myself. I am free—therefore I require none else for my happiness. Alone through eternity—because I was free, am free, and will remain free for ever. This is Vedāntism. I preached the theory so long, but oh, joy! Mary, my dear sister, I am realizing it now every day. Yes, I am. I am free—Alone—Alone. I am the One without a second.

Vivekananda's eyes were looking at the light of another world, his real abode. And how vividly and touchingly he expressed his nostalgic yearning to return to it, in his letter of April 18, 1900, written from Alameda, California, to Miss MacLeod, his ever loyal Joe:

Just now I received your and Mrs. Bull's welcome letter. I direct this to London. I am so glad Mrs. Leggett is on the sure way to recovery.

I am so sorry Mr. Leggett resigned the presidentship.

Well, I keep quiet for fear of making further trouble. You know my methods are extremely harsh, and once roused I may rattle Abhedananda too much for his peace of mind.

I wrote to him only to tell him his notions about Mrs. Bull are entirely wrong.

Work is always difficult. Pray for me, Joe, that my work may stop for ever and my whole soul be absorbed in Mother. Her work She knows.

[36] Referring to Mrs. Hale.

You must be glad to be in London once more—the old friends—give them all my love and gratitude.

I am well, very well mentally. I feel the rest of the soul more than that of the body. The battles are lost and won. I have bundled my things and am waiting for the Great Deliverer.

Śiva, O Śiva, carry my boat to the other shore!

After all, Joe, I am only the boy who used to listen with rapt wonderment to the wonderful words of Ramakrishna under the banyan at Dakshineswar. That is my true nature—works and activities, doing good and so forth, are all superimpositions. Now I again hear his voice, the same old voice thrilling my soul. Bonds are breaking—love dying, work becoming tasteless—the glamour is off life. Now only the voice of the Master calling.—"I come, Lord, I come."—"Let the dead bury the dead. Follow thou Me."—"I come, my beloved Lord, I come."

Yes, I come. Nirvāna is before me. I feel it at times, the same infinite ocean of peace, without a ripple, a breath.

I am glad I was born, glad I suffered so, glad I did make big blunders, glad to enter peace. I leave none bound, I take no bonds. Whether this body will fall and release me or I enter into freedom in the body, the old man is gone, gone for ever, never to come back again!

The guide, the guru, the leader, the teacher, has passed away; the boy, the student, the servant, is left behind.

You understand why I do not want to meddle with Abhedananda. Who am I to meddle with any, Joe? I have long given up my place as a leader—I have no right to raise my voice. Since the beginning of this year I have not dictated anything in India. You know that. Many thanks for what you and Mrs. Bull have been to me in the past. All blessings follow you ever! The sweetest moments of my life have been when I was drifting. I am drifting again—with the bright warm sun ahead and masses of vegetation around—and in the heat everything is so still, so calm—and I am drifting, languidly— in the warm heart of the river. I dare not make a splash with my hands or feet—for fear of breaking the wonderful stillness, stillness that makes you feel sure it is an illusion!

Behind my work was ambition, behind my love was personality, behind my purity was fear, behind my guidance the thirst for power. Now they are vanishing and I drift. I come, Mother, I come, in Thy warm bosom, floating wheresoever Thou takest me, in the voiceless, in the strange, in the wonderland, I come—a spectator, no more an actor.

Oh, it is so calm! My thoughts seem to come from a great, great distance in the interior of my own heart. They seem like faint, distant whispers, and peace is upon everything, sweet, sweet peace—like that one feels for a few moments just before falling into sleep, when things are seen and felt like shadows—without fear, without love, without emotion—peace that one feels alone, surrounded with statues and pictures.— I come, Lord, I come.

The world is, but not beautiful nor ugly, but as sensations without exciting any emotion. Oh, Joe, the blessedness of it! Everything is good and beautiful; for things are all losing their relative proportions to me—my body among the first. Om That Existence!

I hope great things come to you all in London and Paris. Fresh joy—fresh benefits to mind and body.

THE PARIS CONGRESS

But the arrow of Swami Vivekananda's life had not yet finished its flight. Next he was to be seen in Paris participating in the Congress of the History of Religions, held on the occasion of the Universal Exposition. This Congress, compared with the Parliament of Religions of Chicago, was a rather tame affair.

The discussion was limited to technical theories regarding the origin of the rituals of religion; for the Catholic hierarchy, evidently not wanting a repetition of the triumph of Oriental ideas in the American Parliament, did not allow any discussion of religious doctrines. Swami Vivekananda, on account of his failing health, took part in only two sessions. He repudiated the theory of the German orientalist Gustav Oppert that the Śiva lingam was a mere phallic symbol. He described the Vedas as the common basis of both Hinduism and Buddhism, and held that both Krishna and the Bhagavad Gītā were prior to Buddhism. Further, he rejected the theory of the Hellenic influence on the drama, art, literature, astrology, and other sciences developed in India.

In Paris he came to know his distinguished countryman J. C. Bose, the discoverer of the life and nervous system in plants, who had been invited to join the scientific section of the Congress. The Swami referred to the Indian scientist as "the pride and glory of Bengal."

In Paris Swami Vivekananda was the guest of Mr. and Mrs. Leggett, at whose house he met many distinguished people. Among these was the young Duke of Richelieu, a scion of an old and aristocratic family of France. The title had been created by Louis XIII, and one of the ancestors of the Duke had been Premier under Louis XVIII. Born in Paris, educated at a Jesuit school in France, and later graduated from the University of Aix-en-Provence, the Duke of Richelieu became greatly attached to the Swami and visited him frequently. On the eve of Vivekananda's departure from Paris, the Swami asked the Duke if he would renounce the world and become his disciple. The Duke wanted to know what he would gain in return for such renunciation, and the Swami said, "I shall give you the desire for death." When asked to explain, the Swami declared that he would give the Duke such a state of mind that when confronted by death he would laugh at it. But the Duke preferred to pursue a worldly career, though he cherished a life-long devotion to Swami Vivekananda.

During his stay in Paris the Swami met such prominent people as Professor Patrick Geddes of Edinburgh University, Père Hyacinthe, Hiram Maxim, Sarah Bernhardt, Jules Bois, and Madame Emma Calvé. Père Hyacinthe, a Carmelite monk who had renounced his vows, had married an American lady and assumed the name of Charles Loyson. The Swami, however, always addressed him by his old monastic name and described him as endowed with "a very sweet nature" and the temperament of a lover of God. Maxim, the inventor of the gun associated with his name, was a great connoisseur and lover of India and China. Sarah Bernhardt also bore a great love for India, which she often described as "very ancient, very civilized." To visit India was the dream of her life.

Madame Calvé the Swami had met in America, and now he came to know her more intimately. She became one of his devoted followers. "She was born poor," he once wrote of her, "but by her innate talents, prodigious labour and diligence, and after wrestling against much hardship, she is now enormously rich and commands respect from kings and emperors. . . . The rare combination of beauty, youth, talents, and 'divine' voice has assigned Calvé the highest place among the singers of the West. There is, indeed, no better teacher than misery and poverty. That constant fight against the dire poverty, misery, and hardship of the days of her girlhood, which has led to her present triumph over them, has brought into her life a unique sympathy and a depth of thought with a wide outlook."

After the Swami's passing away, Madame Calvé visited the Belur Math, the headquarters of the Ramakrishna Mission. In old age she embraced the Catholic faith and had to give up, officially, her allegiance to Swami Vivekananda. But one wonders whether she was able to efface him from her heart.

Jules Bois, with whom the Swami stayed for a few days in Paris, was a distinguished writer. "We have," the Swami wrote to a disciple, "many great ideas in common and feel happy together."

Most of the Swami's time in Paris was devoted to the study of French culture and especially the language. He wrote a few letters in French. About the culture, his appreciation was tempered with criticism. He spoke of Paris as the "home of liberty"; there the ethics and society of the West had been formed, and its university had been the model of all others. But in a letter to Swami Turiyananda, dated September 1, 1900, he also wrote: "The people of France are mere intellectualists. They run after worldly things and firmly believe God and souls to be mere superstitions; they are extremely loath to talk on such subjects. This is truly a materialistic country."

After the Congress of the History of Religions was concluded, the Swami spent a few days at Lannion in Brittany, as the guest of Mrs. Ole Bull. Sister Nivedita, who had just returned from America, was also in the party. There, in his conversations, the Swami dwelt mostly on Buddha and his teachings. Contrasting Buddhism with Hinduism, he one day said that the former exhorted men to "realize all this as illusion," while Hinduism asked them to "realize that within the illusion is the Real." Of how this was to be done, Hinduism never presumed to enunciate any rigid law. The Buddhist command could only be carried out through monasticism; the Hindu might be fulfilled through any state of life. All alike were roads to the One Real. One of the highest and the greatest expressions of the Faith is put into the mouth of a butcher, preaching, by the orders of a married woman, to a sannyāsin.[37] Thus Buddhism became the religion of a monastic order, but Hinduism, in spite of its exaltation of monasticism, remains ever the religion of faithfulness to daily duty, whatever it may be, as the path by which man may attain to God.

From Lannion, on St. Michael's Day, he visited Mont St. Michel. He was struck by the similarity between the rituals of Hinduism and Roman Catholicism. He said, "Christianity is not alien to Hinduism."

Nivedita took leave of the Swami in Brittany and departed for England in order to raise funds for her work on behalf of Indian women. While giving her his blessings, the Swami said: "There is a peculiar sect of Mohammedans who are reported to be so fanatical that they take each new-born babe and expose it, saying, 'If God made thee, perish! If Ali made thee, live!' Now this which they say to the child, I say, but in the opposite sense, to you, tonight—'Go forth into the world, and there, if I made you, be destroyed! If Mother made you, live!'" Perhaps the Swami remembered how some of his beloved Western dis-

[37] The butcher and the woman, in the story referred to, which is found in one of the Purānas, were householders who had received spiritual illumination through the performance of their respective duties.

ciples, unable to understand the profundity of his life and teachings, had deserted him. He also realized the difficulties Westerners experienced in identifying themselves completely with the customs of India. He had told Nivedita, before they left India, that she must resume, as if she had never broken them off, all her old habits and social customs of the West.

On October 24, 1900, Swami Vivekananda left Paris for the East, by way of Vienna and Constantinople. Besides the Swami, the party consisted of Monsieur and Madame Loyson, Jules Bois, Madame Calvé, and Miss MacLeod. The Swami was Calvé's guest.

In Vienna the Swami remarked, "If Turkey is called 'the sick man of Europe,' Austria ought to be called 'the sick woman of Europe'!"

The party arrived in Constantinople after passing through Hungary, Serbia, Romania, and Bulgaria. Next the Swami and his friends came to Athens. They visited several islands and a Greek monastery. From Athens they sailed to Egypt and the Swami was delighted to visit the museum in Cairo. While in Cairo, he and his women devotees, one day, in the course of sightseeing, unknowingly entered the part of the city in which the girls of ill fame lived, and when the inmates hurled coarse jokes at the Swami from their porches, the ladies wanted to take him away; but he refused to go. Some of the prostitutes came into the street, and the ladies saw from a distance that they knelt before him and kissed the hem of his garment. Presently the Swami joined his friends and drove away.

In Cairo the Swami had a presentiment that something had happened to Mr. Sevier. He became restless to return to India, took the first available boat, and sailed for Bombay alone.

Throughout his European tour the Swami's friends had noticed that he was becoming more and more detached from the spectacle of external things, and buried in meditation. A sort of indifference to the world was gradually overpowering him. On August 14 he had written to a friend that he did not expect to live long. From Paris he wrote to Turiyananda: "My body and mind are broken down; I need rest badly. In addition there is not a single person on whom I can depend; on the other hand, as long as I live, all will be very selfish, depending upon me for everything." In Egypt the Swami had seemed to be turning the last pages of his life-experience. One of the party later remarked, "How tired and world-weary he seemed!" Nivedita, who had had the opportunity of observing him closely during his second trip to the West, writes:

The outstanding impression made by the Swami's bearing during all these months of European and American life, was one of almost complete indifference to his surroundings. Current estimates of value left him entirely unaffected. He was never in any way startled or incredulous under success, being too deeply convinced of the greatness of the Power that worked through him, to be surprised by it. But neither was he unnerved by external failure. Both victory and defeat would come and go. He was their witness. . . . He moved fearless and unhesitant through the luxury of the West. As determinedly as I had seen him in India, dressed in the two garments of simple folk, sitting on the floor and eating with his fingers, so, equally without doubt or shrinking, was his acceptance of the complexity of the means of living in America or France. Monk and king, he said, were the obverse and reverse of a single medal. From the use of the best to the renunciation of all was but one step. India had thrown all her prestige in the past round poverty. Some prestige was in the future to be cast round wealth.

For some time the Swami had been trying to disentangle himself from the responsibilities of work. He had already transferred the property of the Belur Math from his own name to the Trustees of the organization. On August 25, 1900, he had written to Nivedita from Paris:

Now I am free, as I have kept no power or authority or position for me in the work. I also have resigned the Presidentship of the Ramakrishna Mission. The Math etc. belong now to the immediate disciples of Ramakrishna except myself. The Presidentship is now Brahmananda's—next it will fall on Premananda etc., in turn. I am so glad a whole load is off me. Now I am happy. . . .

I no longer represent anybody, nor am I responsible to anybody. As to my friends, I had a morbid sense of obligation. I have thought well and find I owe nothing to anybody —if anything. I have given my best energies, unto death almost, and received only hectoring and mischief-making and botheration. . . .

Your letter indicates that I am jealous of your new friends. You must know once for all I am born without jealousy, without avarice, without the desire to rule—whatever other vices I may be born with.

I never directed you before; now, after I am nobody in the work, I have no direction whatever. I only know this much: So long as you serve "Mother" with a whole heart, She will be your guide.

I never had any jealousy about what friends you made. I never criticized my brethren for mixing up in anything. Only I do believe the Western people have the peculiarity of trying to force upon others whatever seems good to them, forgetting that what is good for you may not be good for others. As such I am afraid you would try to force upon others whatever turn your mind might take in contact with new friends. That was the only reason I sometimes tried to stop any particular influence, and nothing else.

You are free. Have your own choice, your own work. . . .

Friends or foes, they are all instruments in Her hands to help us work out our own karma, through pleasure or pain. As such, "Mother" bless them all.

How did America impress Swami Vivekananda during his second visit to the West? What impressions did he carry to India of the state of things in the New World? During his first visit he had been enthusiastic about almost everything he saw—the power, the organization, the material prosperity, the democracy, and the spirit of freedom and justice. But now he was greatly disillusioned. In America's enormous combinations and ferocious struggle for supremacy he discovered the power of Mammon. He saw that the commercial spirit was composed, for the most part, of greed, selfishness, and a struggle for privilege and power. He was disgusted with the ruthlessness of wealthy business men, swallowing up the small tradespeople by means of large combinations. That was indeed tyranny. He could admire an organization; "but what beauty is there among a pack of wolves?" he said to a disciple. He also noticed, in all their nakedness, the social vices and the arrogance of race, religion, and colour. America, he confided to Miss MacLeod, would not be the instrument to harmonize East and West.

During his trip through Eastern Europe, from Paris to Constantinople, he smelt war. He felt the stench of it rising on all sides. "Europe," he remarked, "is a vast military camp."

But the tragedy of the West had not been altogether unperceived by him even during his first visit. As early as 1895 he said to Sister Christine: "Europe is on the edge of a volcano. If the fire is not extinguished by a flood of spirituality, it will erupt."

One cannot but be amazed at the Swami's prophetic intuition as expressed through the following remarks made to Christine in 1896: "The next upheaval will come from Russia or China. I cannot see clearly which, but it will be either the one or the other." He further said: "The world is in the third epoch, under the domination of the vaiśya. The fourth epoch will be under that of the śudra."[38]

TOWARDS THE END

Swami Vivekananda disembarked in Bombay and immediately entrained for Calcutta, arriving at the Belur Math late in the evening of December 9, 1900. The Swami had not informed anybody of his return. The gate of the monastery was locked for the night. He heard the dinner bell, and in his eagerness to join the monks at their meal, scaled the gate. There was great rejoicing over his home-coming.

At the Math Swami Vivekananda was told about the passing away of his beloved disciple Mr. Sevier at Mayavati in the Himālayas. This was the sad news of which he had had a presentiment in Egypt. He was greatly distressed, and on December 11 wrote to Miss MacLeod: "Thus two great Englishmen[39] gave up their lives for us—us, the Hindus. This is martyrdom, if anything is." Again he wrote to her on December 26: "He was cremated on the bank of the river that flows by his āśrama, à la Hindu, covered with garlands, the brāhmins carrying the body and the boys chanting the Vedas. The cause has already two martyrs. It makes me love dear England and its heroic breed. The Mother is watering the plant of future India with the best blood of England. Glory unto Her!"

The Swami stayed at the Math for eighteen days and left for Mayavati to see Mrs. Sevier. The distance from the railroad station to the monastery at Mayavati was sixty-five miles. The Swami did not give the inmates sufficient time to arrange for his comfortable transportation. He left the railroad station in a hurry in the company of Shivananda and Sadananda. The winter of that year was particularly severe in the Himālayas; there was a heavy snowfall on the way, and in his present state of health he could hardly walk. He reached the monastery, however, on January 3, 1901.

The meeting with Mrs. Sevier stirred his emotions. He was delighted, how-

[38] The vaiśya, or the merchant, and the śudra, or the worker, represent the third and fourth castes in Hindu society. Swami Vivekananda said that the four castes, by turn, governed human society. The brāhmin dominated the thought-current of the world during the glorious days of the ancient Hindu civilization. Then came the rule of the kshattriya, the military, as manifested through the supremacy of Europe from the time of the Roman Empire to the middle of the seventeenth century. Next followed the rule of the vaiśya, marked by the rise of America. The Swami prophesied the coming supremacy of the śudra class. After the completion of the cycle, he said, the spiritual culture would again assert itself and influence human civilization through the power of the brāhmin. Swami Vivekananda often spoke of the future greatness of India as surpassing all her glories of the past.

[39] The other was Mr. Goodwin.

ever, to see the magnificent view of the eternal snow and also the progress of
the work. Because of the heavy winter, he was forced to stay indoors most
of the time. It was a glorious occasion for the members of the āśrama. The
Swami's conversation was inspiring. He spoke of the devotion of his Western
disciples to his cause, and in this connexion particularly mentioned the name
of Mr. Sevier. He also emphasized the necessity of loyalty to the work undertaken, loyalty to the leader, and loyalty to the organization. But the leader,
the Swami said, must command respect and obedience by his character. While
at Mayavati, in spite of a suffocating attack of asthma, he was busy with his
huge correspondence and wrote three articles for the magazine Prabuddha
Bhārata. The least physical effort exhausted him. One day he exclaimed, "My
body is done for!"

The Advaita Āśrama at Mayavati had been founded, as may be remembered,
with a view to enabling its members to develop their spiritual life through the
practice of the non-dualistic discipline. All forms of ritual and worship were
strictly excluded. But some of the members, accustomed to rituals, had set apart
a room as the shrine, where a picture of Śri Ramakrishna was installed and
worshipped daily. One morning the Swami chanced to enter this room while
the worship was going on. He said nothing at that time, but in the evening
severely reprimanded the inmates for violating the rules of the monastery. As
he did not want to hurt their feelings too much, he did not ask them to discon-
tinue the worship, but it was stopped by the members themselves.

One of them, however, whose heart was set on dualistic worship, asked the
advice of the Holy Mother. She wrote: "Śri Ramakrishna was all Advaita and
preached Advaita. Why should you not follow Advaita? All his disciples are
Advaitins."

After his return to the Belur Math, the Swami said in the course of a conversation: "I thought of having one centre at least from which the external
worship of Śri Ramakrishna would be excluded. But I found that the Old Man
had already established himself even there. Well! Well!"

The above incident should not indicate any lack of respect in Swami Vivekananda for Śri Ramakrishna or dualistic worship. During the last few years of
his life he showed a passionate love for the Master. Following his return to
the Belur Math he arranged, as will be seen presently, the birthday festival
of Śri Ramakrishna and the worship of the Divine Mother, according to traditional rituals.

The Swami's real nature was that of a lover of God, though he appeared
outwardly as a philosopher. But in all his teachings, both in India and abroad,
he had emphasized the non-dualistic philosophy. For Ultimate Reality, in the
Hindu spiritual tradition, is non-dual. Dualism is a stage on the way to non-
dualism. Through non-dualism alone, in the opinion of the Swami, can the
different dualistic concepts of the Personal God be harmonized. Without the
foundation of the non-dualistic Absolute, dualism breeds fanaticism, exclusive-
ness, and dangerous emotionalism. He saw both in India and abroad a caricature
of dualism in the worship conducted in the temples, churches, and other places
of worship.

In India the Swami found that non-dualism had degenerated into mere dry intellectual speculation. And so he wanted to restore non-dualism to its pristine purity. With that end in view he had established the Advaita Āsrama at Maya-vati, overlooking the gorgeous eternal snow of the Himālayas, where the mind naturally soars to the contemplation of the Infinite, and there he had banned all vestiges of dualistic worship. In the future, the Swami believed, all religions would receive a new orientation from the non-dualistic doctrine and spread goodwill among men.

On his way to Mayavati Swami Vivekananda had heard the melancholy news of the passing away of the Mahārājā of Khetri, his faithful disciple, who had borne the financial burden of his first trip to America. The Mahārājā had undertaken the repairing of a high tower of the Emperor Akbar's tomb near Agra, and one day, while inspecting the work, had missed his footing, fallen several hundred feet, and died. "Thus," wrote the Swami to Mary Hale, "we sometimes come to grief on account of our zeal for antiquity. Take care, Mary, don't be too zealous about your piece of Indian antiquity."[40] "So you see," the Swami wrote to Mary again, "things are gloomy with me just now and my own health is wretched. Yet I am sure to bob up soon and am waiting for the next turn."

The Swami left Mayavati on January 18, and travelled four days on slippery slopes, partly through snow, before reaching the railroad station. He arrived at the Belur Math on January 24.

Swami Vivekananda had been in this monastery for seven weeks when press-ing invitations for a lecture trip began to pour in from East Bengal. His mother, furthermore, had expressed an earnest desire to visit the holy places situated in that part of India. On January 26 he wrote to Mrs. Ole Bull: "I am going to take my mother on pilgrimage. . . . This is the one great wish of a Hindu widow. I have brought only misery to my people all my life. I am trying to fulfil this one wish of hers."

On March 18, in the company of a large party of his sannyāsin disciples, the Swami left for Dacca, the chief city of East Bengal, and arrived the next day. He was in poor health, suffering from both asthma and diabetes. During an asthmatic attack, when the pain was acute, he said half dreamily: "What does it matter! I have given them enough for fifteen hundred years." But he had hardly any rest. People besieged him day and night for instruction. In Dacca he delivered two public lectures and also visited the house of Nag Mahashay, where he was entertained by the saint's wife.

Next he proceeded to Chandranāth, a holy place near Chittagong, and to sacred Kāmākhyā in Assam. While in Assam he spent several days at Shillong in order to recover his health, and there met Sir Henry Cotton, the chief Government official and a friend of the Indians in their national aspiration. The two exchanged many ideas, and at Sir Henry's request the Government physician looked after the Swami's health.

Vivekananda returned to the Belur Monastery in the second week of May. Concerning the impressions of his trip, he said that a certain part of Assam was endowed with incomparable natural beauty. The people were more sturdy,

---

[40] Referring to himself.

active, and resolute than those of West Bengal. But in religious views they were rather conservative and even fanatical. He had found that some of the gullible people believed in pseudo-Incarnations, several of whom were living at that time in Dacca itself. The Swami had exhorted the people to cultivate manliness and the faculty of reasoning. To a sentimental young man of Dacca he had said: "My boy, take my advice; develop your muscles and brain by eating good food and by healthy exercise, and then you will be able to think for yourself. Without nourishing food your brain seems to have weakened a little." On another occasion, in a public meeting, he had declared, addressing the youths of Bengal, who had very little physical stamina, "You will be nearer to God through football than through the Bhagavad Gita."

The brother disciples and his own disciples were much concerned about the Swami's health, which was going from bad to worse. The damp climate of Bengal did not suit him at all; it aggravated his asthma, and further, he was very, very tired. He was earnestly requested to lead a quiet life, and to satisfy his friends the Swami lived in the monastery for about seven months in comparative retirement. They tried to entertain him with light talk. But he could not be dissuaded from giving instruction to his disciples whenever the occasion arose.

He loved his room on the second storey, in the southeast corner of the monastery building, to which he joyfully returned from his trips to the West or other parts of India. This large room with four windows and three doors served as both study and bedroom. In the corner to the right of the entrance door stood a mirror about five feet high, and near this, a rack with his ochre clothes. In the middle of the room was an iron bedstead with a spring mattress, which had been given to him by one of his Western disciples. But he seldom used it; for he preferred to sleep on a small couch placed by its side. A writing-table with letters, manuscripts, pen, ink, paper, and blotting-pad, a call-bell, some flowers in a metal vase, a photograph of the Master, a deer-skin which he used at the time of meditation, and a small table with a tea-set completed the furnishings.

Here he wrote, gave instruction to his disciples and brother monks, received friends, communed with God in meditation, and sometimes ate his meals. And it was in this room that he ultimately entered into the final ecstasy from which he never returned to ordinary consciousness. The room has been preserved as it was while the Swami was in his physical body, everything in it being kept as on the last day of his life, the calendar on the wall reading July 4, 1902.

On December 19, 1900, he wrote to an American disciple: "Verily I am a bird of passage. Gay and busy Paris, grim old Constantinople, sparkling little Athens, and pyramidal Cairo are left behind, and here I am writing in my room on the Ganges, in the Math. It is so quiet and still! The broad river is dancing in the bright sunshine, only now and then an occasional cargo boat breaking the silence with the splashing of the waves. It is the cold season here, but the middle of the day is warm and bright every day. It is like the winter of southern California. Everything is green and gold, and the grass is like velvet, yet the air is cold and crisp and delightful."

After the Swami's return from East Bengal he lived a relaxed life in the monastery, surrounded by his pet animals: the dog Bāghā, the she-goat Hansi, an antelope, a stork, several cows and sheep and ducks and geese, and a kid called Mātru who was adorned with a collar of little bells, and with whom the Swami ran and played like a child. The animals adored him; Mātru, the little kid, who had been—so he pretended—a relation of his in a previous existence, slept in his room. When it died he grieved like a child and said to a disciple: "How strange! Whomsoever I love dies early." Before milking Hansi for his tea, he always asked her permission. Bāghā, who took part in the Hindu ceremonies, went to bathe in the Ganges with the devotees on sacred occasions, as for instance when the gongs and conchs announced the end of an eclipse. He was, in a sense, the leader of the group of animals at the Math. After his death he was given a burial in the grounds of the monastery.

Referring to his pet animals he wrote to an American disciple on September 7, 1901: "The rains have come down in right earnest, and it is a deluge—pouring, pouring, pouring, night and day. The river is rising, flooding the banks; the ponds and tanks have overflowed. I have just now returned from lending a hand in cutting a deep drain to take off the water from the Math grounds. The rainwater stands at places some feet deep. My huge stork is full of glee and so are the ducks and geese. My tame antelope fled from the Math and gave us some days of anxiety in finding him out. One of my ducks unfortunately died yesterday. She had been gasping for breath more than a week. One of my waggish old monks says, 'Sir, it is no use living in the Kaliyuga, when ducks catch cold from damp and rain, and frogs sneeze!' One of the geese had her plumes falling off. Knowing no other method of treatment, I left her some minutes in a tub of water mixed with mild carbolic, so that it might either kill or heal—and she is all right now."

Thus Swami Vivekananda tried to lead a carefree life at the monastery, sometimes going about the grounds clad in his loin-cloth, sometimes supervising the cooking arrangements and himself preparing some delicacies for the inmates, and sometimes joining his disciples and brother monks in the singing of devotional music. At other times he imparted spiritual instruction to the visitors, or engaged in deep thought whenever his inner spirit was stirred up, occupied himself with serious study in his room, or explained to the members of the Math the intricate passages of the scriptures and unfolded to them his scheme of future work.

Though his body was wearing away day by day, his mind was luminous. At times his eyes assumed a far-away look, showing how tired he was of the world. One day he said, "For one thing we may be grateful: this life is not eternal."

The illness did not show any sign of abatement, but that did not dampen his spirit to work. When urged to rest, he said to a disciple: "My son, there is no rest for me. That which Śri Ramakrishna called 'Kāli' took possession of my body and soul three or four days before his passing away. That makes me work and work and never lets me keep still or look to my personal comfort." Then he told the disciple how the Master, before his passing away, had transmitted his spiritual power to him.[41]

During the later part of 1901 the Swami observed all the religious festivals

41 See p. 34.

at the Math. The Divine Mother was worshipped in strict orthodox fashion during the Durgā-pujā, Lakshmi-pujā, and Kāli-pujā. On the occasion of the Durgā-
pujā the poor were given a sumptuous feast. Thus the Swami demonstrated
the efficacy of religious rituals in the development of the spiritual life. In
February 1902 the birth anniversary of Śri Ramakrishna was celebrated at the
Belur Math, and over thirty thousand devotees gathered for the occasion. But
the Swami was feverish. He was confined to his room by the swelling of his
legs. From the windows he watched the dancing and the music of the devotees.

To the disciple who was attending him the Swami said: "He who has realized
the Ātman becomes a storehouse of great power. From him as the centre a
spiritual force emanates, working within a certain radius; people who come
within this circle become inspired with his ideas and are overwhelmed by them.
Thus without much religious striving they derive benefit from the spiritual
experience of an illumined person. This is called grace."

"Blessed are those," the Swami continued, "who have seen Śri Ramakrishna.
All of you, too, will get his vision. When you have come here, you are very
near to him. Nobody has been able to understand him who came on earth as
Śri Ramakrishna. Even his own nearest devotees have no real clue to it. Only
some have a little inkling of it. All will understand in time."

It is said that the spot immediately beneath a lamp is dark. And so it was
that the orthodox people of the neighbouring villages hardly understood the
ideas and ideals of the Belur Math. The monks there did not in all respects lead
the life of orthodox sannyāsins. Devotees from abroad frequented the monastery. In matters of food and dress the inmates were liberal. Thus they became
the butt of criticism. The villagers invented scandals about them and the passengers on the boats passing along the Ganges would point out the monastery
with an accusing finger.

When the Swami heard all this he said: "That is good. It is a law of nature.
That is the way with all founders of religion. Without persecution superior ideas
cannot penetrate into the heart of society."

But the criticism of the neighbours in time gave place to pride in having in
their midst so many saintly souls.

Many distinguished Indians used to visit the Swami at this time. With some
of them he discussed the idea of founding a Vedic Institution for the promotion
of the ancient Āryan culture and the knowledge of Sanskrit. This was one of
the Swami's favourite thoughts, on which he dwelt even on the last day of his
life on earth.

Towards the end of 1901 two learned Buddhists from Japan came to the Belur
Math to induce the Swami to attend a Congress of Religions that was being contemplated in Japan at that time. One of them was the famous artist and art critic
Okakura, and the other Oda, the abbot of a Buddhist monastery. The Swami
became particularly fond of Okakura and said, "We are two brothers who meet
again, having come from the ends of the earth." Though pressed by the visitors,
he could not accept the invitation to go to Japan, partly because of his failing
health and partly because he was sceptical that the Japanese would appreciate
the monastic ideal of the Non-dualistic Vedānta. In a letter to a Western lady
written in June 1902, the Swami made the following interesting observation

about the connexion between the monastic ideal and fidelity in married life:

In my opinion, a race must first cultivate a great respect for motherhood, through the sanctification and inviolability of marriage, before it can attain to the ideal of perfect chastity. The Roman Catholics and the Hindus, holding marriage sacred and inviolate, have produced great chaste men and women of immense power. To the Arab, marriage is a contract or a forceful possession, to be dissolved at will, and we do not find there the development of the idea of the virgin or the brahmachārin. Modern Buddhism—having fallen among races who had not yet come up to the evolution of marriage—has made a travesty of monasticism. So until there is developed in Japan a great and sacred ideal about marriage (apart from mutual attraction and love), I do not see how there can be great monks and nuns. As you have come to see that the glory of life is chastity, so my eyes also have been opened to the necessity of this great sanctification for the vast majority, in order that a few lifelong chaste powers may be produced.

The Swami used to say that absolute loyalty and devotion between husbands and wives for three successive generations find their expression in the birth of an ideal monk.

Okakura earnestly requested the Swami to accompany him on a visit to Bodh-Gayā, where Buddha had attained illumination. Taking advantage of several weeks' respite from his ailment, the Swami accepted the invitation. He also desired to see Benares. The trip lasted through January and February 1902, and was a fitting end to all his wanderings. He arrived at Bodh-Gayā on the morning of his last birthday and was received with genuine courtesy and hospitality by the orthodox Hindu monk in charge of the temple. This and the similar respect and affection shown by the priests in Benares proved the extent of his influence over men's hearts. It may be remembered that Bodh-Gayā had been the first of the holy places he had visited during Śri Ramakrishna's lifetime. And some years later, when he was still an unknown monk, he had said farewell to Benares with the words: "Till that day when I fall on society like a thunderbolt I shall visit this place no more."

In Benares the Swami was offered a sum of money by a Mahārājā to establish a monastery there. He accepted the offer and, on his return to Calcutta, sent Swami Shivananda to organize the work. Even before Swami Vivekananda's visit to Benares, several young men, under the Swami's inspiration, had started a small organization for the purpose of providing destitute pilgrims with food, shelter, and medical aid. Delighted with their unselfish spirit, the Swami said to them: "You have the true spirit, my boys, and you will always have my love and blessings! Go on bravely; never mind your poverty. Money will come. A great thing will grow out of it, surpassing your fondest hopes." The Swami wrote the appeal which was published with the first report of the "Ramakrishna Home of Service," as the institution came to be called. In later years it became the premier institution of its kind started by the Ramakrishna Mission.

The Swami returned from Benares. But hardly had he arrived at Belur when his illness showed signs of aggravation in the damp air of Bengal. During the last year and a half of his life he was, off and on, under the strict supervision of his physicians. Diabetes took the form of dropsy. His feet swelled and certain parts of his body became hypersensitive. He could hardly close his eyes in sleep.

A native physician made him follow a very strict regime: he had to avoid water and salt. For twenty-one days he did not allow a drop of water to pass through his throat. To a disciple he said: "The body is only a tool of the mind. What the mind dictates the body will have to obey. Now I do not even think of water. I do not miss it at all. . . . I see I can do anything."

Though his body was subjected to a devitalizing illness, his mind retained its usual vigour. During this period he was seen reading the newly published *Encyclopaedia Britannica*. One of his householder disciples remarked that it was difficult to master these twenty-five volumes in one life. But the Swami had already finished ten volumes and was busy reading the eleventh. He told the disciple to ask him any question from the ten volumes he had read, and to the latter's utter amazement the Swami not only displayed his knowledge of many technical subjects but even quoted the language of the book here and there. He explained to the disciple that there was nothing miraculous about it. A man who observed strict chastity in thought and action, he declared, could develop the retentive power of the mind and reproduce exactly what he had heard or read but once, even years before.

The regeneration of India was the ever recurring theme of the Swami's thought. Two of the projects dear to his heart were the establishment of a Vedic College and a convent for women. The latter was to be started on the bank of the Ganges under the direction of the Holy Mother and was to be completely separated from the Belur Monastery. The teachers trained in the convent were to take charge of the education of Indian women along national lines.

But the Swami's heart always went out in sympathy for the poor and neglected masses. During the later part of 1901 a number of Sonthāl labourers were engaged in digging the grounds about the monastery. They were poor and outside the pale of society. The Swami felt an especial joy in talking to them, and listened to the accounts of their misery with great compassion. One day he arranged a feast for them and served them with delicacies that they had never before tasted. Then, when the meal was finished, the Swami said to them: "You are Nārāyanas. Today I have entertained the Lord Himself by feeding you."

He said to a disciple: "I actually saw God in them. How guileless they are!"

Afterwards he said, addressing the inmates of the Belur Math:

"See how simple-hearted these poor, illiterate people are! Will you be able to relieve their miseries to some extent at least? Otherwise of what use is our wearing the ochre robe of the sannyāsin? To be able to sacrifice everything for the good of others is real monasticism. Sometimes I think within myself: 'What is the good of building monasteries and so forth? Why not sell them and distribute the money among the poor, indigent Nārāyanas? What homes should we care for, we who have made the tree our shelter? Alas! How can we have the heart to put a morsel into our mouths, when our countrymen have not enough wherewith to feed or clothe themselves? . . . Mother, shall there be no redress for them?' One of the purposes of my going out to preach religion to the West, as you know, was to see if I could find any means of providing for the people of my country. Seeing their poverty and distress, I think sometimes: 'Let us throw away all the paraphernalia of worship—blowing the conch and ringing the bell and waving the lights before the image. . . . Let us throw away all pride of learning and study of the scriptures and all spiritual disciplines for the attainment of personal liberation. Let us go from village to village, devoting ourselves to the service of the poor. Let us, through the force of our character and spirituality and our austere living, convince the rich about their duties to the masses, and get money and the means wherewith to serve the poor and the distressed. . . . Alas! Nobody in our country thinks for the low, the poor, the miserable! Those who are the backbone of the nation, whose labour produces food, those whose one day's absence from work raises a cry of general distress in the city—where is the man in our country who sympathizes with them, who shares in their joys and sorrows? Look how, for want of sympathy on the part of the Hindus, thousands of pariahs are becoming Christians in the Madras Presidency! Don't think that it is merely the pinch of hunger that drives them to embrace Christianity. It is simply because they do not get your sympathy. You are continually telling them: 'Don't touch me,' 'Don't touch this or that!' Is there any fellow-feeling or sense of dharma left in the country? There is only 'Don't-touchism' now! Kick out all such degrading usages! How I wish to abolish the barriers of 'Don't-touchism' and go out and bring together one and all, crying: 'Come, all ye that are poor and destitute, fallen and downtrodden! We are one in the name of Ramakrishna!' Unless they are elevated, the Great Mother India will never awake! What are we good for if we cannot provide facilities for their food and clothing? Alas, they are ignorant of the ways of the world and hence fail to eke out a living though labouring hard day and night for it. Gather all your forces together to remove the veil from their eyes. What I see clear as daylight is that the same Brahman, the same Śakti, is in them as in me! Only there is a difference in the degree of manifestation—that is all. Have you ever seen a country in the whole history of the world rise unless there was a uniform circulation of the national blood all over the body? Know for certain that not much can be done with that body one limb of which is paralysed, even though the other limbs are healthy."

One of the lay disciples pointed out the difficulty of establishing unity and harmony among the diverse sects in India. Vivekananda replied with irritation:

"Don't come here any more if you think any task too difficult. Through the grace of the Lord, everything becomes easy of achievement. Your duty is to serve the poor and the distressed without distinction of caste and creed. What business have you to consider the fruits of your action? Your duty is to go on working, and everything will set itself right in time, and work by itself. My method of work is to construct, and not to destroy that which is already existing. . . . You are all intelligent boys and profess to be my disciples—tell me what you have done. Couldn't you give away one life for the sake of others? Let the reading of Vedānta and the practice of meditation and the like be left for the next life! Let this body go in the service of others—and then I shall know you have not come to me in vain!"

A little later he said: "After so much tapasyā, austerity, I have known that the highest truth is this: 'He is present in all beings. These are all the manifested forms of Him. There is no other God to seek for! He alone is worshipping God, who serves all beings.' "

In this exhortation is found Vivekananda's message in all its vividness. These words are addressed to India and the Western world alike. The West, too, has its pariahs. He who exploits another man, near or distant, offends God and will pay for it sooner or later. All men are sons of the same God, all bear within them the same God. He who wishes to serve God must serve man—and in the first instance, man in the humblest, poorest, most degraded form. Only by breaking down the barriers between man and man can one usher in the kingdom of heaven on earth.

There were moments when Vivekananda felt gloomy. His body was wasting away, and only a few young men came forward to help him in his work. He wanted more of them who, fired with indomitable faith in God and in them-selves, would renounce everything for the welfare of others. He used to say that with a dozen such people he could divert into a new channel the whole thought-current of the country. Disregarding his physical suffering, he constantly inspired his disciples to cultivate this new faith.

Thus we see him, one day, seated on a canvas cot under the mango tree in the courtyard of the monastery. Sannyāsins and brahmachārins about him were busy doing their daily duties. One was sweeping the courtyard with a big broom. Swami Premananda, after his bath, was climbing the steps to the shrine. Sud-denly Swami Vivekananda's eyes became radiant. Shaking with emotion, he said to a disciple:

"Where will you go to seek Brahman? He is immanent in all beings. Here, here is the visible Brahman! Shame on those who, neglecting the visible Brahman, set their minds on other things! Here is the visible Brahman before you as tangible as a fruit in one's hand! Can't you see? Here—here—here is Brahman!"

These words struck those around him with a kind of electric shock. For a quarter of an hour they remained glued to the spot, as if petrified. The broom in the hand of the sweeper stopped. Premananda fell into a trance. Everyone experienced an indescribable peace. At last the Swami said to Premananda, "Now go to worship."

The brother disciples tried to restrain the Swami's activities, especially instruc-tion to visitors and seekers. But he was unyielding. "Look here!" he said to them one day. "What good is this body? Let it go in helping others. Did not the Master preach until the very end? And shall I not do the same? I do not care a straw if the body goes. You cannot imagine how happy I am when I find earnest seekers after truth to talk to. In the work of waking up Ātman in my fellow men I shall gladly die again and again!"

Till the very end the Swami remained the great leader of the monastery, guiding with a firm hand the details of its daily life, in spite of his own suffering. He insisted upon thorough cleanliness and examined the beds to see that they were aired and properly taken care of. He drew up a weekly time-table and saw that it was scrupulously observed. The classes on the Vedas and the Purānas were held daily, he himself conducting them when his health permitted. He discouraged too much ritualism in the chapel. He warned the monks against exaggerated sentimentalism and narrow sectarianism.

But the leader kept a stern watch on the practice of daily meditation on the part of the inmates of the monastery. The bell sounded at fixed hours for meals, study, discussion, and meditation. About three months before his death he made it a rule that at four o'clock in the morning a hand-bell should be rung from room to room to awaken the monks. Within half an hour all should be gathered in the chapel to meditate. But he was always before them. He got up at three and went to the chapel, where he sat facing the north, meditating motionless for more than two hours. No one was allowed to leave his seat before the Swami set the example. As he got up, he chanted softly, "Śiva! Śiva!" Bowing to the image of Śri Ramakrishna, he would go downstairs and pace the courtyard, singing a song about the Divine Mother or Śiva. Naturally his presence in the chapel created an intense spiritual atmosphere. Swami Brahmananda said: "Ah! One at once becomes absorbed if one sits for meditation in company with Naren! I do not feel this when I sit alone."

Once, after an absence of several days on account of illness, he entered the chapel and found only two monks there. He became annoyed; in order to discipline the absentees he forbade them to eat their meals at the monastery. They had to go out and beg their food. He did not spare anyone, even a beloved brother disciple for whom he cherished the highest respect and who happened to be absent from the chapel that morning.

Another day, he found a brother disciple, Swami Shivananda, in bed at the hour of meditation. He said to the latter: "Brother! I know you do not need meditation. You have already realized the highest goal through the grace of Śri Ramakrishna. But you should daily meditate with the youngsters in order to set an example to them."

From that day on, Shivananda, whether ill or well, always communed with God during the early hours of the morning. In his old age, when it became physically impossible for him to go to the chapel, he used to sit on his bed for meditation.

But the Swami, preoccupied as he was with the training of his Indian disciples, never forgot his Western ones. Their welfare, too, was always in his thought and prayer.

To Miss MacLeod he wrote on June 14, 1901:

Well, Joe, keep health and spirits up. . . . *Gloire et honneur* await you—and mukti. The natural ambition of woman is, through marriage, to climb up leaning upon a man; but those days are gone. You shall be great without the help of any man, just as you are, plain, dear Joe—our Joe, everlasting Joe. . . .

We have seen enough of this life not to care for any of its bubbles, have we not, Joe? For months I have been practising to drive away all sentiments; therefore I stop here, and good-bye just now. It was ordained by Mother that we should work together; it has been already for the good of many; it shall be for the good of many more. So let it be. It is useless planning useless high flights; Mother will find her own way . . . rest assured.

To Mary Hale, on August 27, 1901, he wrote with his usual wit:

I would that my health were what you expected—at least to be able to write you a long letter. It is getting worse, in fact, every day—and so many complications and botherations without that, I have ceased to notice it at all.

I wish you all joy in your lovely *Suisse* chalet—splendid health, good appetite, and a light study of Swiss or other antiquities just to liven things up a bit. I am so glad that you are breathing the free air of the mountains, but sorry that Sam is not in the best of health. Well, there is no anxiety about it; he has naturally such a fine physique.

"Woman's moods and man's luck—the gods themselves do not know, not to speak of men." My instincts may be very feminine—but what I am exercised with just this moment is that you get a little bit of manliness about you. Oh! Mary, your brain, health, beauty, everything, is going to waste just for the lack of that one essential—assertion of individuality. Your haughtiness, spirit, etc. are all nonsense—only mockery. You are at best a boarding-school girl—no backbone! no backbone!

Alas! this life-long leading-string business! This is very harsh, very brutal—but I can't help it. I love you, Mary—sincerely, genuinely. I can't cheat you with namby-pamby sugar candies. Nor do they ever come to me.

Then again, I am a dying man; I have no time to fool in. Wake up, girl! I expect now from you letters of the right slashing order. Give it right straight—I need a good deal of rousing. . . .

I am in a sense a retired man. I don't keep much note of what is going on about the Movement. Then the Movement is getting bigger and it is impossible for one man to know all about it minutely. I now do nothing—except try to eat and sleep and nurse my body the rest of the time.

Good-bye, dear Mary. Hope we shall meet again somewhere in this life—but meeting or no meeting, I remain ever your loving brother, VIVEKANANDA.

To his beloved disciple Nivedita he wrote on February 12, 1902: "May all powers come unto you! May Mother Herself be your hands and mind! It is immense power—irresistible—that I pray for you, and, if possible, along with it infinite peace. . . .

"If there was any truth in Śri Ramakrishna, may He take you into His leading, even as He did me, nay, a thousand times more!"

And again, to Miss MacLeod: "I can't, even in imagination, pay the immense debt of gratitude I owe you. Wherever you are you never forget my welfare; and there, you are the only one that bears all my burdens, all my brutal outbursts. . . ."

MAHĀSAMĀDHI

The sun, enveloped in a golden radiance, was fast descending to the horizon. The last two months of the Swami's life on earth had been full of events foreshadowing the approaching end. Yet few had thought the end so near.

Soon after his return from Benares the Swami greatly desired to see his sannyāsin disciples and he wrote to them to come to the Belur Math, even if only for a short time. "Many of his disciples from distant parts of the world," writes Sister Nivedita, "gathered round the Swami. Ill as he looked, there was none probably who suspected how near the end had come. Yet visits were paid and farewells exchanged that it had needed voyages half round the world to make."

More and more the Swami was seen to free himself from all responsibilities, leaving the work to other hands. "How often," he said, "does a man ruin his disciples by remaining always with them! When men are once trained, it is essential that their leader leave them, for without his absence they cannot develop themselves." "Plants," he had said some time before, "always remain small under a big tree." Yet the near and dear ones thought that he would certainly live three or four years more.

He refused to express any opinion on the questions of the day. "I can no more enter into outside affairs," he said; "I am already on the way." On another occasion he said: "You may be right; but I cannot enter any more into these matters. I am going down into death." News of the world met with but a far-away rejoinder from him.

On May 15, 1902, he wrote to Miss MacLeod, perhaps for the last time: "I am somewhat better, but of course far from what I expected. A great idea of quiet has come upon me. I am going to retire for good—no more work for me. If possible, I will revert to my old days of begging. All blessings attend you, Joe; you have been a good angel to me."

But it was difficult for him to give up what had been dearer to him than his life: the work. On the last Sunday before the end he said to one of his disciples: "You know the work is always my weak point. When I think that might come to an end, I am all undone." He could easily withdraw from weakness and attachment, but the work still retained its power to move him.

Śri Ramakrishna and the Divine Mother preoccupied his mind. He acted as if he were the child of the Mother or the boy playing at the feet of Śri Rama-krishna at Dakshineswar. He said, "A great tapasyā and meditation has come upon me, and I am making ready for death."

His disciples and spiritual brothers were worried to see his contemplative mood. They remembered the words of Śri Ramakrishna that Naren, after his mission was completed, would merge for ever into samādhi, and that he would refuse to live in his physical body if he realized who he was. A brother monk asked him one day, quite casually, "Do you know yet who you are?" The unexpected reply, "Yes, I now know!" awed into silence everyone present. No further question was asked. All remembered the story of the great nirvikalpa samādhi of Naren's youth, and how, when it was over, Śri Ramakrishna had said: "Now the Mother has shown you everything. But this realization, like the jewel locked in a box, will be hidden away from you and kept in my custody. I will keep the key with me. Only after you have fulfilled your mission on this earth will the box be unlocked, and you will know everything as you have known now."

They also remembered that in the cave of Amarnāth, in the summer of 1898, he had received the grace of Śiva—not to die till he himself should will to do so. He was looking death in the face unafraid as it drew near.

Everything about the Swami in these days was deliberate and significant, yet none could apprehend its true import. People were deceived by his outer cheerfulness. From the beginning of June he appeared to be regaining his health.

One day, about a week before the end, he bade a disciple bring him the Bengali almanac. He was seen several times on subsequent days studying the book intently, as if he was undecided about something he wanted to know. After the passing away, the brother monks and disciples realized that he had been debating about the day when he should throw away the mortal body. Ramakrishna, too, had consulted the almanac before his death.

Three days before the mahāsamādhi, Vivekananda pointed out to Swami Premananda a particular spot on the monastery grounds where he wished his body to be cremated.

On Wednesday the Swami fasted, following the orthodox rule: it was the eleventh day of the moon. Sister Nivedita came to the monastery to ask him some questions about her school; but he was not interested and referred her to some other Swamis. He insisted, however, on serving Nivedita the morning meal. To quote the Sister's words:

Each dish, as it was offered—boiled seeds of the jack-fruit, boiled potatoes, plain rice, and ice-cold milk—formed the subject of playful chat; and finally, to end the meal, he himself poured the water over her hands, and dried them with a towel.

"It is I who should do these things for you, Swamiji! Not you for me!" was the protest naturally offered. But his answer was startling in its solemnity—"Jesus washed the feet of his disciples!"

Something checked the answer, "But that was the last time!" as it rose to the lips, and the words remained unuttered. This was well. For here also, the last time had come.

There was nothing sad or grave about the Swami during these days. Efforts were made not to tire him. Conversations were kept as light as possible, touching only upon the pet animals that surrounded him, his garden experiments, books, and absent friends. But all the while one was conscious of a luminous presence of which the Swami's bodily form seemed only a shadow or symbol. The members of the monastery had never felt so strongly as now, before him, that they stood in the presence of an infinite light; yet none was prepared to see the end so soon, least of all on that Friday, July the Fourth, on which he appeared so much stronger and healthier than he had been for years.

On the supreme day, Friday, he rose very early. Going to the chapel, alone, he shut the windows and bolted the doors, contrary to his habit, and meditated for three hours. Descending the stairs of the shrine, he sang a beautiful song about Kāli:

> Is Kāli, my Mother, really black?
> The Naked One, though black She seems,
> Lights the Lotus of the heart.
> Men call Her black, but yet my mind
> Does not believe that She is so:
> Now She is white, now red, now blue;
> Now She appears as yellow, too.
>
> I hardly know who Mother is,
> Though I have pondered all my life:
> Now Purusha, now Prakriti,
> And now the Void, She seems to be.
> To meditate on all these things
> Confounds poor Kamalākānta's wits.

Then he said, almost in a whisper: "If there were another Vivekananda, then he would have understood what this Vivekananda has done! And yet—how many Vivekanandas shall be born in time!"

He expressed the desire to worship Mother Kāli at the Math the following day, and asked two of his disciples to procure all the necessary articles for the ceremony. Next he asked the disciple Suddhananda to read a passage from the Yajur-Veda with the commentary of a well-known expositor. The Swami said that he did not agree with the commentator and exhorted the disciple to give a new interpretation of the Vedic texts.

He partook of the noon meal with great relish, in company with the members of the Math, though usually, at that time, he ate alone in his room because of his illness. Immediately afterwards, full of life and humour, he gave lessons to the brahmacharins for three hours on Sanskrit grammar. In the afternoon he took a walk for about two miles with Swami Premananda and discussed his plan to start a Vedic College in the monastery.

"What will be the good of studying the Vedas?" Premananda asked.

"It will kill superstition," Swami Vivekananda said.

On his return the Swami inquired very tenderly concerning every member of the monastery. Then he conversed for a long time with his companions on the rise and fall of nations. "India is immortal," he said, "if she persists in her search for God. But if she goes in for politics and social conflict, she will die."

At seven o'clock in the evening the bell rang for worship in the chapel. The Swami went to his room and told the disciple who attended him that none was to come to him until called for. He spent an hour in meditation and telling his beads, then called the disciple and asked him to open all the windows and fan his head. He lay down quietly on his bed and the attendant thought that he was either sleeping or meditating.

At the end of an hour his hands trembled a little and he breathed once very deeply. There was a silence for a minute or two, and again he breathed in the same manner. His eyes became fixed in the centre of his eyebrows, his face assumed a divine expression, and eternal silence fell.

"There was," said a brother disciple of the Swami, "a little blood in his nostrils, about his mouth, and in his eyes." According to the Yoga scriptures, the life-breath of an illumined yogi passes out through the opening on the top of the head, causing the blood to flow in the nostrils and the mouth.

The great ecstasy took place at ten minutes past nine. Swami Vivekananda passed away at the age of thirty-nine years, five months, and twenty-four days, thus fulfilling his own prophecy: "I shall not live to be forty years old."

The brother disciples thought that he might have fallen into samādhi, and chanted the Master's name to bring back his consciousness. But he remained on his back motionless.

Physicians were sent for and the body was thoroughly examined. In the doctor's opinion life was only suspended; artificial respiration was tried. At midnight, however, Swami Vivekananda was pronounced dead, the cause, according to medical science, having been apoplexy or sudden failure of the heart. But the monks were convinced that their leader had voluntarily cast off his body in samādhi, as predicted by Śri Ramakrishna.

In the morning people poured in from all quarters. Nivedita sat by the body and fanned it till it was brought down at 2 p.m. to the porch leading to the courtyard. It was covered with ochre robes and decorated with flowers. Incense was burnt and a religious service was performed with lights, conchshells, and bells. The brother monks and disciples took their final leave and the procession started, moving slowly through the courtyard and across the lawn, till it reached the vilva tree near the spot where the Swami himself had desired his body to be cremated.

The funeral pyre was built and the body was consigned to the flames kindled with sandalwood. Across the Ganges, on the other bank, Ramakrishna had been cremated sixteen years before.

Nivedita began to weep like a child, rolling on the ground. Suddenly the wind blew into her lap a piece of the ochre robe from the pyre, and she received it as a blessing. It was dusk when the flames subsided. The sacred relics were gathered and the pyre was washed with the water of the Ganges. The place is now marked by a temple, the table of the altar standing on the very spot where the Swami's body rested in the flames.

Gloom and desolation fell upon the monastery. The monks prayed in the depths of their hearts: "O Lord! Thy will be done!" But deep beneath their grief all felt that this was not the end. The words of the leader, uttered long before his death, rang in their ears:

"It may be that I shall find it good to get outside my body—to cast it off like a worn-out garment. But I shall not cease to work. I shall inspire men everywhere, until the world shall know that it is one with God."

And: "May I be born again and again, and suffer thousands of miseries, so that I may worship the only God that exists, the only God I believe in, the sum total of all souls."

For centuries to come people everywhere will be inspired by Swami Vivekananda's message: O Man! first realize that you are one with Brahman—aham Brahmāsmi—and then realize that the whole universe is verily the same Brahman—sarvam khalvidam Brahma.

VIVEKANANDA, THE WANDERING MONK

VIVEKANANDA TEMPLE AT THE BELUR MATH

THE BELUR MATH

APPENDIX

APPENDIX[1]

RELIGION

EACH SOUL is potentially divine. The goal is to manifest this divinity within by controlling nature, external and internal. Do this either by work, or worship, or psychic control, or philosophy—by one, or more, or all of these—and be free. This is the whole of religion. Doctrines, or dogmas, or rituals, or books, or temples, or forms, are but secondary details.

Religion is its own end. That religion which is only a means to worldly well-being is not religion, whatever else it may be.

True religion is entirely transcendental. Every being that is in the universe has the potentiality of transcending the senses; even the little worm will one day transcend the senses and reach God. No life will be a failure; there is no such thing as failure in the universe.

He alone can be religious who dares to say, as the mighty Buddha once said under the Bo-tree: "Death is better than a vegetating, ignorant life; it is better to die on the battlefield than to live a life of defeat." This is the basis of religion. When a man takes this stand, he is on the way to finding the truth, he is on the way to God. That determination is the first impulse towards becoming religious.

Man must realize God, feel God, see God, talk to God. That is religion. All the ancient books and scriptures are the writings of persons who came into direct contact with spiritual facts. They say that there is such a thing as realization even in this life, and that it is open to everyone; and religion begins with the opening of this faculty, if I may call it so.

That is religion which makes us realize the Unchangeable One; and that is the religion for everyone. He who realizes transcendental truths, he who realizes the Ātman in his own nature, he who comes face to face with God, sees God in everything, has become a rishi. And there is no religious life for you until you

[1] This appendix contains a number of Swami Vivekananda's important statements on religion and philosophy. They have been selected from two volumes: *Swami Vivekananda on Religion and Philosophy*, published by the Ramakrishna Mission Students' Home, Calcutta, and *Teachings of Swami Vivekananda*, published by the Advaita Āśrama, Mayavati, Himālayas. We wish to express our indebtedness to the publishers.

have become a rishi. Then alone does religion begin for you; now is only the preparation.

No man is born into any religion; he has religion in his own soul.

Now, in my little experience I have collected this knowledge: In spite of all the devilry that religion is blamed with, religion is not at all at fault; no religion ever persecuted men, no religion ever burnt witches, no religion ever did any of these things. What then incited people to do these things? Politics, but never religion. And if such politics takes the name of religion, whose fault is it?

To the Hindu, man is not travelling from error to truth, but from truth to truth—from lower truth to higher truth. To him all religions, from the lowest fetishism to the highest absolutism, mean so many attempts of the human soul to grasp and realize the Infinite, each determined by the conditions of its birth and association; and each of these attempts marks a stage of progress.

Religious quarrels are always over the husks. When purity, when spirituality, goes, leaving the soul dry, then quarrels begin, and not before.

Man has an idea that there can be only one religion, that there can be only one Prophet, that there can be only one Incarnation; but that idea is not true. By studying the lives of all these great Messengers, we find that each was destined to play a part, as it were, and a part only; that the harmony consists in the sum total, and not in one note.

There never was my religion or yours, my national religion or your national religion. There never existed many religions; there is only one Religion. One infinite Religion has existed all through eternity and will ever exist, and this Religion is expressing itself in various countries in different ways.

There is one principle which underlies all the various manifestations of religion and which has already been mapped out for us. Every science must end where it finds a unity, because we cannot go any farther. When a perfect unity is reached, then science has nothing more of principles to tell us. So with religion. The gigantic principle, the scope, the plan, of religion was already discovered ages ago, when man found the last words, as they are called in the Vedas, "I am He"—that there is One in whom this whole universe of matter and mind finds its unity, whom they call God, or Brahman, or Allah, or Jehovah, or by any other name. We cannot go beyond that.

The end of all religions is the realizing of God in the soul. If there is one universal truth in all religions, I place it here, in realizing God. Ideals and methods may differ, but that is the central point. There may be a thousand different radii, but they all converge upon the one centre, and that is the realization of God—something behind this world of the senses, this world of eternal eating and drinking and talking nonsense, this world of false shadows and selfishness.

I accept all the religions that were in the past, and worship them all; I worship God with every one of them, in whatever form they worship Him. I shall go to the mosque of the Mohammedan; I shall enter the Christian church and kneel before the Crucifix; I shall enter the Buddhist temple, where I shall take refuge in Buddha and his Law. I shall go into the forest and sit down in meditation with the Hindu, who is trying to see the Light which enlightens the hearts of everyone. Not only shall I do these things, but I shall keep my heart open for all that may come in the future.

If there is ever to be a Universal Religion, it must be one which will have no location in place or time; which will be infinite as the God it will preach, and whose sun will shine upon the followers of Krishna and Christ, on saints and sinners, alike; which will not be Brāhmanical or Buddhist, Christian or Mohammedan, but the sum total of all these, and still have infinite space for development; which in its catholicity will embrace in its infinite arms, and find a place for, every human being, from the lowest, grovelling savage, not far removed from the brute, to the highest man, towering by the virtues of his head and heart almost above humanity, making society stand in awe of him and doubt his human nature. It will be a religion which will have no place for persecution or intolerance in its polity, which will recognize divinity in every man and woman, and whose whole scope, whose whole force, will be centred in aiding humanity to realize its own true, divine nature.

GOD

THE SUM TOTAL of this whole universe is God Himself. Is God then matter? No, certainly not; for matter is God perceived by the five senses. God perceived through the inner organ is mind; and seen through the Spirit, He is Spirit. He is not matter, but whatever is real in matter is He.

The Universal Intelligence is what we call God. Call It by any other name, it is absolutely certain that in the beginning there was that infinite Cosmic Intelligence.

The highest ideal of every man is called God. Ignorant or wise, saint or sinner, man or woman, educated or uneducated, cultivated or uncultivated—to every human being the highest ideals of beauty, of sublimity, and of power give us the complete conception of the loving and lovable God. These ideals exist, in some shape or other, in every mind naturally; they form part and parcel of all our minds. All the active manifestations of human nature are the struggles of these ideals to become realized in practical life.

The child rebels against law as soon as it is born. Its first utterance is a cry, a protest against the bondage in which it finds itself. This longing for freedom produces the idea of a Being who is absolutely free. The concept of God is a fundamental element in the human constitution. Satchidānanda (Existence-Knowledge-Bliss Absolute) is, in Vedānta, the highest concept of God possible to the mind. It is by Its nature the Essence of Knowledge and the Essence of Bliss.

The religions of the unthinking masses all over the world teach, and have always taught, of a God who is outside the universe, who lives in heaven, who governs from that place, who is the punisher of the bad and the rewarder of the good, and so on. As man advances spiritually, he begins to feel that that God is omnipresent, that He is not a distant God, but clearly the Soul of all souls. And a few individuals, who have developed enough and are pure enough, go still farther and find at last that they and the Father are one.

No man can really see God except through human manifestations. Whenever we try to think of God as He is, in His absolute perfection, we invariably meet with the most miserable failure, because as long as we are men, we cannot conceive Him as anything higher than man. The time will come when we shall transcend our human nature and know Him as He is.

There are two ideas of God in our scriptures: the one, the Personal, and the other, the Impersonal. The idea of the Personal God is that He is the omnipresent Creator, Preserver, and Destroyer of everything, the eternal Father and Mother of the universe, but One who is eternally separate from us and from all souls. Liberation consists in coming near to Him and living in Him. Then there is the other idea, that of the Impersonal, where all these adjectives are taken away as superfluous, as illogical, and there remains an impersonal, omnipresent Being. He cannot be called a knowing being, because knowledge belongs only to the human mind. He cannot be called a thinking being, because thinking is a process of the weak only. He cannot be called a reasoning being, because reasoning too is a sign of weakness. He cannot be called a creating being, because none creates except in bondage. What bondage has He? None works except it be to supply some wants; what wants has He? In the Vedas it is not the word He that is used, but It, for He would make an invidious distinction, as if God were a man.

A generalization ending in the Personal God can never be universal, for to conceive of a Personal God we must say that He is all merciful, all good. But this world is a mixed thing—some good, some bad. And you will always find that the idea of a Personal God has to carry with it the idea of a Personal Devil. That is how we clearly see that the idea of a Personal God is not a true generalization. We have to go beyond, to the Impersonal. In That the universe exists with all its joys and miseries; for whatever exists in it has all come from the Impersonal.

Brahman is One, but is at the same time appearing to us as many on the relative plane. Name and form are at the root of this relativity. For instance, what do you find when you abstract name and form from a jar? Only earth, which is its essence. Similarly, through delusion you are thinking of and seeing a cloth, a monastery, and so on. The phenomenal world depends on this nescience, which obstructs knowledge and has no real existence. One sees variety—such as wife, children, body, mind—only in the world created by nescience, by means of name and form. As soon as this nescience is removed, there takes place the realization of Brahman, which eternally exists.

You are also that undivided Brahman. This very moment you can realize It, if you think yourself truly and absolutely to be so. It is all mere want of direct perception. . . . Being again and again entangled in the intricate maze of delusion and hard hit by sorrows and afflictions, the eye will turn of itself to one's own real nature, the Inner Self. It is owing to the presence of the desire for bliss, in the heart, that man, getting hard shocks one after another, turns his eye inward—to his own Self. A time is sure to come to everyone, without exception, when he will do so; to one it may be in this life, to another, after thousands of incarnations.

Suppose we all go with vessels in our hands to fetch water from a lake. One has a cup, another a jar, another a bucket, and so forth, and we all fill our vessels. The water in each case naturally takes the form of the vessel carried by each of us. So it is with religion. Our minds are like those vessels. God is like the water filling the different vessels. And in each vessel the vision of God comes in the form of the vessel. Yet He is One; He is God in every case.

The Personal God is as much an entity for Himself as we are for ourselves, and no more. God can also be seen as a form, just as we are seen. As men we must have God; as God we need none. This is why Sri Ramakrishna saw the Divine Mother ever present with him, more real than any other thing around him; but in samādhi all disappeared but the Self. The Personal God comes nearer and nearer, until He melts away and there is no more Personal God and no more "I"—all is merged in the Self.

After so much austerity I have understood this as the real truth: God is present in every jiva; there is no other God besides that. He who serves the jiva serves God indeed.

He reveals Himself to the pure heart; the pure and the stainless see God, yea, even in this life. Then all doubt ceases. So the best proof a Hindu sage gives about God is: "I have seen God."

I have been asked many times, "Why do you use that word God?" Because it is the best word for our purpose. You cannot find a better word than that; all the hopes, aspirations, and happiness of humanity have been centred in that word. It is impossible now to change that word. A word like this is first coined by a great saint, who realizes its import and understands its meaning. But as it becomes current in society, ignorant people take up the word, and the result is that it loses its spirit and glory. The word God has been used from time immemorial, and the idea of the Cosmic Intelligence, and all that is great and holy, is associated with it.

Today God is being abandoned by the world because He does not seem to be doing enough for the world. So they say, "Of what good is He?" Shall we look upon God as a mere municipal authority?

He neither punishes nor rewards any. His infinite mercy is open to everyone, at all times, in all places, under all conditions—unfailing, unswerving.

The wind is blowing; those vessels whose sails are unfurled catch it and go forward on their way, but those which have their sails furled do not catch the wind. Is that the fault of the wind? Is it the fault of the Merciful Father, whose wind of mercy is blowing without ceasing, day and night, whose mercy knows no end—is it His fault that some of us are happy and some unhappy?

Be strong and stand up and seek the God of Love. This is the highest strength. What power is higher than the power of purity? Love and purity govern the world. This love of God cannot be reached by the weak; therefore be not weak, either physically, mentally, morally, or spiritually.

The Lord alone is real; everything else is unreal. Everything else should be rejected for the sake of the Lord. Vanity of vanities, all is vanity! Serve the Lord and Him alone.

God is the inexplicable, inexpressible essence of love—to be known, but never defined.

DIVINE INCARNATION

GOD UNDERSTANDS human failings and becomes man to do good to humanity. "Whenever virtue subsides and wickedness prevails I manifest Myself. To establish virtue, to destroy evil, to save the good, I come in every age." "Fools deride Me who have assumed the human form, without knowing My real nature as the Lord of the universe." Such are Śri Krishna's declarations in the Gitā on Incarnation. "When a huge tidal wave comes," says Śri Ramakrishna, "all the little brooks and ditches become full to the brim without any effort or consciousness on their own part; so when an Incarnation comes, a tidal wave of spirituality breaks upon the world, and people feel spirituality in the very air."

It has been said: "No man hath seen God at any time, but through the Son." And that is true. Where shall we see God but in the Son? It is true that you and I, and the poorest of us, the meanest, even, embody that God, even reflect that God. The vibration of light is everywhere, omnipresent. But we have to light the lamp before we can see the light. The omnipresent God of the universe cannot be seen until He is reflected in these giant lamps of the earth—the Prophets, the God-men, the Incarnations.

"Whenever extraordinary spiritual power is manifested by man, know that I am there; it is from Me that the manifestation comes." That leaves the door open for the Hindu to worship the Incarnations of all the religions in the world. The Hindu can worship any sage and any saint from any country whatsoever.

It is absolutely necessary to worship God as man, and blessed are those races which have such God-men to worship. Christians have such a God-man in Christ. That is the natural way to see God; see God in man. All our ideas of God are concentrated there.

The Absolute cannot be worshipped; so we must worship a manifestation, such a one as has our nature. Jesus had our nature; he became the Christ. So can we and so must we. Christ and Buddha are the names of a state to be attained; Jesus and Gautama were the persons to attain it.

Our salutations go to all the past Prophets, whose teachings and lives we have inherited, whatever may have been their race, clime, or creed. Our salutations go to all those God-like men and women who are working at present to help humanity, whatever be their birth, colour, or race. Our salutations go to those who are coming in the future—living Gods—to work unselfishly for our descendants!

THE ĀTMAN, OR SOUL

WHAT IS IT that gives unity to the changing elements of our being? What is it that keeps up the identity of the thing called individuality, moving from moment to moment? What is it by which all our different impressions are pieced together, upon which the perceptions come together, as it were, reside, and form a united whole? This something upon which the mind is painting all these pictures, this something upon which our sensations, carried by the mind, are placed and grouped and formed into a unity, is what is called the Soul of man.

The mind and the body are like two layers in the same substance, moving at different rates of speed. One being slower and the other quicker—relatively speaking—we can distinguish between the two motions. But still something else is necessary. Motion can only be perceived when there is something else which is not moving. Behind this never-ending chain of motion is the Soul, changeless, colourless, pure. All these impressions are merely reflected upon It, as images are thrown upon a screen by a magic lantern without in any way tarnishing it.

The feeling of freedom which possesses us all shows there is something in us besides mind and body. The Soul that reigns within is free and creates the desire for freedom.

The Hindu believes that man is Spirit. Him the sword cannot pierce, Him fire cannot burn, Him water cannot melt, Him the air cannot dry. The Hindu believes that every soul is a circle whose circumference is nowhere, but whose centre is located in the body, and that death means the change of this centre from body to body. The soul is not bound by the conditions of matter. In its very essence it is free, unlimited, holy, pure, and perfect. But somehow or other it finds itself tied down to matter and thinks of itself as matter.

We all hold in India that the Soul is by Its nature pure and perfect, infinite in power, and blessed. According to the dualist, this natural blissfulness of the Soul has become contracted by past bad work, and through the grace of God It is again going to open out and show Its perfection; while according to the non-dualist, even this idea of contraction is a partial mistake; it is the veil of māyā that causes us to think the Soul has lost Its powers; but the powers are there, fully present.

In every man and in every animal, however weak or wicked, great or small, resides the same omnipresent, omniscient Soul. The difference is not in the Soul, but in the degree of manifestation.

Everything in time, space, and causation is bound. The Soul is beyond all time, all space, all causation. That which is bound is nature, not the Soul. Therefore proclaim your freedom and be what you are—ever free, ever blessed.

You are free, free, free! "Oh, blessed am I! Free am I! I am infinite! In my soul I can find no beginning and no end. All is my Self." Say this unceasingly.

Vedānta teaches that Nirvāna can be attained here and now, that we do not have to wait for death to reach it. Nirvāna is the realization of the Self; and after having once known that, if only for an instant, never again can one be deluded by the mirage of personality.

There is no "I" and no "you"; it is all one. It is either all "I" or all "you." This idea of duality, of two, is entirely false, and the whole universe, as we ordinarily know it, is the result of this false knowledge. When discrimination comes, and man finds there are not two, but One, he finds that he himself is this universe.

The seeing of many is the great sin of the world. See all as the Self and love all; let the idea of separateness go.

Man, after his vain search for God outside himself, completes the circle and comes back to the point from which he started—the human soul; and he finds that the God whom he was searching for over hill and dale, whom he was seeking in every brook, in every temple, in churches and heavens, that God whom he was imagining as sitting in heaven and ruling the world, is his own Self. I am He, and He is I. None is God but I, and this little "I" never existed.

Cry for help and you will get it; and at last you will find that the one crying for help has vanished and so has the Helper, and the play is over. Only the Self remains.

THE GURU

THE SOUL can only receive impulses from another soul, and from nothing else. We may study books all our lives, we may become very intellectual; but in the end we shall find that we have not developed at all spiritually. . . . This inadequacy of books to quicken spiritual growth is the reason why, although almost every one of us can speak most wonderfully on spiritual matters, when it comes to action and the living of a spiritual life, we find ourselves awfully deficient. To quicken the spirit, the impulse must come from another soul. The person from whose soul such an impulse comes is called the guru, the teacher; and the person to whose soul the impulse is conveyed is called the śishya, the student.

He is the guru "who has himself crossed the terrible ocean of life, and without any thought of gain to himself helps others also to cross the ocean." This is the guru, and mark that none else can be a guru.

It is a mysterious law of nature that as soon as the field is ready, the seed must come; as soon as the soul wants religion, the transmitter of religious force must come. "The seeking sinner meeteth the seeking Saviour."

There are great dangers in regard to the transmitter, the guru. There are many who, though immersed in ignorance, yet, in the pride of their hearts, fancy they know everything, and not only do not stop there, but offer to take others on their shoulders; and thus, the blind leading the blind, both fall into the ditch. The world is full of these. Everyone wants to be a teacher, every beggar wants to make a gift of a million dollars! Just as these beggars are ridiculous, so are these teachers.

Get the mercy of God and of His greatest children. These are the two chief ways to God. The company of these children of light is very hard to get; five minutes in their company will change a whole life, and if you really want it enough, one will come to you. The presence of those who love God makes a place holy, such is the glory of the children of the Lord. They are He; and when they speak, their words are scriptures. The places where they live are filled with their vibrations, and those going there feel them and tend to become holy also.

FAITH IN ONESELF

THROUGHOUT the history of mankind, if any one motive power has been more potent than others in the lives of great men and women, it is that of faith in themselves. Born with the consciousness that they were to be great, they became great.

Let a man go down as low as possible, there must come a time when out of sheer desperation he will take an upward curve and learn to have faith in himself. But it is better for us that we should know it from the very first. Why should we have all these bitter experiences in order to gain faith in ourselves?

It is generally said that he is an atheist who does not believe in God. Vedānta says that he is an atheist who does not believe in himself. But this is not selfish faith, because Vedānta, again, is the doctrine of Oneness. It means faith in all because you are all.

Do you know how much energy, how many powers, how many forces, are still lurking behind that frame of yours? What scientist has known all that is in man? Millions of years have passed since man came here, and yet but one infinitesimal part of his powers has been manifested. Therefore you must not say that you are weak. How do you know what possibilities lie behind that degradation on the surface? You know but little of that which is within you; for behind you is the ocean of infinite power and blessedness.

Be not afraid of anything. You will do marvellous work. The moment you fear, you are nobody. It is fear that is the great cause of misery in the world. It is fear that is the greatest of superstitions. It is fear that is the cause of our woes. And it is fearlessness that brings heaven in a moment.

If a man, day and night, thinks he is miserable, low, and nothing, nothing he becomes. If you say, "Yea, yea, I am, I am," so shall you be; and if you say, "I am not," think that you are not, and day and night meditate upon the fact that you are nothing, ay, nothing shall you be. That is the great fact which you ought to remember. We are the children of the Almighty; we are sparks of the infinite Divine Fire. How can you be nothing? We are everything, we can do everything—and man must do everything.

Losing faith in oneself means losing faith in God. Do you believe in that infinite, good Providence working in and through you? If you believe that this Omnipresent One is present in every atom, is in everything, through and through, penetrating your body, mind, and soul, how can you lose heart?

Men are taught from childhood that they are weak and that they are sinners. Teach them that they are all glorious children of immortality, even those who are the weakest in manifestation. Let positive, strong, helpful thoughts enter into their brains from their very childhood. Lay yourself open to these thoughts, and not to weakening and paralysing ones. Say to your own minds, "I am He, I am He." Let it ring day and night in your minds like a song, and at the point of death declare, "I am He." That is the truth. The infinite strength of the world is yours.

Those that blame others—and alas! the number of them is increasing every day—are generally miserable, with helpless brains. They have brought themselves to that pass through their own mistakes, and blame others; but this does not alter their position. It does not serve them in any way. This attempt to throw the blame upon others only weakens them the more. Therefore blame none for your faults; stand upon your own feet and take the whole responsibility upon yourselves. Say, "This misery that I am suffering is of my own doing, and that very thing proves that it will have to be undone by me alone." That which I have created I can demolish; that which is created by someone else I shall never be able to destroy. Therefore stand up, be bold, be strong!

All the strength and succour you want is within yourselves. Therefore make your own future. Let the dead past bury its dead. The infinite future is before you, and you must always remember that each word, thought, and deed lays up a store for you, and that as the bad thoughts and bad deeds are ready to spring upon you like tigers, so also there is the inspiring hope that the good thoughts and good deeds are ready, with the power of a hundred thousand angels, to defend you always and for ever.

What makes a man stand up and work? Strength. Strength is goodness, weakness is sin. If there is one word that you find coming out like a bomb from the Upanishads, bursting like a bomb-shell upon masses of ignorance, it is the word *fearlessness*. And the only religion that ought to be taught is the religion of fearlessness. Either in this world or in the world of religion, it is true that fear is the sure cause of degradation and sin. It is fear that brings misery, fear that brings death, fear that breeds evil. And what causes fear? Ignorance of our own nature.

KARMA-YOGA

WHAT IS KARMA-YOGA? It is the knowledge of the secret of work. Instead of being knocked about in this universe and after long delay and thrashing getting to know things as they are, we learn from karma-yoga the secret of work, the method of work, the organizing power of work. A vast mass of energy may be spent in vain if we do not know how to utilize it. Karma-yoga makes a science of work; you learn by it how best to utilize all the activities of this world. Work is inevitable; it must be so. But we should work to the highest purpose.

Work incessantly, but give up all attachment to work. Do not identify yourself with anything. Hold your mind free. All this that you see, the pains and miseries, are but the necessary conditions of this world. Poverty and wealth and happiness are but momentary; they do not belong to our real nature at all. Our nature is far beyond misery and happiness, beyond every object of the senses, beyond the imagination; and yet we must go on working all the time. Misery comes through attachment, not through work. As soon as we identify ourselves with the work we do, we feel miserable; but if we do not identify ourselves with it, we do not feel that misery.

Each wave in the mind that says "I" and "mine" immediately puts a chain round us and makes us slaves; and the more we say "I" and "mine," the more our slavery grows, the more our misery increases. Therefore karma-yoga tells us to enjoy the beauty of all things in the world, but not to identify ourselves with any one of them.

Non-attachment does not mean anything that we may do in relation to our external body; it is all in the mind. If we have no link with the body and with the things of the senses, we are non-attached, wherever and whatever we may be. A man may be on the throne and perfectly non-attached; another man may be in rags and still very much attached. First we have to attain this state of non-attachment, and then to work incessantly. Karma-yoga gives us the method that will help us in giving up all attachment, though it is very hard.

Here are two ways of giving up attachment. The one is for those who do not believe in God or in any outside help. They are left to their own devices; they have simply to work with their own will, with the powers of their mind and discrimination, saying, "I must be non-attached." For those who believe in God there is another way, which is much less difficult. They give up the fruit of work unto the Lord; they work and are never attached to the results. Whatever they see, feel, hear, or do is for Him. Let us not claim any praise or benefit for whatever work we may do. It is the Lord's; give up the fruit unto Him.

Karma-yoga teaches us how to work for work's sake, unattached, without caring who is helped, and it also teaches us why we should work. The karma-yogi works because it is his nature, because he feels it is good for him to do so, and he has no object beyond that. His position in the world is that of a giver, and he never cares to receive anything. He knows that he is giving, and does not ask for anything in return, and therefore he eludes the grasp of misery.

The karma-yogi need not believe in any doctrine whatever. He may even not believe in God, may not ask what his soul is or indulge in any metaphysical speculation. He has his own special method of realizing selflessness, and he has to work it out himself. Every moment of his life must be realization, because he has to solve by mere work, without the help of doctrine or theory, the very same problem to which the jnāni applies his reason, and the bhakta his love.

I have been told many times that a man cannot work if he does not have the passion which we generally feel for work. I also thought that way years ago; but as I am growing older and getting more experience, I find that it is not true. The less passion there is, the better we work. The calmer we are, the better it is for us and the greater is the amount of work we can do. When we let loose our feelings we waste so much energy, shatter our nerves, disturb our minds, and accomplish very little. The energy which ought to have gone into work is spent as mere feeling, which counts for nothing. It is only when the mind is very calm and collected that the whole of its energy is spent in doing good work. And if you read the lives of the great workers whom the world has produced, you will find that they were wonderfully calm men. Nothing could throw them off their balance. That is why the man who becomes angry never does a great amount of work, and the man whom nothing can make angry accomplishes so much. The man who gives way to anger or hatred or any other passion cannot work; he only breaks himself to pieces and does nothing practical. It is the calm, forgiving, equable, well-balanced mind that does the greatest amount of work.

BHAKTI, OR LOVE OF GOD

BHAKTI-YOGA is a real, genuine search after the Lord, a search beginning, continuing, and ending in love. One single moment of the madness of extreme love of God brings us eternal freedom.

"Bhakti is intense love of God." "When a man gets it he loves all, hates none; he becomes satisfied for ever." This love cannot be reduced to any earthly benefit, because so long as worldly desires last, this kind of love does not come.

There is bhakti within you, only a veil of lust-and-wealth covers it, and as soon as that is removed, bhakti will manifest by itself.

One way of attaining bhakti is by repeating the name of God a number of times. Mantras have an effect—the mere repetition of words. . . . To obtain bhakti, seek the company of holy men who have bhakti, and read books like the Gitā and The Imitation of Christ. Always think of the attributes of God.

The daily necessary thoughts can all be associated with God: Eat to Him, drink to Him, sleep to Him, see Him in all. Talk of God to others; this is most beneficial.

Bhakti-yoga does not say, "Give up"; it only says, "Love; love the Highest." And everything low naturally falls away from him the object of whose love is the Highest.

If a man does not get food one day, he is troubled; if his son dies, how agonizing it is to him! The true bhakta feels the same pangs in his heart when he yearns for God. The great quality of bhakti is that it cleanses the mind; and bhakti for the Supreme Lord, firmly established, is alone sufficient to purify the mind.

Bhakti differs from the Western idea of religion in that bhakti admits no element of fear, no Being to be appeased or propitiated. There are even bhaktas who worship God as their own child so that there may remain no feeling even of awe or reverence. There can be no fear in true love; so long as there is the least fear, bhakti cannot even begin. In bhakti there is also no place for begging or bargaining with God. The idea of asking God for anything is sacrilege to a bhakta. He will not pray for health or wealth or even to go to heaven.

"Lord, they build high temples in Thy name; they make gifts in Thy name. I am poor; I have nothing; so I take this body of mine and place it at Thy feet. Do not give me up, O Lord!" Such is the prayer proceeding out of the depths of the bhakta's heart. To him who has experienced it, this eternal sacrifice of the self unto the beloved Lord is higher by far than all wealth and power, than all soaring thoughts of renown and enjoyment.

When the devotee has realized his Ideal, he is no more impelled to ask whether God can be demonstrated or not, whether He is omnipotent and omniscient or not. To him He is only the God of Love. He is the highest ideal of love, and that is sufficient for all his purposes. God, as love, is self-evident; it requires no proof to demonstrate the existence of the beloved to the lover. The magistrate God of other forms of religion may require a good deal of proof to demonstrate, but the bhakta does not and cannot think of such a God at all. To him God exists entirely as love.

The perfected bhakta no more goes to see God in temples and churches; he knows no place where he will not find Him. He finds Him outside the temple as well as in the temple; he finds Him in the wicked man's wickedness as well as in the saint's saintliness, because he has Him already seated in glory in his own heart as the one almighty, inextinguishable Light of Love, which is ever shining and eternally present.

We all have to begin as dualists in the religion of love. God is to us a separate Being, and we feel ourselves to be separate beings also. Love then comes in between, and man begins to approach God; and God also comes nearer and nearer to man. Man takes up all the various relationships of life, such as those of father, mother, son, friend, master, and lover, and projects them on his ideal of love, on his God. To him God exists as all these. And the last point of his progress is reached when he feels that he has become absolutely merged in the object of his worship.

I know one whom the world used to call mad, and this was his answer: "My friends, the whole world is a lunatic asylum: some are mad after worldly love, some after name, some after fame, some after money, some after salvation and going to heaven. In this big lunatic asylum I too am mad; I am mad after God. You are mad; so am I. I think my madness is after all the best."

MEDITATION

THE MEDITATIVE STATE is the highest state of existence. So long as there is desire no real happiness can come. It is only the contemplative, witness-like study of objects that brings to us real enjoyment and happiness. The animal has its happiness in the senses, man in his intellect, and the god in spiritual contemplation. It is only to the soul that has attained to this contemplative state that the world really becomes beautiful. To him who desires nothing, and does not mix himself up with them, the manifold changes of nature are one panorama of beauty and sublimity.

First the practice of meditation has to proceed with some one object before the mind. Once I used to concentrate my mind on a black point. In the end, I could not see the point any more or feel that the point was before me at all; the mind had ceased to exist; no wave or mental state would arise—as if it were all an ocean without any breath of air. In that state I used to experience glimpses of supersensuous truth. So, I think, the practice of meditation even on some trifling external object leads to mental concentration. But it is true that the mind very easily attains calmness when one practises meditation on something on which one's mind is most apt to settle down. This is why we have in India so much worship of gods and goddesses. . . . The fact is, however, that the objects of meditation can never be the same with all men. People have proclaimed and preached to others only those external objects to which they themselves held in order to become perfected in meditation. Oblivious of the fact that these objects are merely aids to the attainment of perfect mental calmness, men have extolled them, later, beyond everything else. They have wholly concerned themselves with the means, remaining comparatively unmindful of the end. The real aim is to make the mind functionless; but this cannot be done unless one first becomes absorbed in some object.

You must keep the mind fixed on one object; meditation should be like an unbroken stream of oil. The ordinary man's mind is scattered on different objects, and at the time of meditation, too, the mind is at first apt to wander. Let any desire whatever arise in the mind; sit calmly and watch what sorts of ideas are coming. By continuing to watch in that way, the mind becomes calm and there are no thought-waves in it. These waves represent the thought-activity of the mind. Those things that you have previously thought about too deeply have transformed themselves into a subconscious current, and therefore they come up in the mind in meditation. The rise of these waves, or thoughts, during meditation is evidence that your mind is tending towards concentration.

Think always that you are the omnipresent Ātman. "I am neither the body nor the mind nor the buddhi (the determinative faculty), neither the gross nor the subtle body"—by this process of elimination immerse your mind in the transcendental Knowledge which is your real nature. Kill the mind by thus plunging it repeatedly in this Knowledge. Then only will you realize the Essence of Intelligence and be established in your real nature. Knower and

known, meditator and object meditated upon, will then become one, and the
cessation of all phenomenal superimpositions will follow. . . . There is no relative or conditional knowledge in this state. When the Ātman is the only knower,
by what means can you possibly know It? The Ātman is knowledge, the Ātman
is intelligence, the Ātman is Satchidānanda.

How has all the knowledge in the world been gained but by the concentration of the powers of the mind? The world is ready to give up its secrets if we
only know how to knock, how to give it the necessary blow. The strength and
force of the blow come through concentration. There is no limit to the power of
the human mind. The more concentrated it is, the more power is brought to
bear on one point; that is the secret.

How are we to know that the mind has become concentrated? The idea
of time will vanish. The more time passes unnoticed, the more concentrated we
are. In common life we see that when we are interested in a book we do not
note the time at all, and when we leave the book we are often surprised to find
how many hours have passed. All time will have the tendency to stand in the
present. So the definition is given: when the past and present become one, the
mind is said to be concentrated.

Concentration is the essence of all knowledge; nothing can be done without
it. Ninety per cent of his thought-force is wasted by the ordinary human being,
and therefore he is constantly committing blunders; the trained man or mind
never makes a mistake.

MIND AND THOUGHT

WHEN YOUR MIND has become controlled you have control over the whole
body; instead of being a slave to this machine, the machine is your slave. Instead
of the machine's being able to drag the soul down, it becomes its greatest
helpmate.

When the mind is free from activity or functioning, it vanishes and the
Self is revealed. This state has been described by the commentator Śankara
as aparokshānubhuti, or supersensuous experience.

We are what our thoughts have made us; so take care what you think.

Every vicious thought will rebound, every thought of hatred which you have
thought, even in a cave, is stored up and will one day come back to you with
tremendous power in the form of some misery here. If you project hatred and
jealousy, they will rebound on you with compound interest. No power can
avert them; when once you have put them in motion, you will have to bear
their fruit. Remembering this will prevent you from doing wicked things.

We are heirs to all the good thoughts of the universe if we open ourselves to them.

ONENESS

HE INDEED IS A YOGI who sees himself in the whole universe and the whole universe in himself.

Not one atom in the universe can move without dragging the whole world along with it. There cannot be any progress without the whole world's following in its wake; and it is becoming clearer every day that the solution of any problem can never be attained on racial or national or any narrow grounds.

I am thoroughly convinced that no individual or nation can live by holding itself apart from the community of others; whenever such an attempt has been made, under the false notion of greatness, policy, or holiness, the result has always been disastrous to the one who thus secluded himself.

Each is responsible for the evil anywhere in the world.

All that unites with the universal is virtue. All that separates is sin.

Not one can be happy until all are happy.

When you hurt anyone you hurt yourself, for you and your brother are one.

DUTY

To GIVE AN objective definition of duty is entirely impossible. Yet there is duty from the subjective side. Any action that makes us go Godward is a good action and is our duty; any action that takes us away from God is evil and is not our duty.

By doing well the duty which is nearest to us, the duty which is in our hands now, we make ourselves stronger; and improving ourselves in this manner, step by step, we may even reach a state in which it will be our privilege to do the most coveted and honoured duties in life and in society.

No man can long occupy satisfactorily a position for which he is not fitted. There is no use in grumbling against nature's adjustment. He who does the lower work is not therefore a lower man. No man is to be judged by the mere nature of his duties; but all should be judged by the manner and the spirit in which they perform them.

It is the worker attached to results who grumbles about the nature of the duty which has fallen to his lot; to the unattached worker all duties are equally good, and form efficient instruments with which selfishness and sensuality may be killed and the freedom of the soul secured.

Duty is seldom sweet. It is only when love greases its wheels that it runs smoothly; it is a continuous friction otherwise. How else could parents do their duty to their children, husbands to their wives, and vice versa? Do we not meet with cases of friction every day in our lives? Duty is sweet only through love.

Duty, as it is commonly understood, becomes a disease with us; it drags us ever onward. It catches hold of us and makes our whole life miserable. It is the bane of human life. This idea of duty is like the midday summer sun; it scorches the innermost soul of mankind. Look at those poor slaves to duty! Duty leaves them no time to say prayers, no time to bathe. Duty is ever on them. They go out and work—duty is on them! They come home and think of the work for the next day—duty is on them! It is living a slave's life, and at last dropping down in the street and dying in harness, like a horse. This is duty as it is understood. The only true duty is to be unattached and to work as free beings, to give up all works unto God.

Every duty is holy, and devotion to duty is the highest form of worship of God.

SERVICE

This is the gist of all worship: to be good and to do good to others. He who sees Śiva in the poor, in the weak, and in the diseased really worships Śiva; and if he sees Śiva only in the image, his worship is but preliminary. He who has served and helped one poor man, seeing Śiva in him, without thinking of his caste or creed or race, or anything, with him Śiva is more pleased than He is with the man who sees Him only in temples.

Selfishness is the chief sin: thinking of ourselves first. He who thinks, "I will eat first, I will have more money than others, and I will possess everything"; he who thinks, "I will go to heaven before others, I will get mukti before others," is the selfish man. The unselfish man says, "I will be last; I do not care to go to heaven; I will go to hell if by doing so I can help my brothers." This unselfishness is the test of religion.

Do you love your fellow men? Where should you go to seek for God—are not all the poor, the miserable, the weak, Gods? Why not worship them first? Why go to dig a well on the bank of the Ganges?

It is our privilege to be allowed to be charitable, for only so can we grow. The poor man suffers that we may be helped. Let the giver kneel down and give thanks; let the receiver stand up and permit. See the Lord back of every being and give to Him.

Selfishness is the Devil incarnate in every man. Every bit of self is of the Devil. Take away self on one side and God enters by the other.

The highest ideal is eternal and entire self-abnegation, where there is no "I" but all is "Thou."

Are you unselfish? That is the question. If you are, you will be perfect without reading a single religious book, without going into a single church or temple.

NON-INJURY

NEVER PRODUCING PAIN by thought, word, or deed, in any living being, is what is called ahimsā, non-injury. There is no virtue higher than non-injury. There is no happiness higher than that which a man obtains by this attitude of non-offensiveness to all creation.

The test of ahimsā is absence of jealousy. Any man may do a good deed or make a good gift on the spur of the moment or under the pressure of some superstition or priestcraft; but the real lover of mankind is he who is jealous of none. The so-called great men of the world are seen to become jealous of each other for a small name, for a little fame, and for a few bits of gold. So long as this jealousy exists in a heart, it is far away from the perfection of ahimsā. . . . The man who will mercilessly cheat widows and orphans, and do the vilest deeds for money, is worse than any brute, even if he lives entirely on vegetables. The man whose heart never cherishes even the thought of injury to anyone, who rejoices at the prosperity of even his greatest enemy, that man is a bhakta, he is a yogi, he is the guru of all, even though he lives every day on the flesh of swine. Therefore we must always remember that external practices have value only as they help to develop internal purity. It is better to have internal purity alone, when minute attention to external observances is not practicable. But woe unto the man and woe unto the nation that forgets the real, internal, spiritual essentials of religion and mechanically clutches with death-like grasp external forms and never lets them go!

Non-injury has to be attained by him who would be free. No one is more powerful than he who has attained perfect non-injury. No one could fight, no one could quarrel, in his presence. Yes, his very presence means peace, means love, wherever he may be. Nobody could be angry or fight in his presence. Even animals, ferocious animals, would be peaceful before him.

KARMA AND REBIRTH

ANY WORD, any action, any thought that produces an effect is called karma. Thus the law of karma means the law of causation, of inevitable cause and effect. Whatever we see or feel or do, whatever action there is anywhere in the universe, while being the effect of past work on the one hand, becomes, on the other, a cause in its turn and produces its own effect. Each one of us is the effect of an infinite past. The child is ushered into the world not as something flashing from the hands of nature, as poets delight so much to depict, but he has the burden of an infinite past; for good or evil he comes to work out his own past deeds. This makes the differentiation. This is the law of karma. Each one of us is the maker of his own fate.

The idea of rebirth runs parallel with the doctrine of the eternity of the human soul. Nothing that ends at one point can be without a beginning, and nothing that begins at one point can be without an end.

How is it that one man is born of good parents, receives a good education, and becomes a good man, while another comes from besotted parents and ends on the gallows? How do you explain this inequality without implicating God? Then, too, what becomes of my freedom if this is my first birth? If I come into this world without experience of a former life, my independence would be gone, for my path would be marked out by the experience of others. If I cannot be the maker of my own fortune, then I am not free. But if this is not my first birth, I can take upon myself the blame for the misery of this life, which is the result of the evil I have committed in another, and say I will unmake it. This, then, is our philosophy of the migration of the soul: We come into this life with the experience of another, and the fortune or misfortune of this existence is the result of our acts in a former existence; and thus we are always becoming better till at last perfection is reached.

There is no other way to vindicate the glory and the liberty of the human soul and to reconcile the inequalities and the horrors of this world, than to place the whole burden upon the legitimate cause—our own independent actions, or karma. Not only so, but every theory of the creation of the soul from nothing inevitably leads to fatalism and pre-ordination, and instead of a Merciful Father, places before us a hideous, cruel, and ever angry God to worship.

EDUCATION

EDUCATION is the manifestation of the perfection already in man.

A child teaches itself. But you can help it to go forward in its own way. What you can do is not of a positive nature, but of a negative. You can take away the obstacles, but knowledge comes from within the child itself. . . . You have come to hear me. When you go home, reflect on what you have learnt, and you will find that you yourself have thought out the same thing; I have only given it expression. I can never teach you anything; you will have to teach yourself; but I can help you, perhaps, in giving expression to that thought.

To me the very essence of education is concentration of mind, not the collecting of facts. If I had to receive my education over again, and had any voice in the matter, I would develop the power of concentration and detachment, and then with a perfect instrument I could collect facts at will.

Education is not the amount of information that is put into your brain and runs riot there, undigested, all your life. We must have life-building, man-making, character-forming assimilation of ideas. If you have assimilated five ideas and made them your life and character, you have more education than a man who has got by heart a whole library.

All the knowledge that the world has ever received comes from the mind; the infinite library of the universe is in your own mind. The external world is simply the suggestion, the occasion, which sets you to studying your own mind; but the object of your study is always your own mind. The falling of an apple gave the suggestion to Newton, and he studied his own mind; he rearranged all the previous links of thought in his mind and discovered a new link among them, which we call gravitation. It was not in the apple or in anything in the centre of the earth.

HAPPINESS

CAN ANY PERMANENT HAPPINESS be given to the world? In the ocean we cannot raise a wave without causing a hollow somewhere else. The sum total of the good things in the world has been the same throughout in its relation to man's need and greed. It cannot be increased or decreased. Take the human race as we know it today. Do we not find the same miseries and the same happiness, the same pleasures and pains, the same differences in position, as in the past? Are not some rich, some poor, some high, some low, some healthy, some unhealthy? All this was the same with the Egyptians, the Greeks, and the Romans in ancient times as it is with the Americans today. So far as history is known, it has always been the same.

We cannot add happiness to this world; similarly, we cannot add pain to it either. The sum total of pleasure and pain displayed here on earth will be the same throughout. We just push it from this side to the other side, and from that side to this, but it will remain the same, because to remain so is its very nature. This ebb and flow, this rising and falling, is the world's very nature; it would be as logical to hold otherwise as to say that we may have life without death.

Philosophy insists that there is a Joy which is absolute, which never changes. That Joy cannot be the same as the joys and pleasures we have in this life, and yet Vedānta shows that everything that is joyful in this life is but a particle of that Real Joy, because that is the only joy there is. Every moment we are enjoying the Absolute Bliss, though covered up, misunderstood, and caricatured. Wherever there is any blessing, blissfulness, or joy—even the joy of the thief in stealing—it is a manifestation of that Absolute Bliss, only it has become obscured, muddled up, as it were, with all sorts of extraneous conditions, and misunderstood.

After every happiness comes misery; they may be far apart or near. The more advanced the soul, the more quickly does one follow the other. What we want is neither happiness nor misery. Both make us forget our true nature; both are chains, one iron, one gold. Behind both is the Ātman, who knows neither happiness nor misery.

The miseries of the world cannot be cured by physical help only. Until man's nature changes, these physical needs will arise and miseries will always be felt, and no amount of physical help will cure them completely. . . . Let men have light, let them be pure and spiritually strong and educated, then alone will misery cease in the world, and not before.

BUDDHA

BUDDHA NEVER bowed down to anything, neither to Vedas, nor caste, nor priest, nor custom. He fearlessly reasoned so far as reason could take him. Such a fearless search for truth and such love for every living thing in the world has never been seen.

Buddha was the first who dared to say: "Believe not because some old manuscripts tell you it is so; believe not because it is your national belief, because you have been made to believe it from your childhood. But reason it all out, and after you have analysed it, then, if you find that it will do good to one and all, believe it, live up to it, and help others to live up to it."

Buddha is the only Prophet who said: "I do not care to know your various theories about God. What is the use of discussing all the subtle doctrines about the soul? Do good and be good. And this will take you to freedom and to whatever truth there is."

Buddha said about himself: "Buddha is the name of infinite knowledge, infinite as the sky. I, Gautama, have reached that state; you will reach it too if you struggle for it."

CHRIST AND CHRISTIANITY

THAT SOUL IS STRONG which has become one with the Lord; none else is strong. What do you think was the cause of the strength of Jesus of Nazareth, that immense, infinite strength which laughed at traitors and blessed those that were willing to murder him? It was his knowledge that "I and my Father are one";

it was his prayer, "Father, just as I am one with You, so make them one with me."

If I, as an Oriental, have to worship Jesus of Nazareth, there is only one way left to me, and that is to worship him as God, and nothing else.

Let the churches preach doctrines, theories, philosophies, to their hearts' content, but when it comes to worship, the real practical part of religion, it should be as Jesus says: "When thou prayest, enter into thy closet; and when thou hast shut the door, pray to thy Father which is in secret."

"Watch and pray, for the kingdom of heaven is at hand"—which means, purify your minds and be ready. . . . You recollect that the Christians are, even in the darkest days, even in the most superstitious Christian countries, always trying to prepare themselves for the coming of the Lord by trying to help others, building hospitals, and so on. So long as the Christians keep to that ideal, their religion lives.

All religions are, at bottom, alike. This is so, although the Christian church, like the Pharisee in the parable, thanks God that it alone is right and thinks that all other religions are wrong and in need of Christian light. Christianity must become tolerant before the world will be willing to unite with the Christian church in a common charity. God has not left Himself without a witness in any heart, and men, especially men who follow Jesus Christ, should be willing to admit this. In fact, Jesus Christ was willing to welcome every good man to the family of God. It is not the man who believes a certain thing, but the man who does the will of the Father in heaven, who is right. On this basis—being right and doing right—the whole world can unite.

MOHAMMED AND ISLĀM

MOHAMMED WAS the Prophet of equality, of the brotherhood of man, the brotherhood of all Mussulmans.

Mohammed showed, by his life, that amongst Mohammedans there should be perfect equality and brotherhood. There was no question of race, caste, colour, or sex. The Sultan of Turkey may buy a negro from the mart of Africa and bring him in chains to Turkey; but should he become a Mohammedan and have sufficient merit and abilities, he might even marry the daughter of the Sultan. Compare this with the way in which the negroes and the American Indians are treated in America! And what do the Hindus do? If a low-caste Hindu chances to touch the food of one belonging to a higher caste, the latter throws it away. Notwithstanding our grand philosophy, you note our weakness in practice; but there you see the greatness of the Mohammedan, beyond other faiths, showing itself in equality, perfect equality, regardless of race or colour.

As soon as a man becomes a Mohammedan, the whole of Islām receives him as a brother, with open arms, without making any distinction, which no other religion does. If one of your American Indians becomes a Mohammedan, the Sultan of Turkey would have no objection to dining with him. If he has brains, no position is barred to him. In America I have never yet seen a church where the white man and the negro can kneel side by side to pray.

For our own motherland a junction of the two great systems, Hinduism and Islām—Vedāntic brain and Islāmic body—is the only hope. . . . I see in my mind's eye the future perfect India rising out of this chaos and strife, glorious and invincible, with Vedāntic brain and Islāmic body.

THE HINDUS AND HINDUISM

In India there never was any religious persecution by the Hindus, but only that wonderful reverence which they have for all the religions of the world. They sheltered a portion of the Hebrews when the latter were driven out of their own country; and the Malabar Jews remain as a result. The Hindus received, at another time, the remnant of the Persians when they were almost annihilated; and these remain, to this day, as a part of us and loved by us, as the modern Parsees of Bombay. There were Christians who claimed to have come with St. Thomas, the disciple of Jesus Christ; they were allowed to settle in India and hold their own opinions; and a colony of them is even now in existence in India. And this spirit of tolerance has not died out. It will not and cannot die there.

You may be a dualist, and I may be a monist; you may believe that you are the eternal servant of God, and I may declare that I am one with God Himself— yet both of us are good Hindus. How is that possible? Read then: "That which exists is One; sages call It by various names."

From the high spiritual flights of the Vedānta philosophy, of which the latest discoveries of science seem like echoes, to the low ideas of idolatry with its multifarious mythology, the agnosticism of the Buddhists, and the atheism of the Jains, each and all have a place in the Hindu's religion.

The religion of the Hindus does not consist in struggles and attempts to believe a certain doctrine or dogma, but in realizing; not in believing, but in becoming. Thus the whole object of their system is by constant struggle to become perfect, to become divine, to reach God and see God; and this reaching God, seeing God, becoming perfect as the Father in heaven is perfect, constitutes the religion of the Hindus.

THE GITĀ

The greatness of little things, that is what the Gitā teaches, bless the old book!

We read in the Bhagavad Gītā again and again that we must all work incessantly. All work is by nature composed of good and evil. We cannot do any work which will not do some good somewhere; there cannot be any work which will not cause some harm somewhere. Every action must necessarily be a mixture of good and evil; yet we are commanded to work incessantly. Good and evil will both have their results. Good action will entail upon us a good effect; bad action, a bad. But good and bad are both bondages of the soul. The solution reached in the Gītā in regard to this bondage-producing nature of work is that if we do not attach ourselves to the work we do, it will not have any binding effect on our soul.

This is the one cause of our misery: we are attached, we are being caught. Therefore, says the Gītā, work constantly. Work but be not attached, be not caught. Reserve unto yourself the power of detaching yourself from everything, however beloved, however much the soul might yearn for it; however great the pangs of misery you feel if you are going to leave it, still, reserve the power of leaving it whenever you want.

The heart's love is due to only one. To whom? To Him who never changes. Śri Krishna says in the Gītā: The Lord is the only one who never changes. His love never fails. Wherever we are and whatever we do, He is ever and ever the same merciful, the same loving heart. He never changes. . . . We must love Him—and everyone that lives, only in and through Him. This is the key-note.

Ay, if there is anything in the Gītā that I like, it is the two verses, coming out strong as the very gist, the very essence, of Krishna's teaching: "He who sees the Supreme Lord dwelling alike in all beings, the Imperishable in things that perish, he sees indeed. For, seeing the Lord as the same, everywhere present, he does not destroy the self by the self, and thus he goes to the highest goal."

THE UPANISHADS

In modern language, the theme of the Upanishads is to find an ultimate unity of things. Knowledge is nothing but finding unity in the midst of diversity. Every science is based upon this; all human knowledge is based upon the finding of unity in the midst of diversity. And if it is the task of small fragments of human knowledge, which we call our sciences, to find unity in the midst of a few different phenomena, the task becomes stupendous when the theme before us is to find unity in the midst of this marvellously diversified universe, where prevail unnumbered differences in name and form, in matter and spirit—each thought differing from every other thought, each form differing from every other form. Yet to harmonize these many planes and unending spheres, to find unity in the midst of this infinite variety, is the theme of the Upanishads.

"The sun does not shine there, nor the moon and the stars, nor these lightnings—not to speak of this fire." What poetry in the world can be more sublime than this? Such poetry you find nowhere else.

INDIA

THE DEBT which the world owes to India is immense. There is not one race on this earth to which the world owes so much as it owes to the patient Hindu, the mild Hindu.

Gifts of political knowledge can be made with the blast of trumpets and the march of cohorts. Gifts of secular knowledge and social knowledge can be made with fire and sword. But spiritual knowledge can only be given in silence, like the dew, which falls unseen and unheard, and yet brings into bloom masses of roses. This has been the gift of India to the world again and again.

The one characteristic of Indian thought is its silence, its calmness. The tremendous power that is behind it is never expressed by violence.

Shall India die? Then from the world all spirituality will be extinct; all moral perfection will be extinct; all sweet-souled sympathy for religion will be extinct; all ideality will be extinct; and in their place will reign the duality of lust and luxury as the male and female deities, with money as its priest; fraud, force, and competition its ceremonies; and the human soul its sacrifice. Such a thing can never be. The power of suffering is infinitely greater than the power of doing; the power of love is of infinitely greater potency than the power of hatred.

CAUSES OF INDIA'S DOWNFALL

I CONSIDER that the great national sin is the neglect of the masses, and that is one of the causes of our downfall. No amount of politics will be of any avail until the masses in India are once more well educated, well fed, and well cared for.

Our nation is totally lacking in the faculty of organization. It is this one drawback which produces all sorts of evil. We are altogether averse to making a common cause for anything. The first requisite for organization is obedience.

No man, no nation, can hate others and live. India's doom was sealed the very day they invented the word mlechcha and stopped from communion with others. Take care how you foster that idea. It is easy to talk about Vedānta, but how hard to carry out even its least precepts!

THE WAY TO INDIA'S REGENERATION

THE MORE THE Hindus study the past, the more glorious will be their future, and whoever tries to bring the past to the door of everyone is a great benefactor to his nation. The degeneration of India came not because the laws and customs of the ancients were bad, but because they were not allowed to be carried to their legitimate conclusions.

Nowadays everybody blames those who constantly look back to the past. It is said that so much looking back to the past is the cause of all India's woes. To me, on the contrary, it seems that the opposite is true. So long as they forgot the past, the Hindu nation remained in a state of stupor; and as soon as they have begun to look into the past, there is on every side a fresh manifestation of life. It is out of this past that the future has to be moulded; this past will become the future.

Our method is very easily described. It simply consists in reasserting the national life. Buddha preached renunciation; India heard, and in six centuries she reached her greatest height. The secret lies there. The national ideals of India are renunciation and service. Intensify her in those channels, and the rest will take care of itself. The banner of the spirit cannot be raised too high in this country. In it alone is salvation.

First bread and then religion. We stuff them too much with religion, when the poor fellows have been starving. No dogmas will satisfy the cravings of hunger. There are two curses here: first, our physical weakness, secondly, our jealousy, our dried-up hearts. You may talk doctrines by the millions, you may have sects by the hundreds of millions; ay, but it is all nothing until you have the heart to feel. Feel for them, as your Veda teaches you, till you find they are parts of your bodies, till you realize that you and they, the poor and the rich, the saint and the sinner, are all parts of one infinite Whole, which you call Brahman.

You must all set your shoulders to the wheel! Your duty at present is to go from one part of the country to another, from village to village, and make the people understand that mere sitting about idly won't do any more. Make them understand their real condition, and say: "O ye brothers all, arise! Awake! How much longer will you remain asleep?" Go and advise them how to improve their own condition, and make them comprehend the sublime truths of the scriptures by presenting them in a lucid and popular way. Also instruct them, in simple words, about the necessities of life, and in trade, commerce, agriculture, and so on. If you cannot do this, then fie upon your education and culture, and fie upon your study of the Vedas and Vedānta!

Religion for a long time has come to be static in India; what we want is to make it dynamic. I want it to be brought into the life of everybody. Religion, as it has always been in the past, must enter the palaces of kings as well as the homes of the poorest peasants in the land. Religion, the common inheritance, the universal birthright of the race, must be brought free to the door of everybody. Religion in India must be made as free and as easy of access as is God's air. And this is the kind of thing we have to bring about in India—but not by getting up little sects and fighting on points of difference. Let us preach where we all agree, and leave the differences to remedy themselves. As I have said again and again, if there is the darkness of centuries in a room, and we go into the room and begin to cry, "Oh, it is dark, it is dark!"—will the darkness go? Bring in light and the darkness will vanish at once.

We have to learn from others. You put the seed in the ground and give it plenty of earth and air and water to feed upon; when the seed grows into the plant, and into a gigantic tree, does it become the earth, does it become the air, or does it become the water? It becomes the mighty plant, the mighty tree, after its own nature, having absorbed everything that was given to it. Let that be your position. We have indeed many things to learn from others; yea, that man who refuses to learn is already dead.

Then only will India awake when hundreds of large-hearted men and women, giving up all desire of enjoying the luxuries of life, shall long and exert themselves to the utmost for the well-being of the millions of their countrymen who are gradually sinking lower and lower in the vortex of destitution and ignorance. I have experienced even in my insignificant life that good motives, sincerity, and infinite love can conquer the world. One single soul possessed of these virtues can destroy the dark designs of millions of hypocrites and brutes.

Let the New India arise—out of the cottage of the peasant grasping the plough, out of the huts of the fisherman, the cobbler, and the sweeper. Let her spring from the grocer's shop, from beside the oven of the fritter-seller. Let her emanate from the factory, from marts and from markets. Let her emerge from the groves and forests, from hills and mountains. These common people have suffered oppression for thousands of years—suffered it without a murmur—and as a result have got wonderful fortitude. They have suffered eternal misery, which has given them unflinching vitality. Living on a handful of oatmeal they can convulse the world; give them only half a piece of bread, and the whole world will not be big enough to contain their energy. And besides, they have got the wonderful strength that comes of a pure and moral life which is not to be found anywhere else in the world. Such peacefulness, such contentment, such love, such power of silent and incessant work, and such a manifestation of a lion's strength in times of action—where else will you find these?

Do you know what my idea is? By preaching the profound secrets of the Vedānta religion in the Western world, we shall attract the sympathy and regard of these mighty nations, maintaining for ourselves the position of their teacher in spiritual matters; let them remain our teachers in all material concerns. . . . Nothing will come of crying day and night before them, "Give me this!" or "Give me that!" When there grows a link of sympathy and regard between both nations by this give-and-take intercourse, there will be then no need for these noisy cries. They will do everything of their own accord. I believe that by this cultivation of religion and the wider diffusion of Vedānta, both this country and the West will gain enormously. To me the pursuit of politics is a secondary means in comparison with this. I will lay down my life to carry out this belief practically. If you believe in any other way of accomplishing the good of India, well, you may go on working in your own way.

MISCELLANEOUS

IN THE FIRST PLACE, I would ask mankind to recognize this maxim: Do not destroy. Break not, pull not anything down, but build. Help if you can. Do not injure if you cannot render help. Secondly, take a man where he stands, and from there give him a lift.

Remember the words of Christ: "Ask and it shall be given unto you, seek and you shall find, knock and it shall be opened unto you." These words are literally true, not figures or fiction. They were the outflow of the heart's blood of one of the greatest sons of God who ever came to this world of ours—words which came as the fruit of realization from a man who had felt and seen God, who had spoken with God a hundred times more intensely than you or I see this building.

Truth has such a face that anyone who sees that face becomes convinced. The sun does not require any torch to show it; the sun is self-sufficient. If truth requires evidence, what will evidence that evidence?

The yogis say that man can go beyond his direct sense perception and beyond his reason also. Man has in him the faculty, the power, of transcending even his intellect, a power which is in every being, every creature. By the practice of yoga that power is aroused, and then man transcends the ordinary limits of reason and directly perceives things which are beyond all reason.

"Blessed are the pure in heart, for they shall see God." In that one sentence lies the gist of all religions. . . . It alone could save the world were all the other scriptures lost. A vision of God, a glimpse of the Beyond, never comes until the soul is pure.

He who comes with a pure heart and a reverent attitude will have his heart opened; the doors will open for him and he will see the Truth.

It is very easy to say, "Don't be personal"; but the same man who says so is generally most personal. His attachment for particular men and women is very strong; it does not leave him when they die; he wants to follow them beyond death. That is idolatry; it is the seed, the very cause, of idolatry; and the cause being there, it will come out in some form or other. Is it not better to have a personal attachment to an image of Christ or Buddha than to an ordinary man or woman?

Two sorts of persons do not require any image: the human animal, who never thinks of any religion, and the perfected being, who has passed through the disciplinary stages. Between these two points, all of us require some sort of image, outside or inside.

All these forms and ceremonies, these prayers and pilgrimages, these books, bells, candles, and priests, are the preparations; they take off the impurities of the soul; and when the soul becomes pure, it naturally wants to get to the mine of purity, God Himself.

No great work can be achieved by humbug. It is through love, a passion for truth, and tremendous energy, that all undertakings are accomplished. Therefore manifest your manhood.

Vedānta says that you are pure and perfect, and that there is a state beyond good and evil, and that that is your own nature. It is higher than good. Good is only a lesser differentiation than evil. We have no theory of evil. We call it ignorance.

One characteristic idea of Vedānta is that we must allow infinite variation in religious thought, and not try to bring everybody to the same opinion, because the goal is the same. The Vedāntist says in his poetical language: "As so many rivers, having their source in different mountains, roll down, crooked or straight, and at last come into the ocean, so, O Lord, all these various creeds and religions, taking their start from different standpoints and running through courses crooked or straight, at last come unto Thee."

Materialism says that the voice of freedom is a delusion. Idealism says that the voice that tells of bondage is a delusion. Vedānta says that you are free and not free at the same time: never free on the earthly plane, but ever free on the spiritual.

Ye are the children of God, the sharers of Immortal Bliss, holy and perfect beings. Ye divinities on earth—sinners! It is a sin to call a man so; it is a standing libel on human nature.

You may invent an image through which to worship God; but a better image already exists—the living man. You may build a temple in which to worship God, and that may be good; but a better one, a much higher one, already exists—the human body.

GLOSSARY

GLOSSARY

āchārya Religious teacher.

Advaita Non-duality; a school of Vedānta philosophy teaching the oneness of God, soul, and universe, whose chief exponent was Śankarāchārya (A. D. 788-820).

ahimsā Non-injury.

Ānanda Bliss.

Annapurnā A name of the Divine Mother as the Giver of Food.

Arjuna A hero of the epic Mahābhārata and a friend and disciple of Krishna.

Ārya Samāj An orthodox Hindu movement founded by Swami Dayananda (A. D. 1824-1883).

āśrama Hermitage; also any one of the four stages of life: the celibate student stage (brahmacharya), the married householder stage (gārhasthya), the stage of retirement and contemplation (vānaprastha), and the stage of religious mendicancy (sannyāsa).

Ātman The Self or Soul; denotes both the Supreme Soul and the individual soul, which, according to Non-dualistic Vedānta, are ultimately identical.

Avatār Incarnation of God.

Bhagavad Gitā An important Hindu scripture, comprising eighteen chapters of the epic Mahābhārata and containing the teachings of Śri Krishna.

bhakta Devotee of God.

bhakti Love of God.

bhakti-yoga The path of devotion followed by dualistic worshippers.

bhakti-yogi A follower of the path of devotion.

bhoga Enjoyment.

bodhisattva A Buddhist saint on his way to the attainment of Nirvāna, or final illumination; this state is reached through a long series of unselfish deeds.

Bo-tree The famous tree under which Buddha attained illumination.

brahmachārin A celibate student belonging to the first stage of life. See āśrama.

brahmachārini A woman observing the vow of chastity.

brahmacharya The first of the four stages of life; the life of an unmarried student. See āśrama.

Brahman The Absolute; the Supreme Reality of the Vedānta philosophy.

Brāhmana That portion of the Vedas which gives the rules for the employment of the hymns at the various sacrifices, their origin and detailed explanation, etc. It is distinct from the Mantra portion of the Vedas.

brāhmin A member of the priestly caste, the highest caste in Hindu society.

Brāhmo A member of the Brāhmo Samāj.

Brāhmo Samāj A liberal Hindu religious movement founded by Rājā Rammohan Roy (A. D. 1774-1883).

211

buddhi   The determinative faculty of the mind, which makes decisions; sometimes translated as "intellect."

Chaitanya   A prophet born in A. D. 1485, who lived at Navadvip, Bengal, and
emphasized the path of divine love for the realization of God.
chandāla   Untouchable.

Dakshineswar   A village near Calcutta where Ramakrishna lived and communed with God.
darśanas   The six systems of orthodox Hindu philosophy, namely, the Sāmkhya
of Kapila, the Yoga of Patanjali, the Vaiśeshika of Kanāda, the Nyāya of
Gautama, the Purva Mimāmsā of Jaimini, and the Vedānta or Uttara
Mimāmsā of Vyāsa.
Dhammapāda   A famous treatise of the Buddhists.
dharma   Righteousness, duty; the inner constitution of a thing, which governs
its growth.
Diwan   Prime Minister of the ruler of a Native State.
durātman   Wicked soul.
Durgā   A name of the Divine Mother.

garden house   A rich man's country house set in a garden.
Gitā   Same as Bhagavad Gitā.
gopis   The cowherd girls of Vrindāvan, playmates of Krishna.
gunas   A term of the Sāmkhya philosophy, according to which prakriti (nature
or matter), in contrast with Purusha (Soul), consists of three gunas—usually
translated as "qualities"—known as sattva, rajas, and tamas. Tamas stands
for inertia, rajas for activity and restlessness, and sattva for balance or wisdom.
guru   Spiritual preceptor.

Hāldārpukur   A lake in Kāmārpukur, Śri Ramakrishna's birthplace.
Hari   An epithet of the Godhead.
Holy Mother   The wife of Śri Ramakrishna.

Jains   The followers of Jainism, an important religious sect of India.
japa   Repetition of the Lord's name or of a sacred formula given by the spiritual
teacher.
jiva   (Lit., living being.) The individual soul, which in essence is one with
the Universal Soul.
jivanmukta   One who has attained liberation while living in the body.
jivanmukti   Liberation while living in the body.
jnāna   Knowledge of Reality arrived at through reasoning and discrimination;
also the process of reasoning by means of which Ultimate Truth is attained.
jnāna-yoga   A form of spiritual discipline mainly based upon philosophical
discrimination between the real and the unreal, and the renunciation of the
unreal.
jnāna-yogi   A follower of jnāna-yoga.

jnāni   One who follows the path of reasoning and discrimination to realize Ultimate Truth; generally used to denote a non-dualist.

Jumnā   A sacred river of India.

Kāli   (Lit., the Black One.) An epithet of the Divine Mother; the Primal Energy.

Kālidāsa   The great Sanskrit poet and author of *Sakuntalā*.

Kaliyuga   The fourth of the cycles or world periods. According to Hindu mythology the duration of the world is divided into four yugas, namely, Satya, Tretā, Dwāpara, and Kali. In the first, also known as the Golden Age, there is a great preponderance of virtue among men, but with each succeeding yuga virtue diminishes and vice increases. In the Kaliyuga there is a minimum of virtue and a great excess of vice. The world is said to be now passing through the Kaliyuga.

Kamalākānta   A mystic poet of Bengal.

karma   Action in general; duty. The Vedas use the word chiefly to denote ritualistic worship and humanitarian action.

karma-yoga   A spiritual discipline, mainly discussed in the Bhagavad Gitā, based upon the unselfish performance of duty.

karma-yogi   A follower of karma-yoga.

Keshab Chandra Sen   See Sen, Keshab Chandra.

Krishna   An Incarnation of God described in the *Mahābhārata* and the *Bhāgavata*.

kshattriya   A member of the second or warrior caste in Hindu society.

Kundalini   (Lit., coiled-up serpent.) The word refers to the spiritual power dormant in all living beings. When awakened through the practice of spiritual disciplines, it rises through the spinal column, passes through various centres, and at last reaches the brain, when the yogi experiences samādhi or total absorption in the Godhead.

Kurukshetra   A place near modern Delhi, where the great battle described in the *Mahābhārata* was fought.

Lakshmi   The Consort of Vishnu and Goddess of Fortune.

lingam   The phallic symbol associated with Śiva.

Madhva   Same as Madhvāchārya.

Madhvāchārya   The chief exponent of Dualistic Vedānta (A. D. 1199-1276).

Mahābhārata   A celebrated Hindu epic.

mahāsamādhi   The highest state of God-consciousness; the word also signifies the death of an illumined person.

mahātmā   Great soul.

mahātman   Great soul.

Malabar   The southwestern part of India.

mantra   Sacred word by which the spiritual teacher initiates his disciple; sacred word in general; Vedic hymn. Of the two main sections of the Vedas, the Mantra and Brāhmana, the Mantra section describes the hymns used in the sacrifices.

math   Monastery.

māyā   A term of Vedānta philosophy denoting ignorance obscuring the vision of Reality; the cosmic illusion on account of which the One appears as many, the Absolute as the relative.

Meru   A mythical mountain abounding in gold and precious stones. The abode of Brahmā, the Creator, and a meeting-place for the gods, demigods, rishis, and other supernatural beings, Meru is regarded as the axis around which the planets revolve.

Mirābāi   A celebrated woman saint of India.

mlechcha   A non-Hindu, a barbarian. This is a term of reproach applied by orthodox Hindus to foreigners, who do not conform to the established usages of Hindu religion and society. The word corresponds to the "heathen" of the Christians and the "kafir" of the Mussulmans.

mukti   Liberation from the bondage of the world, which is the goal of spiritual practice.

Nārāyana   An epithet of Vishnu, or the Godhead.

Nimbārka   A great Hindu philosopher.

Nirvāna   Final absorption in Brahman, or the All-pervading Reality, through the annihilation of the individual ego.

nirvikalpa samādhi   The highest state of samādhi, in which the aspirant realizes his total oneness with Brahman.

ojas   Virility.

Om   The most sacred word of the Vedas; also written Aum. It is a symbol both of the Personal God and of the Absolute.

Panchavati   A group of five sacred trees planted by Śri Ramakrishna in the temple garden at Dakshineswar for his practice of spiritual discipline.

pandit   Scholar.

Pānini   The famous Sanskrit grammarian; also the grammar written by Pānini.

paramahamsa   One belonging to the highest order of sannyāsins.

Patanjali   The author of the Yoga system, one of the six systems of orthodox Hindu philosophy, dealing with concentration and its methods, control of the mind, and similar matters.

prakriti   Primordial nature; the material substratum of the creation, consisting of sattva, rajas, and tamas. See gunas.

prāna   The vital breath, which sustains life in a physical body; the primal energy or force, of which other physical forces are manifestations. In the books on Yoga, prāna is described as having five modifications, according to its five different bodily functions: (1) prāna (which controls the breath), (2) apāna (which carries downward unassimilated food and drink), (3) vyāna (which pervades the entire body), (4) udāna (by which the contents of the stomach are ejected through the mouth, and by which the soul is conducted from the body at death), and (5) samāna (which carries nutrition throughout the body). Prāna is also a name of Saguna Brahman, or Brahman with attributes.

puja Ritualistic worship.

Puranas Books of Hindu mythology.

Purusha (Lit., person.) A term of Samkhya philosophy denoting the individual conscious principle. In Vedanta the term *Purusha* denotes the Self.

rajas The principle of restlessness or activity in nature. See gunas.

raja-yoga A system of yoga ascribed to Patanjali, dealing with concentration and its methods, control of the mind, samadhi, and similar matters.

Rama The hero of the *Ramayana*, regarded by the Hindus as a Divine Incarnation.

Ramakrishna A great saint of Bengal, regarded as a Divine Incarnation (A. D. 1836-1886).

Ramanuja Same as Ramanujacharya.

Ramanujacharya A great saint of Southern India, the foremost interpreter of the school of Qualified Non-dualistic Vedanta (A. D. 1017-1137).

Ramayana A famous Hindu epic.

rishi A seer of Truth to whom the wisdom of the Vedas was revealed; a general name for saint or ascetic.

Sakti Power, generally the Creative Power of Brahman; a name of the Divine Mother.

samadhi Ecstasy, trance, communion with God.

Samkhya One of the six systems of orthodox Hindu philosophy, founded by Kapila; it teaches that the universe evolves as the result of the union of prakriti (nature) and Purusha (Spirit).

Sankara Same as Sankaracharya.

Sankaracharya One of the greatest saints and philosophers of India, the foremost exponent of Advaita Vedanta (A. D. 788-820).

sannyasa The monastic life; the last of the four stages of life. See asrama.

sannyasin A Hindu monk who has renounced the world in order to realize God.

santih Peace.

Sarasvati The Goddess of Learning.

Satchidananda (Lit., Existence-Knowledge-Bliss Absolute.) A name of Brahman, or Ultimate Reality.

sattva The principle of balance or righteousness in nature. See gunas.

Sen, Keshab Chandra A leader of the Brahmo Samaj (A. D. 1838-1884).

sishya Disciple.

Sita The wife of Rama.

Siva The Destroyer God; the Third Person of the Hindu Trinity, the other two being Brahma, the Creator, and Vishnu, the Preserver.

Sonthals A primitive tribe of Central India.

Sri The word is often used as an honorific prefix to the names of deities and eminent persons, or of celebrated books generally of a sacred character; also used as an auspicious sign at the commencement of letters, manuscripts, etc; often used as an equivalent of the English term *Mr.*

sudra A member of the fourth or labouring caste in Hindu society.

sutra Aphorism.
Swami (Lit., lord.) A title of the monks belonging to the Vedānta school.
Swamiji A term of endearment and respect by which a Swami is addressed.

tamas The principle of dullness or inertia in nature. See gunas.
Tantra A system of religious philosophy in which the Divine Mother, or Power, is the Ultimate Reality; also the scriptures dealing with this philosophy.
tapasyā Austerity.

Upanishads The well-known Hindu scriptures containing the philosophy of the Vedas. They are one hundred and eight in number, of which eleven are called major Upanishads.

vaiśya One belonging to the third caste in Hindu society, the members of which engage in agriculture, commerce, and cattle-rearing.
Vedānta (Lit., the essence or the concluding part of the Vedas.) A system of philosophy mainly based upon the teachings of the Upanishads, the Bhagavad Gitā, and the Vedānta Sutras.
Vedānta Sutras An authoritative treatise on Vedānta, ascribed to Vyāsa.
Vedas The revealed scriptures of the Hindus, consisting of the Rig-Veda, Sāma-Veda, Yajur-Veda, and Atharva-Veda.
Vidyā Knowledge leading to liberation, i.e. to the realization of Ultimate Reality.
Virāt Consciousness limited or conditioned by the upādhi, or limiting adjunct, of the aggregate of gross bodies; an epithet of the Cosmic Soul.
Vishnu (Lit., the All-pervading Spirit.) The Preserver God; the Second Person of the Hindu Trinity, the other two being Brahmā, the Creator, and Śiva, the Destroyer; also a name of the Supreme Lord.
Viśwanāth An epithet of Śiva.
viveka Discrimination between the real and the unreal.
Vrindāvan A town on the bank of the Jumnā river, associated with Śri Krishna's childhood.

Yajur-Veda One of the four Vedas. See Vedas.
yoga Union of the individual soul and the Supreme Soul; the discipline by which such union is effected. The Yoga system of philosophy, ascribed to Patanjali, is one of the six systems of orthodox Hindu philosophy, and deals with the realization of Truth through concentration of the mind.
yogi One who practises yoga.